Lotus
SmartSuite 97
explained

BOOKS AVAILABLE

By both authors:

BP306 A Concise Introduction to Ami Pro 3
BP327 DOS one step at a time
BP337 A Concise User's Guide to Lotus 1-2-3 for Windows
BP341 MS-DOS explained
BP343 A Concise Introd'n to Microsoft Works for Windows
BP346 Programming in Visual Basic for Windows
BP351 WordPerfect 6 explained
BP352 Excel 5 explained
BP353 WordPerfect 6.0 for Windows explained
BP354 Word 6 for Windows explained
BP362 Access one step at a time
BP372 CA-SuperCalc for Windows explained
BP387 Windows one step at a time
BP388 Why not personalise your PC
BP399 Windows 95 one step at a time*
BP400 Windows 95 explained*
BP402 MS Office one step at a time
BP405 MS Works for Windows 95 explained
BP406 MS Word 95 explained
BP407 Excel 95 explained
BP408 Access 95 one step at a time
BP409 MS Office 95 one step at a time
BP415 Using Netscape on the Internet
BP419 Using Microsoft Explorer on the Internet
BP420 E-mail on the Internet
BP426 MS-Office 97 explained
BP428 MS-Word 97 explained
BP429 MS-Excel 97 explained
BP430 MS-Access 97 one step at a time
BP448 Lotus SmartSuite 97 explained

By Noel Kantaris:

BP232 A Concise Introduction to MS-DOS
BP258 Learning to Program in C
BP259 A Concise Introduction to UNIX*
BP261 A Concise Introduction to Lotus 1-2-3
BP264 A Concise Advanced User's Guide to MS-DOS
BP274 A Concise Introduction to SuperCalc 5
BP284 Programming in QuickBASIC
BP325 A Concise User's Guide to Windows 3.1

Lotus SmartSuite 97 explained

by

**N. Kantaris
and
P.R.M. Oliver**

**BERNARD BABANI (publishing) LTD
THE GRAMPIANS
SHEPHERDS BUSH ROAD
LONDON W6 7NF
ENGLAND**

PLEASE NOTE

Although every care has been taken with the production of this book to ensure that any projects, designs, modifications and/or programs, etc., contained herewith, operate in a correct and safe manner and also that any components specified are normally available in Great Britain, the Publishers and Author(s) do not accept responsibility in any way for the failure (including fault in design) of any project, design, modification or program to work correctly or to cause damage to any equipment that it may be connected to or used in conjunction with, or in respect of any other damage or injury that may be so caused, nor do the Publishers accept responsibility in any way for the failure to obtain specified components.

Notice is also given that if equipment that is still under warranty is modified in any way or used or connected with home-built equipment then that warranty may be void.

© 1998 BERNARD BABANI (publishing) LTD

First Published - May 1998
Reprinted - December 1998
Reprinted - April 1999

British Library Cataloguing in Publication Data:

A catalogue record for this book is available from the British Library

ISBN 0 85934 448 7

Cover Design by Gregor Arthur
Cover illustration by Adam Willis
Printed and Bound in Great Britain by Cox & Wyman Ltd, Reading

ABOUT THIS BOOK

Lotus SmartSuite 97 explained has been written to help users to get to grips with the integrated components of this package, namely, the word processor *Word Pro*, the spreadsheet *123*, the presentation graphics *Freelance*, the database *Approach*, the *Organizer*, and the new desktop manager *SmartCenter*. All these components were specifically designed for the *Windows 95,* and *NT* environments.

The book does not describe how to install and use Microsoft Windows. If you need to know more about Windows, then may we suggest you select an appropriate level book for your needs from the 'Books Available' list - the books are loosely graduated in complexity with the less demanding *One step at a time* series, to the more detailed *Explained* series. They are all published by BERNARD BABANI (publishing) Ltd.

The individual applications which make up SmartSuite 97 are designed to work together and have the same look and feel, which makes it easy to learn. For example, the majority of menus, toolbar buttons, and dialogue boxes are the same in each application, which gives them a consistent interface, and makes it easier to share information between them.

The package improves on previous Lotus SmartSuite capabilities, such as the abilities to

- create and edit hyperlinks from within any of its applications to any SmartSuite document, HTML file, or any file on internal or external Web or FTP sites,
- use browser-style query techniques to search text in both HTML and SmartSuite documents on local networks and the Internet,
- share documents with other users within a company's network.

Below we list some of the new features to this latest version of SmartSuite:

- The Ask the Expert; an online, natural language interface to help you with the tasks in Word Pro.
- Command Bars; an enhanced user interface which provides a unified system of toolbars and menus across all applications of SmartSuite 97.
- Tools which give a consistent interface to a number of graphics and drawing facilities across Word Pro, 1-2-3, and Freelance Graphics.
- The Lotus Organizer 97, specifically designed to help users manage e-mail, contact lists, calendars, to do lists, and documents.
- Improved Help features which guide you, no matter which application you are using.

The various applications within SmartSuite 97 can either be used by themselves or made to share information. This book introduces each application by itself, with sufficient detail to get you working, then discusses how to share information between them. No prior knowledge of these packages is assumed.

The book was written with the busy person in mind. It is not necessary to learn all there is to know about a subject, when reading a few selected pages can usually do the same thing quite adequately. With the help of this book, it is hoped that you will be able to come to terms with SmartSuite 97 and get the most out of your computer in terms of efficiency, productivity and enjoyment, and that you will be able to do it in the shortest, most effective and informative way.

If you would like to purchase a Companion Disc for any of the listed books by the same author(s), apart from the ones marked with an asterisk, containing the file/program listings which appear in them, then fill in the form at the back of the book and send it to Phil Oliver at the stipulated address.

ABOUT THE AUTHORS

Noel Kantaris graduated in Electrical Engineering at Bristol University and after spending three years in the Electronics Industry in London, took up a Tutorship in Physics at the University of Queensland. Research interests in Ionospheric Physics, led to the degrees of M.E. in Electronics and Ph.D. in Physics. On return to the UK, he took up a Post-Doctoral Research Fellowship in Radio Physics at the University of Leicester, and then in 1973 a lecturing position in Engineering at the Camborne School of Mines, Cornwall, (part of Exeter University), where between 1978 and 1997 he was also the CSM Computing Manager. At present he is IT Director of FFC Ltd.

Phil Oliver graduated in Mining Engineering at Camborne School of Mines in 1967 and since then has specialised in most aspects of surface mining technology, with a particular emphasis on computer related techniques. He has worked in Guyana, Canada, several Middle Eastern countries, South Africa and the United Kingdom, on such diverse projects as: the planning and management of bauxite, iron, gold and coal mines; rock excavation contracting in the UK; international mining equipment sales and international mine consulting for a major mining house in South Africa. In 1988 he took up a lecturing position at Camborne School of Mines (part of Exeter University) in Surface Mining and Management.

ACKNOWLEDGEMENTS

We would like to thank colleagues at CSM and FFC for the helpful tips and suggestions which assisted us in the writing of this book.

TRADEMARKS

Arial and **Times New Roman** are registered trademarks of The Monotype Corporation plc.

HP and LaserJet are registered trademarks of Hewlett Packard Corporation.

IBM is a registered trademark of International Business Machines, Inc.

Intel is a registered trademark of Intel Corporation.

Windows and **Windows NT** are either registered trademarks or trademarks of Microsoft Corporation.

PostScript is a registered trademark of Adobe Systems Incorporated.

TrueType is a registered trademark of Apple Corporation.

All other brand and product names used in the book are recognised as trademarks, or registered trademarks, of their respective companies.

CONTENTS

1. **PACKAGE OVERVIEW** 1
   Hardware and Software Requirements 4
   Installing SmartSuite 97 5
      Adding or Removing SmartSuite Applicat'ns 10
   The Mouse Pointers 10
   Using the Help Menu 12

2. **LOTUS WORD PRO BASICS** 17
   Starting the Program 17
      The Word Pro Screen 19
      The Status Bar 22
   Creating Word Pro Documents 24
      Entering Text 24
   Moving Around a Document 25
   Templates and Paragraph Styles 26
      Changing Paragraph Styles 26
   Document Screen Displays 27
      Changing Display Views 28
      The Special Views Feature 30
   Changing Default Options 31
      Modifying Page Layout 31
      Changing the Print Options 32
      Changing Other Default Options 33
   Saving to a File 34
      Closing a Document 36

3. **EDITING WORD PRO DOCUMENTS** 37
   Selecting Text 39
   Copying Blocks of Text 41
   Moving Blocks of Text 42
   Deleting Blocks of Text 43
   The Undo Command 43
   Finding and Changing Text 44
   Page Breaks 46
   Using the Spell Checker 47
   Using the Thesaurus 48
   Printing Documents 49

4. FORMATTING DOCUMENTS 55

- Formatting Text 55
- SmartIcons Setup 58
- Text Enhancements 60
    - Paragraph Alignment 60
    - Line and Paragraph Spacing 61
    - Indenting Text 62
    - Hanging Indents 63
    - Inserting Bullets 65
    - Inserting Date and Time 67
    - Inserting Annotations 68
- Formatting with Page Tabs 69
- Formatting with Styles 70
    - Paragraph Styles 71
- Document SmartMaster Template 73
    - Creating a SmartMaster Template 73
- Special Formatting Features 76
    - Inserting Drop Capitals 76
    - Inserting Special Characters and Symbols 77
    - Inserting Other Formatting Characters ... 78

5. DOCUMENT ENHANCEMENTS 79

- Page Numbering 79
- Using Headers and Footers 81
- Using Footnotes 83
- Using Multiple Columns on a Page 84
- Frames and Drawing 86
    - Creating a Frame 86
    - Moving a Frame 88
    - Placing Text in a Frame 91
- Importing a Graphic 92
- The Drawing Tools 93
    - Creating a Drawing 94
    - Editing a Drawing 94
    - Using Layered Drawings 95

6. USING TABLES AND GRAPHS 97
- Creating a Table 98
  - Navigating Around a Table 99
  - Changing Column Width and Row Height   100
  - Entering Expressions 101
  - Editing a Table 104
- Using the Chart Facility 106
  - Pre-defined Chart Types 109
  - Improving a Chart 111

7. THE LOTUS 1-2-3 SPREADSHEET 113
- Starting the Lotus 1-2-3 Program 113
- The Lotus 1-2-3 Screen 115
- Workbook Navigation 117
  - Moving Between Sheets 119
  - Renaming Sheets 120
  - Grouping Sheets 121
  - Selecting a Range of Cells 122
  - Shortcut Menus 122
- Viewing Multiple Workbook Sheets 123
- Entering Information 124
  - Changing Text Alignment and Fonts 126
- Saving a Workbook 128
- Opening a Workbook 129
- Exiting Lotus 1-2-3 130

8. FILLING IN A WORKSHEET 131
- Formatting Entries 132
  - Filling a Range by Example 133
  - Entering Text, Numbers and Formulae ... 134
- Using Functions 135
  - Using the AutoSum Icon 136
- Printing a Worksheet 138
  - Page Preview 140
- Enhancing a Worksheet 141
  - Header and Footer Icons and Codes 142
- 3-Dimensional Worksheets 144
  - Copying Sheets in a Workbook 144
- Linking Worksheets 146

Relative and Absolute Cell Addresses 147
Freezing Panes on Screen 149
Linking Files 150

9. SPREADSHEET CHARTS 151
Preparing for a Bar Chart 151
The Chart Command 153
    Saving and Naming Charts 156
Quick Menus 157
Customising a Chart 159
    Drawing a Multiple Bar Chart 159
    Drawing a Pie Chart 162
    Annotating a Chart 164

10. FREELANCE GRAPHICS 165
Starting the Freelance Program 165
The Freelance Screen 166
Freelance Views Tabs 167
    The Current Page Tab 168
    The Page Sorter Tab 170
    The Outliner Tab 171
    Notes Pages 172
    Adding a Clip Art Image or Diagram 173
    Adding a Drawing and Text 174
Screen Show 175
    Enhancing a Screen Show 176
Printing a Presentation 177

11. THE APPROACH DATABASE 179
Starting the Approach Program 181
Parts of the Approach Screen 183
Using Help in Approach 184
Creating a Database Application 186
    Browsing and Sorting a Database 192
    Applying a Filter to a Sort 193
Find Using a Database Form 195
Working with Data 196
    Printing a Database 198

12. RELATIONAL DATABASE DESIGN 199
Creating a Join 201
Creating a Report 203
   Searching a Report 205
Creating an Additional Database 208
Creating a Crosstab View 210

13. THE LOTUS ORGANIZER 215
Starting the Organizer Program 215
   Parts of the Organizer Screen 216
The Toolbox Icons 218
Using Help in Organizer 219
Viewing Appointments 220
   Entering Appointments 222
   Printing Information 225
Other Organizer Facilities 226
   To Do List 227
   Address 229
   Calls 231
   Planner 232
   Notepad 233
   Anniversary 234

14. SHARING INFORMATION 235
Copying or Moving Information 236
   Source File Available without Application . 236
   Source File and Application Available 238
Object Linking and Embedding 239
   Example of Linking or Embedding 240
   Linking or Embedding Selected Information 242
   Linking or Embedding into Approach 243
   Editing an Embedded Object 244
Hypertext Links 245
Mail Merging Lists 247
   Getting an Address List 249
   Creating an Address List in Word Pro 250
   Selecting a Letter to Merge 252

APPENDIX - GLOSSARY OF TERMS 255
INDEX 269

1. PACKAGE OVERVIEW

Lotus SmartSuite 97 is a collection of powerful, full-featured, programs with the same look and feel that work together as if they were a single program. SmartSuite 97 was specifically designed to allow you to work with your information data, either by yourself or in collaboration with others, quickly and efficiently.

Lotus SmartSuite 97 includes Word Pro, Lotus 1-2-3, Approach, Freelance Graphics, Organizer, and ScreenCam. With the package you also get SmartCenter 97, a desktop information and command centre. All SmartSuite 97 applications have a built-in consistency which makes them easier to use. For example, they all have standardised toolbars and consistent menus, commands, and dialogue boxes. Once you become familiar with one application, it is far easier to learn and use the others.

All SmartSuite 97 components are 32-bit applications and include new Internet features. For example, you can access news, weather, and Stock Market quotes directly from SmartCenter. Furthermore, SmartSuite is the only office suite that is uniquely designed to take advantage of Lotus Notes. Finally, all SmartSuite 97 applications support LotusScript, a cross-platform, BASIC-compatible, object-oriented programming language which allows you to write macros to carry out repetitive work or build your own custom solutions.

Lotus 1-2-3 and Organizer are the most updated applications in SmartSuite 97, with the largest number of new features, followed by some extras in Word Pro.

The Lotus 1-2-3 97 spreadsheet includes the following new features:

- Team Consolidate - a powerful new feature for spreadsheet collaboration that facilitates group planning, forecasting, and budgeting. Data can easily be requested from colleagues and consolidated into one summary workbook.

- Outlining - allows you to automatically expand and collapse groups of rows and columns, and to view or print only the required data.
- HTML Publishing - allows you to publish 1-2-3 tables directly to the Internet in HTML (Hypertext Markup Language) format.
- Full Object Linking and Embedding (OLE 2.0) Support - both as a container and server. It will also support drag & drop and automation support for cross application scripting.
- AutoTotal - detects the word 'Total' and automatically analyses the spreadsheet data and totals the figures in the column or row.
- InfoBox - a common tool for inspecting, formatting or changing the properties of any object in 1-2-3. With the InfoBox, all editing is 'live' with formatting changes being displayed in the spreadsheet as you make them.

The personal information manager Lotus Organizer 97 includes the following new features:

- Drag and drop appointments - as the duration of each appointment is represented graphically in the Calendar section, it can be changed via drag and drop.
- Call rollover - calls logged in your Calls section as tasks, will automatically roll over to the next day, to prevent missed calls, until they are marked as completed.
- Embed objects in Notepad - the Notepad section is a Notepad container. You can link or embed OLE objects such as workbooks, documents, presentations, and metafiles, on Notepad pages for in-place editing of this information. You can manage related information by organising it in the Notepad section that automatically generates a table of contents.

- TAPI support - resulting in easier and more streamlined autodialling capabilities for the Calls and Address sections.
- Rich text formatting - the Notepad section supports rich text formatting so you can format your text with bold, italic, underline, font size and type, as well as colour.
- Links to the Internet - allows access to the Lotus customer support on the Web, and the ability to launch a web page from the Organizer Notepad.
- Support for international addresses - allows the printing of address labels and envelopes of 25 international address formats.

The word processor Lotus Word Pro 97 includes the following new features:
- Cross references - allows you to reference a page, section number, or title in a document from another location within that document.
- Drop caps - allows you to insert a drop capital (large first letter of a paragraph) into your document.
- Internet capability - allows Web authoring, the use of HTML SmartMaster templates, automating the process for creating links, previewing HTML documents in a Browser, publishing HTML documents as Web pages, and viewing source code.
- Linked frames - allows the creation of documents where text automatically flows from one frame to the next when in edit mode.
- Booklet printing - allows you to set up and print a document so that pages can be folded in half and stapled together.
- Watermarks - allows you to use default or your own pictures as a background graphic.

Hardware and Software Requirements

If SmartSuite 97 is already installed on your computer, you can safely skip this and the next section of this chapter.

To install and use SmartSuite 97 you need an IBM-compatible PC equipped with Intel's 80486 (or higher) processor. In addition, you need the following:

- Windows 95, or Windows NT 4.0, or later versions of these programs.

- Random access memory (RAM): 8MB; 12MB recommended when running multiple programs in Windows 95, or 16MB with Windows NT.

- Hard disc space required for SmartSuite 97: 82MB for installing the minimum features of all the SmartSuite applications, 133MB for the default installation, and 220MB for installing all the features, tours, templates, sample files, and Help.

- Video adapter: VGA or higher resolution. If you are using Freelance Graphics, you will need a 256-colour video adapter.

- Pointing device: Microsoft Mouse or compatible.

Realistically, to run SmartSuite 97 with reasonable sized applications, you will need a Pentium PC with at least 16MB of RAM. To run SmartSuite 97 from a network, you must also have a network compatible with your Windows operating environment.

If you are connected to the Internet, you can take advantage of the Lotus SmartCenter, or one of the SmartSuite 97 applications to open files on an FTP (File Transfer Protocol) or Web server. You can also save a document to an FTP server. Finally, you can use Word Pro's advanced editing and formatting features to compile a message which is then sent as an attachment using your current e-mail program.

Installing SmartSuite 97

Installing SmartSuite on your computer's hard disc is made very easy with the use of the Install program, which even configures SmartSuite automatically to take advantage of the computer's hardware. One of Install's functions is to convert compressed SmartSuite files from the distribution discs, or CD-ROM, prior to copying them onto your hard disc.

Note: If you are using a virus detection utility, disable it before running Install, as it might conflict with it.

To install SmartSuite, click the **Start** button and select the **Run** command, as shown below left. Selecting this command, opens the **Run** dialogue box, as shown below right.

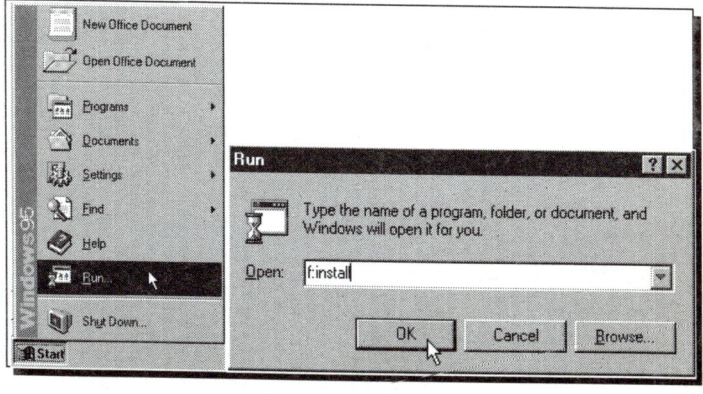

If the application was distributed on diskettes, insert disc #1 into the A: drive and type in the **Command Line** box:

```
a:\install
```

In our case we used the CD-ROM in the F: drive. Clicking the **OK** button, starts the installation of SmartSuite 97.

If you have a CD-ROM drive and have inserted the SmartSuite CD in it prior of starting Windows, then the Autorun program starts automatically and displays the following screen:

Clicking the black rectangle with the word 'Lotus' in it (pointed to above) lets you see the SmartSuite Tour.

We suggest that you first look at the SmartSuite Tour before proceeding with the installation.

Starting the Install program either from the Autorun screen or using the **Start, Run** command, causes SmartSuite to verify your authenticity, and to allow you to specify the drive and main folder under which you want to install the package. In our case, we selected drive E: and called the main folder 'Lotus'. The program then displays the following screen, so that you know where the various program files are being placed.

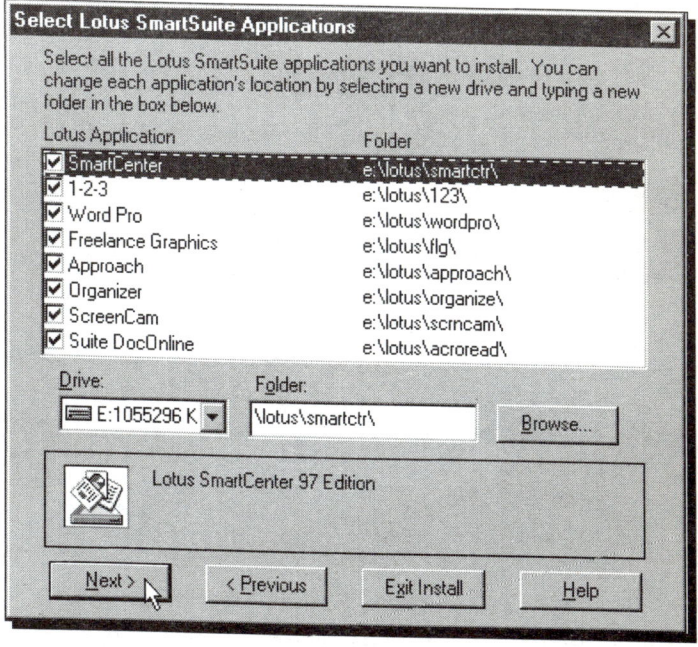

Next, you are asked to select one of three types of installation; default, minimum, or custom. The default installation includes the typical SmartSuite features used by most people. The minimum installation is primarily for laptop users with minimum disc space, while the custom installation allows you to make your own choice of the features you want to use.

Having selected the type of installation, the Install program displays additional dialogue boxes prompting you to:

- Select whether you want previous Windows 3.x versions of SmartSuite removed from your hard disc, which will free disc space,.
- Select the program folder for the application shortcuts.

Next, installation begins and the following dialogue box is displayed:

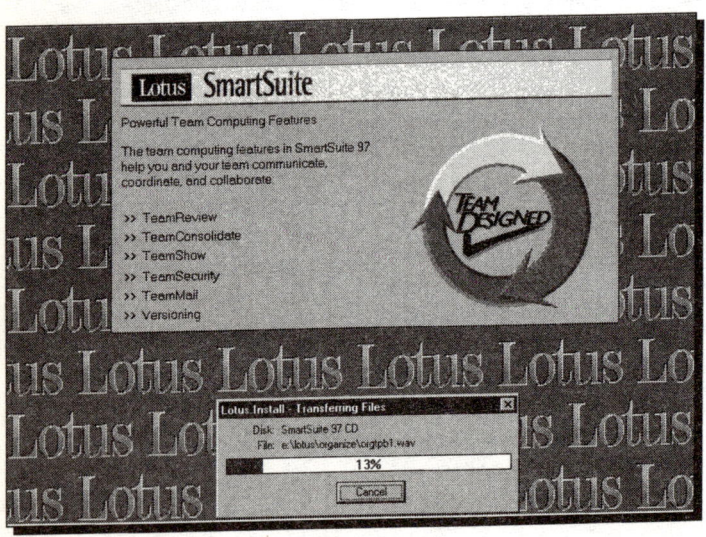

Throughout installation, the Install program informs you on what it is doing and what percentage of the total file transfer it has covered, as shown at the lower half of the above screen dump. Once installation is complete, and if you have a modem, you are asked to register SmartSuite electronically with appropriate forms being displayed on your screen for your use.

Finally, two tools are installed automatically. These are:

- The **SuiteStart** on the right-hand corner of the Windows Task bar, as shown below.

Pointing and left-clicking once on any of the above icons, starts the selected SmartSuite application. To find out which icon goes with which application, let the mouse pointer rest on an icon and the application name will appear on a small banner.

- The **SmartCenter** that appears at the top of your screen, as shown below.

Unfortunately, Lotus SmartCenter 97 loads automatically on switching on your PC. It also (most annoying) attempts to connect you to the Internet, whether you want to or not! SmartCenter takes over your PC, as Lotus assumes that you are only using their software! To OutSmart SmartCenter and stop this from happening, do the following:

- Click on the **Start** button and select **Setting, Taskbar**.

- Click the Start Menu Programs tab of the displayed **Taskbar Properties** dialogue box and click the **Remove** button.

- Double-click the **StartUp** folder within the **Programs** folder.

- Select 'Lotus SmartCenter 97' shortcut and click the **Remove** button then the **Close** button.

- Open the Recycle Bin and drag the Lotus SmartCenter shortcut icon onto your desktop.

To load SmartCenter, when you want it, double-click its shortcut icon on your desktop.

Adding or Removing SmartSuite Applications:

To add or remove a SmartSuite application:

- Close all open applications.
- Point to **Settings** on the Windows **Start** menu, and click Control Panel. Next, double-click the Add/Remove Programs icon, shown here, and then click the Install/Uninstall tab.

- From the list, choose 'Lotus SmartSuite 97'.
- Click the **Add/Remove** button.
- Select the application you want to remove and click **OK**.

The Mouse Pointers

In SmartSuite applications, as with all other graphical based programs, the use of a mouse makes many operations both easier and more fun to carry out.

SmartSuite makes use of the mouse pointers available in Windows, some of the most common of which are illustrated below. When a SmartSuite application is initially started up the first you will see is the hourglass, which turns into an upward pointing hollow arrow once the individual application screen appears on your display. In Word Pro, if you are pointing in the text area, then it turns into an I beam. Other shapes depend on the type of work you are doing at the time. The most common pointers are:

 The hourglass which displays when you are waiting while performing a function.

◪ The arrow which appears when the pointer is placed over menus, scrolling bars, and buttons.

I   The I-beam which appears when you enter or edit data.

⇩   The vertical pointer which appears when pointing over a column in a Word Pro table and used to select the column.

⇨   The horizontal pointer which appears when pointing at a row in a Word Pro table and used to select the row.

◄║►   The vertical split arrow which appears when pointing over the area separating two columns and used to size a column in 1-2-3.

≑   The horizontal split arrow which appears when pointing over the area separating two rows and used to size a row in 1-2-3.

+   The frame cross which you drag to create a frame, or the draw pointer which appears when you are drawing freehand.

✋   The hand which appears when you crop an entire drawing or are about to grab the contents of a cell in order to move them.

✊   The clenched hand that appears when you are actually moving the contents of a cell.

✥   The large 4-headed arrow which appears after choosing the **Control, Move/Size** command(s) for moving or sizing windows.

↔   The double arrows which appear when over the border of a window, used to drag the side and alter the size of the window.

☝   The Help hand which appears in the Help windows, and is used to access 'hypertext' type links.

Using the Help Menu

An easy way to get help in a SmartSuite application is to left-click the **Help** menu option at the top of the application window, and select the **Help Topics** option of the displayed submenu, shown here. This displays the dialogue box shown below.

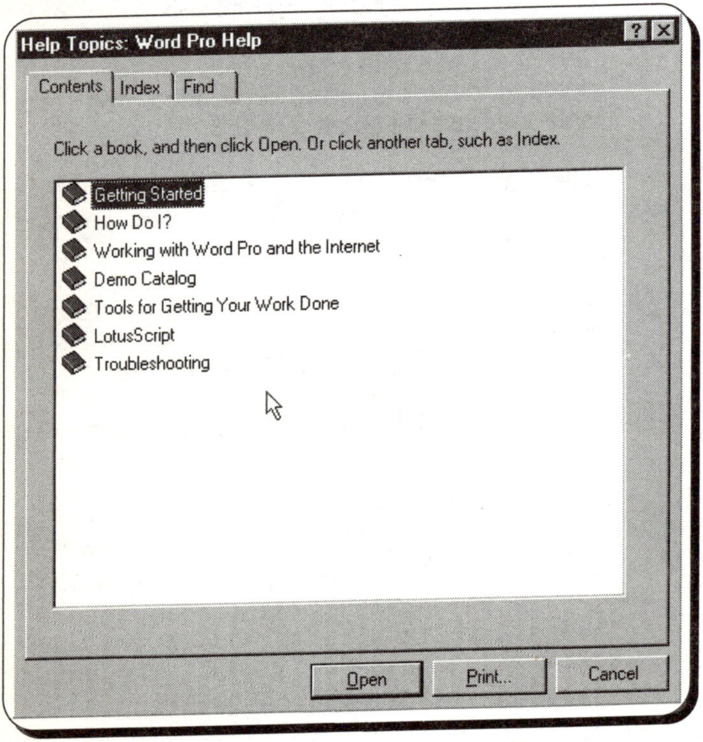

You can either view selected information on the screen or print it on paper.

Left-clicking the Find tab, displays a dialogue box with three areas for typing, selecting and displaying information, as shown below.

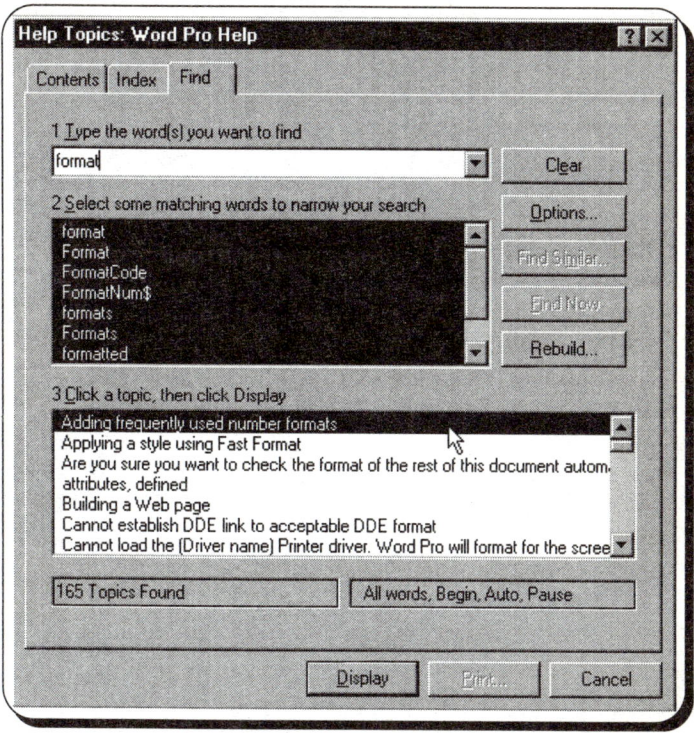

Typing, for example, the words *format* in the first 'Find' box, causes a list of related topics to appear automatically in the second 'Select' box. Selection of one or more matching words from the displayed list narrows down the selection of topics appearing in the third 'Display' box.

Finally, selecting a topic from the third display box by left-clicking it to highlight it and pressing the **Display** button at the bottom of the dialogue box, produces information on your selection.

If the topic you want to select is not visible within the display area of the third box, use the scroll bar to get to it.

As an exercise, click the Index tab of the **Help Topics** dialogue box and type the word 'open' in the first text box. Immediately the topic 'Opening' appears in the second text box, as shown below.

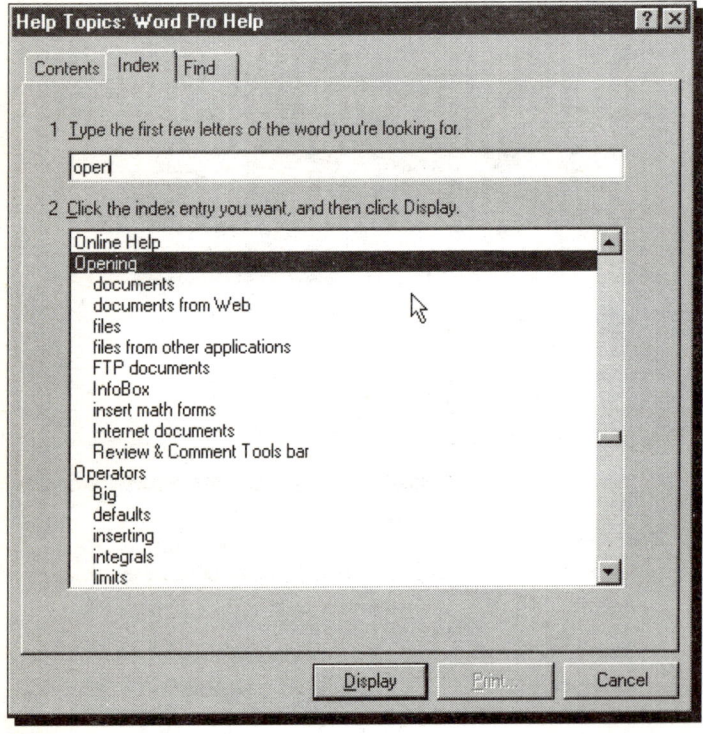

Next, double-click on the item of your choice to display all you need to know about it. Similar searches can be carried out from other SmartSuite 97 applications.

The above help screen can also be displayed by simply pressing the **F1** function key.

Another way of getting help is to use the **Ask the Expert** option from the **Help** sub-menu which adds the following Ask the Expert Toolbar to your document.

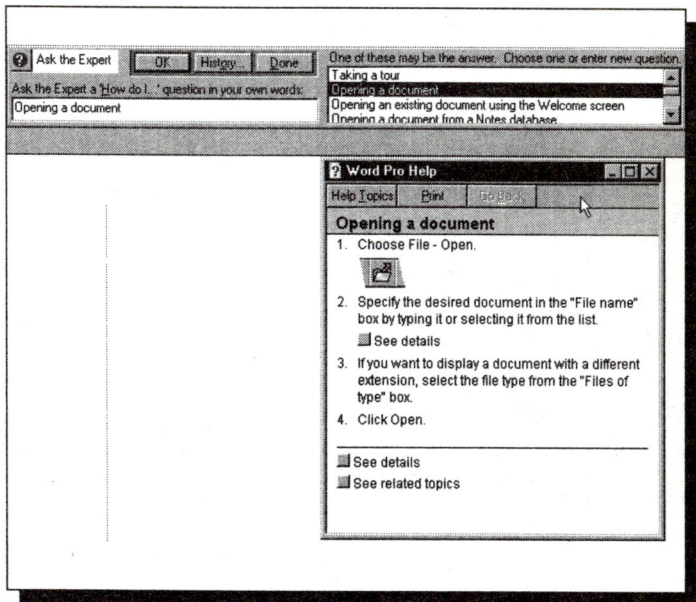

Typing a request, such as 'opening a document' in the 'How do I ...' text box displays a list of related topics to the right of it. Selecting one of these topics and pressing the '?' on the left of the new toolbar displays relevant information on the selected topic. To remove the **Ask the Expert** help screen, simply click the **Done** button.

Some dialogue boxes in SmartSuite applications display a '?' button (for an example, see the **Help Topics** dialogue boxes) as shown below.

Clicking this button changes the mouse pointer from its usual inclined arrow shape to the 'What's this?' shape, as shown below.

Pointing to an object in the dialogue box or window and clicking, gives additional information. To illustrate this, apply the procedure to the 'First' find box of the **Help Topics** dialogue box, as shown below.

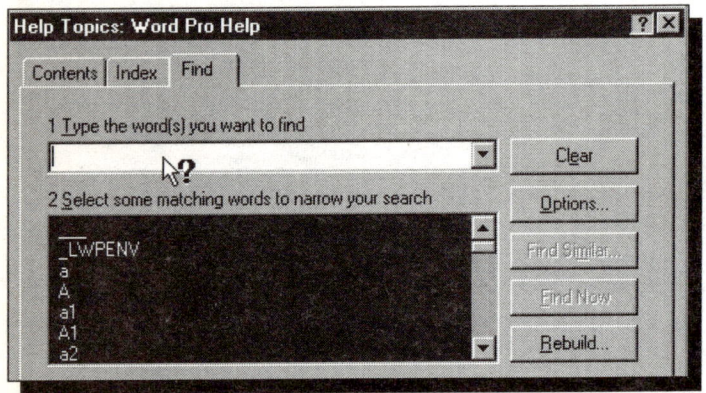

Clicking the left mouse button displays the following additional information.

> Provides a space for you to type the word(s) or phrase you want to find in the Help topics. You can type a few characters and use the word list below to see if any words match what you type.
>
> If you want to specify more than one word, separate them with a space. If you specify uppercase characters, then only words that are uppercase will be found. However, if you specify lowercase characters, both upper and lowercase words will be found.
>
> To change the search options, click Options.

2. LOTUS WORD PRO BASICS

Starting the Program

Word Pro 97 is started in Windows either by clicking the **Start** button then selecting **Programs, Lotus SmartSuite** and clicking on the 'Lotus Word Pro 97' icon on the cascade menu, as shown below,

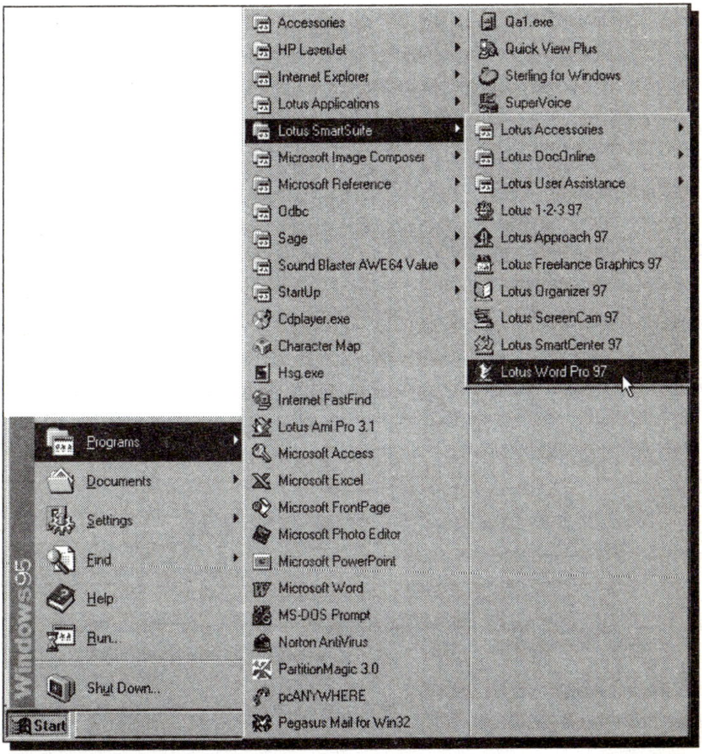

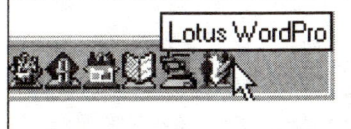 or by clicking the Word Pro 97 icon on the Task Bar, shown to the left.

In either case, Word Pro 97 starts to load and after the 'Welcoming' screen, the following dialogue box is displayed.

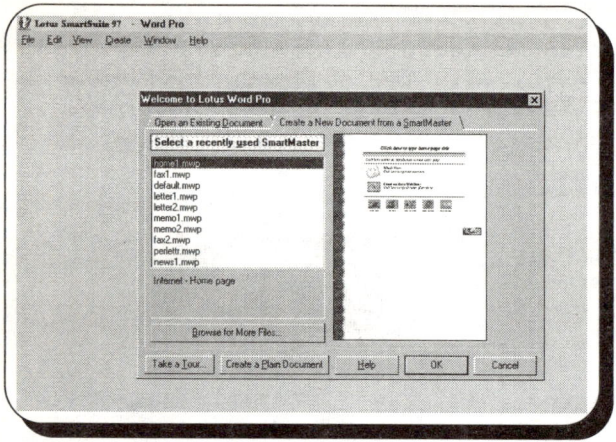

As you can see, Word Pro offers you the possibility of using one of its SmartMasters when the appropriate tab is pressed, as shown above, or select a document to open when the Open an Existing Document tab is clicked, as shown below.

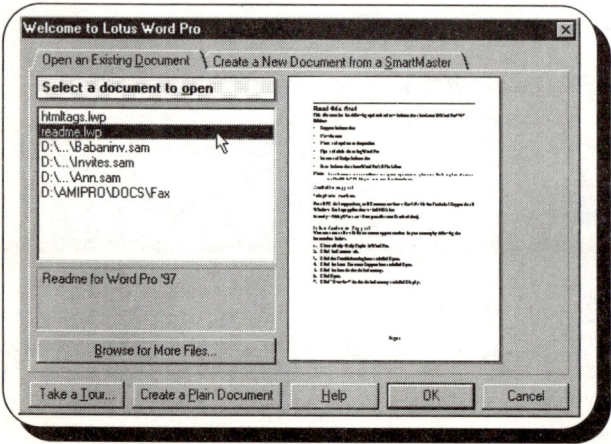

Note that from either of these two screens of the **Welcoming** dialogue box you can select to **Browse for More Files**, **Take a Tour** (you need the distribution CD in the CD-ROM drive for this option), or **Create a Plain Document**.

If you have used a previous version of Word Pro or Ami Pro, we strongly suggest that you first open the **readme.lwp** document. In it you will find information relating to customer support, new features in Word Pro 97, and more importantly, all about the new Word Pro file format and backward compatibility, and what you should do if you use both Word Pro and Ami Pro at the same time. Do spend sometime reading this document; it is important.

The Word Pro Screen:

The opening 'blank' screen of Word Pro 97 is shown below.

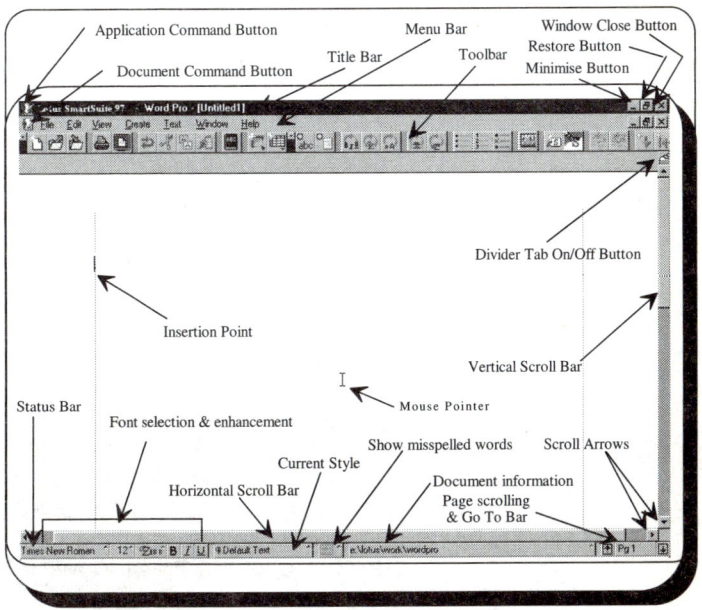

It is perhaps worth spending some time looking at the various parts that make up this screen. Word Pro follows the usual Windows conventions and if you are familiar with these you can skip through this section. Otherwise a few minutes might be well spent here.

The window as shown takes up the full screen area available. If you click on the application restore button, the top one of the two restore buttons at the top right of the screen, you can make Word show in a smaller window. This can be useful when you are running several applications at the same time and you want to transfer between them with the mouse.

Note that the Word Pro window, which in this case displays an empty document with the title 'Untitled1', has a solid 'Title bar', indicating that it is the active application window. Although multiple windows can be displayed simultaneously, you can only enter data into the active window (which will always be displayed on top). Title bars of non active windows appear a lighter shade than that of the active one.

The Word Pro screen is divided into several areas which have the following functions:

Area	*Function*
Command Buttons	Clicking on the top command button, (see upper-left corner of the Word Pro window), displays a pull-down menu which can be used to control the program window. It includes commands for restoring, moving, sizing, maximising, minimising, and closing the window. The lower command button controls the current document window in the same manner.

Title Bar	The bar at the top of a window which displays the application name and the name of the current document.
Minimise Button	When clicked on, this button minimises a document to an icon, or the application to the Windows Taskbar.
Restore Button	When clicked on, this button restores the active window to the position and size that was occupied before it was maximised. The restore button is then replaced by a Maximise button, as shown here, which is used to set the window to full screen size.
Close Button	The extreme top right button that you click to close a window.
Menu Bar	The bar below the Title bar which allows you to choose from several menu options. Clicking on a menu item displays the pull-down menu associated with that item.
Toolbar	The bar below the Menu bar which contains buttons that give you mouse click access to the functions most often used in the program. These are grouped according to function.
Divider Tabs Button	The button you click to see all related documents that make up the current document.

Insertion Pointer	The pointer used to specify the place of text insertion.
Scroll Bars	The areas on the screen (extreme right and bottom of each window) that contain scroll boxes in vertical and horizontal bars. Clicking on these bars allows you to control the part of a document which is visible on the screen.
Scroll Arrows	The arrowheads at each end of each scroll bar which you click to scroll the screen up and down one line, or left and right 10% of the screen, at a time.

The Status Bar:

The Status bar always appear at the bottom of the Word Pro screen. It provides current information relating to your document and lets you change settings such as text fonts, sizes, and attributes.

The first three boxes on the Status bar, shown to the left, are the Font box, the Size box, and the Colour box which show which font, size and colour of characters are currently being used. Following these boxes are the three buttons which allow you to change the attributes of a font to bold, italic or underlined.

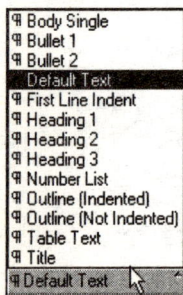

Next comes the Style box which displays the current text or object style being used. Clicking on the Style box displays a list of available styles, shown here, for specific divisions within a document, such as headings, paragraphs, objects, etc. Styles can be created from scratch or by modifying existing ones.

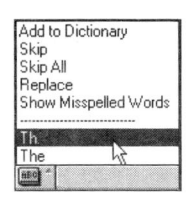

To the right of the Style box you will find the Show Misspelled Words box which lights up when the cursor rests on a misspelled word. Clicking on the box displays a list of possible corrections, as shown here.

Next in line on the Status bar comes the Document Information box which when clicked lists information relevant to the open document. This lists the time and date the document was created, in which folder it is to be found, who created it, and what version of the document is displayed.

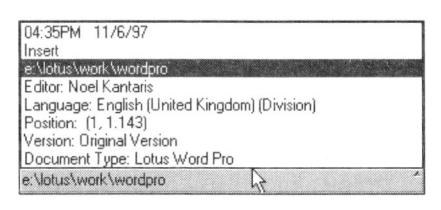

Finally, the Page Scrolling buttons are to be found at the extreme right of the Status bar. Clicking on the downward arrow scrolls the display to the next page, while clicking the upward arrow scrolls the display to the previous page. Clicking on the actual page number, opens up the **Go To** dialogue box, as shown below, in which you can specify either the page number or the document part to go to.

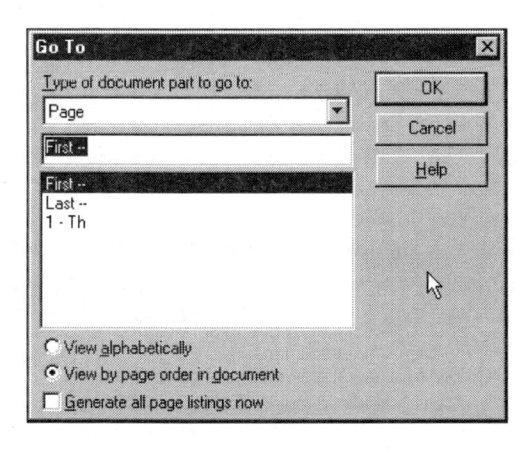

23

Creating Word Pro Documents

When the program is first used, all Word Pro's features default to those shown on page 19, provided you chose to create a plain document. It is quite possible to use Word Pro in this mode, without changing any main settings, but obviously it is possible to customise the package to your exact needs, as we shall see later.

Entering Text:

In order to illustrate some of Word Pro's capabilities, you need to have a short text at hand. We suggest you type the memo displayed below into a new document. At this stage, don't worry if the length of the lines below differ from those on your display.

As you type in text, any time you want to force a new line, or paragraph, just press <Enter>. While typing within a paragraph, Word Pro sorts out line lengths automatically (known as 'word wrap'), without you having to press any keys to move to a new line. If you make a mistake while typing, press the <BkSp> key enough times to erase the mistake and start again.

MEMO TO PC USERS

Networked Computers

The microcomputers in the Data Processing room are a mixture of IBM compatible PCs with either 486 or Pentium processors. They all have 3.5" floppy drives of 1.44MB capacity, and some also have CD-ROM drives. The PCs are connected to various printers via a network; the Laser printers available giving best output.

The computer you are using will have at least an 1,200MB capacity hard disc on which a number of software programs, including the latest version of Windows, have been installed. To make life easier, the hard disc is highly structured with each program installed in a separate folder (directory).

Moving Around a Document

You can move the cursor around a document with the mouse or with the normal direction keys, and with the key combinations listed below.

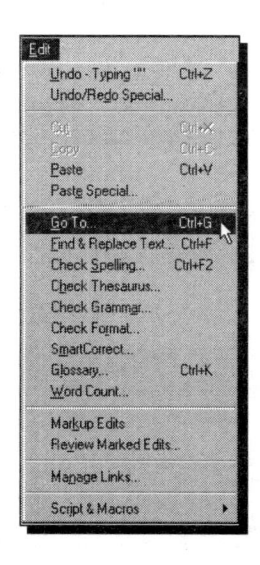

To move	*Press*
Left one character	←
Right one character	→
Up one line	↑
Down one line	↓
Left one word	Ctrl+←
Right one word	Ctrl+→
To beginning of line	Home
To end of line	End
To paragraph beginning	Ctrl+↑
To paragraph end	Ctrl+↓
Up one screen	PgUp
Down one screen	PgDn
To top of previous page	Ctrl+PgUp
To top of next page	Ctrl+PgDn
To beginning of file	Ctrl+Home
To end of file	Ctrl+End

In a multi-page document, click the **Go To** button on the Status bar, or use the **Edit**, **Go To** command (or <Ctrl+G>), shown here, to jump to a specified page number.

Obviously, you need to become familiar with the above methods of moving the cursor around a document, particularly if you are not using a mouse and you spot an error in a document which needs to be corrected, which is the subject of the latter half of this chapter.

Templates and Paragraph Styles

When you start Word Pro for the first time, you are offered the option of creating and formatting a new document using a SmartMaster template (style sheet), or to create a plain document. The plain document option uses the **default.mwp** SmartMaster template.

If you choose to use a SmartMaster template, as you highlight the template, a preview displays the format of each selection so you can see it before you click **OK**. A SmartMaster template contains, both the document page settings and a set of formatting instructions which can be applied to text (paragraph styles).

Changing Paragraph Styles:

To change the style of a paragraph, do the following:

- Place the cursor (insertion pointer) on the paragraph in question, say the title line
- Left click the Style Status button, and select the **Heading 1** style.

The selected paragraph reformats instantly in bold, and in Arial Black typeface of point size 14.

With the cursor in the second line of text, select **Heading 2** which reformats the line in Arial 12. Your memo should now look presentable, as shown below.

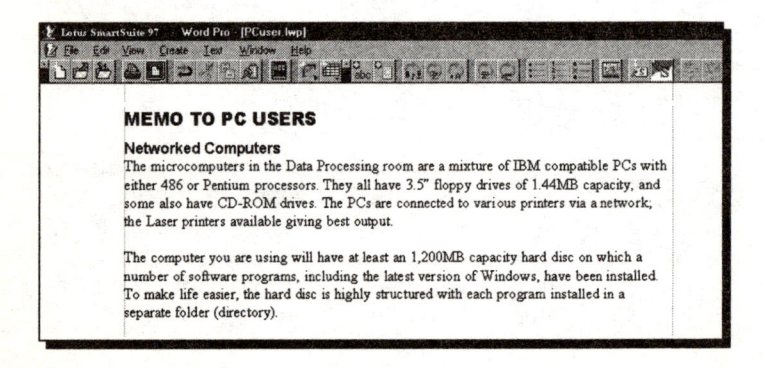

MEMO TO PC USERS

Networked Computers
The microcomputers in the Data Processing room are a mixture of IBM compatible PCs with either 486 or Pentium processors. They all have 3.5" floppy drives of 1.44MB capacity, and some also have CD-ROM drives. The PCs are connected to various printers via a network; the Laser printers available giving best output.

The computer you are using will have at least an 1,200MB capacity hard disc on which a number of software programs, including the latest version of Windows, have been installed. To make life easier, the hard disc is highly structured with each program installed in a separate folder (directory).

Document Screen Displays

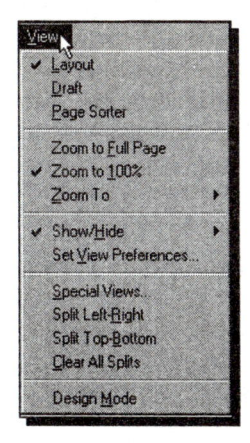

Word Pro provides three main display modes, **Layout**, **Draft**, and **Page Sorter**. In addition, each of these display modes can be displayed at several different Zoom enlargements and Split levels. You control all these viewing options with the **View** sub-menu, shown here, and when a document is displayed you can switch freely between them. When first loaded the screen displays in **Layout** mode.

The various display options have the following effect:

Layout   Provides a WYSIWYG (what you see is what you get) view of a document. The text displays in the typefaces and point sizes you specify, and with the selected attributes (alignment, indention, spacing, etc.). All text frames, tables, graphics, headers, footers, and footnotes appear on the screen as they will in the final printed document.

Draft   A view that optimises the layout of a document to make reading easier. For example, text wraps to fit the window, rather than the way it would actually print. All text frames, tables and graphics are displayed left aligned on the page. Headers, footers, and footnotes do not display in this mode.

Page Sorter A view used to organise your document into groups of pages based on where the page breaks, divisions, or sections are to be found in the document. If you want to move a group of pages, collapse the pages into a page range - shown with a small hollow '+' sign at the top of the group, as shown here, before dragging them to the new location. When you drag and drop pages in Page Sorter view, Word Pro moves all the pages in a grouping.

Zoom Allows you to change the viewing magnification factor from full page, through 100%, to the **Zoom To** sub-menu options shown here.

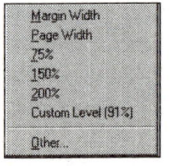

Changing Display Views:

The **View** sub-menu provides two options for changing what you see on your display. You can, for example, select **Show/Hide** which enables you to display a variety of options. Left-clicking an option activates that option and places a tick against it. To deselect an option, left-click it once more. If you choose the **Clean Screen** option, Word Pro presents you with a clean, uncluttered screen; the Menu bar, Toolbar icons, Scroll bars, and Status bar are removed. To return to the usual screen, click the icon, shown here, which appears at the bottom-right of your screen when in this mode.

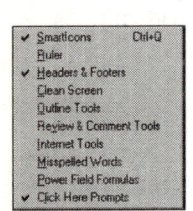

The second option for changing what you see on the screen is the **Set View Preferences** which displays the following dialogue box:

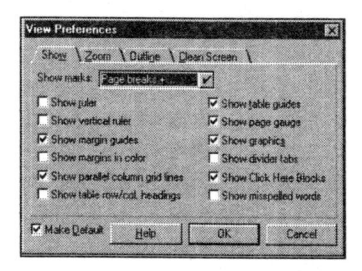

From here you have precise control on what you want to **Show** on screen, what the **Zoom** options should be, whether to show your document in **Outline** mode, and what precisely should be displayed when you choose **Clean Screen**. All these options are reached by clicking the appropriate tab of the **View Preferences** dialogue box.

For example, clicking the **Outline** tab and left-clicking the **Show outline** box, pointed to below, while the PCusers document is on screen, provides a collapsible view of the document, which enables you to see its organisation at a glance. Below, we show both the **View Preferences** dialogue box open, and the effect it has on your document after you press the **OK** button. To return your document to its former view, deselect the **Show outline** box.

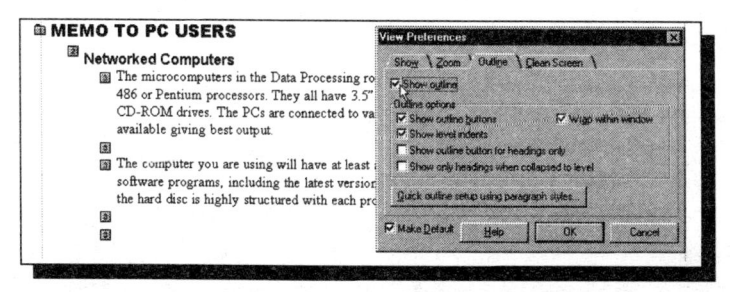

Using this mode, allows you to quickly rearrange large sections of text. Some people like to create an outline of their document first, consisting of all the headings, then to sort out the document structure and finally fill in the text.

The Special Views Feature:

The **View, Special Views** option, opens up the following dialogue box:

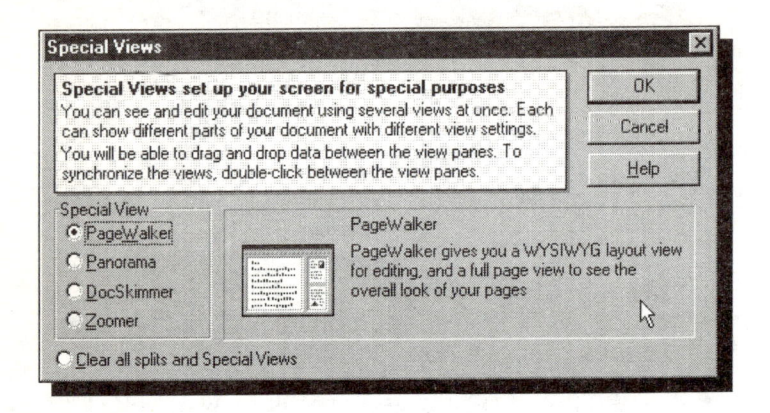

This allows you to look at a document from several perspectives by dividing one document into several panes (windows). When you choose a special view, Word Pro removes all the splits you previously created.

Word Pro provides four pre-defined Special Views which allow you to edit a document. These are: PageWalker, Panorama, DocSkimmer, and Zoomer. As you select each one of these views on the above dialogue box, an explanation of its function is given at the bottom right of the dialogue box. You can adjust the sizes of the panes using the mouse and, as you do so, Word Pro automatically resizes them so they all fit in your workspace.

The various Special Views can be used to see information in different parts of the same document so that it facilitates editing of the document. One of these editing techniques involves the use of drag and drop (more about this in the next chapter), which requires different parts of your document to be displayed on your screen simultaneously in two different panes.

Changing Default Options

Modifying Page Layout:

To change the standard page margins for your entire document from the cursor position onward, or for selected text (more about this later), use the **File, Document Properties, Page** command to display the following dialogue box.

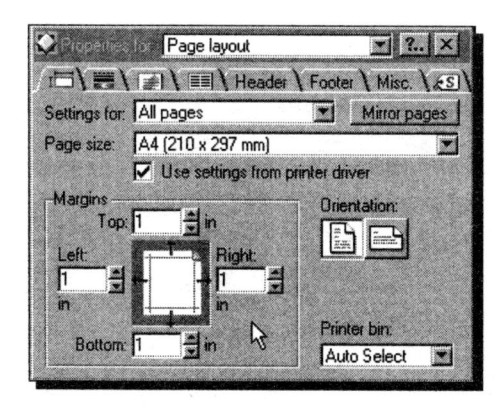

From here, amongst other options, you can set the paper size, the page margins, and the orientation of the print-out on the page. The other tabs on the dialogue box (from left to right) allow you to do the following:

- Change the colour, pattern, and line style
- Apply a watermark to the pages of your document
- Format a document in newspaper columns
- Change the header margin settings
- Change the footer margin settings
- Change the tab settings, alignment and grid
- Apply a style to a current selection.

Changing the Print Options:

To change the default print options from those set during installation, select the **File, Print** command which opens the following dialogue box:

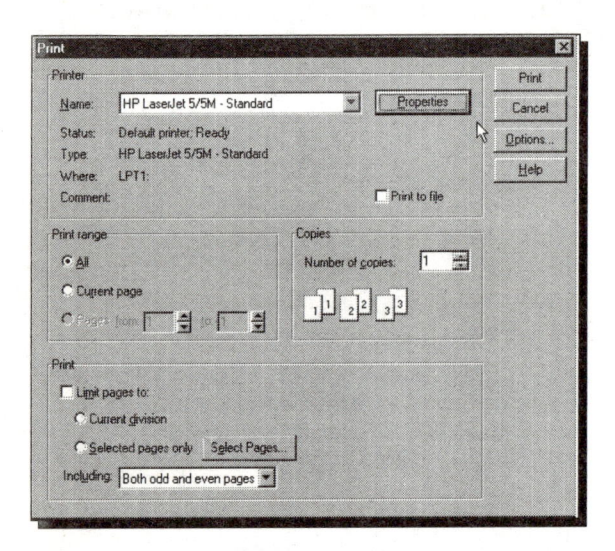

From here you can do the following:

- Change the default printer by clicking the down arrow to the right of the **Name** box and selecting an alternative printer, provided such a printer has been installed previously with the use of the **Start, Settings, Printers** command.

- Click the **Options** button on the **Print** dialogue box to change the print order, print without pictures, or print as a booklet, to mention but a few of the available options, in the **Print Options** dialogue box.

- Click the **Properties** button on the **Print** dialogue box to change the paper size, print orientation, paper source, print quality, and other options.

Changing Other Default Options:

You can also change the default options available to you in Word Pro 97, by selecting the **File, Word Properties** command. Using the displayed dialogue box shown below, you can, amongst other things, do the following:

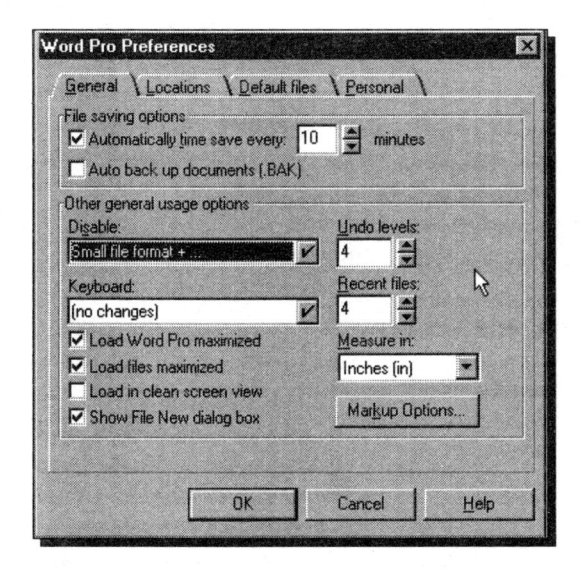

- Change the file saving options, the number of undo operations, the number of recent files shown at the bottom of the **File** sub-menu, change the units of measurement, and other display options.
- Change the location of your documents.
- Change the default plain document SmartMaster, dictionary, glossary, and file open types.
- Change personal details.

Saving to a File

To save a document to a file on disc, use either of the following two commands:

- **File, Save** (or click the Save toolbar icon) which is used when a document has previously been saved to disc in a named file; using this command automatically saves your work under the existing filename without prompting you.

- **File, Save As** command which is used when you want to save your document with a different name from the one you gave it already.

Using the **File, Save As** command (or the very first time you use the **File, Save** command when a document has no name), causes the following dialogue box to appear on your screen:

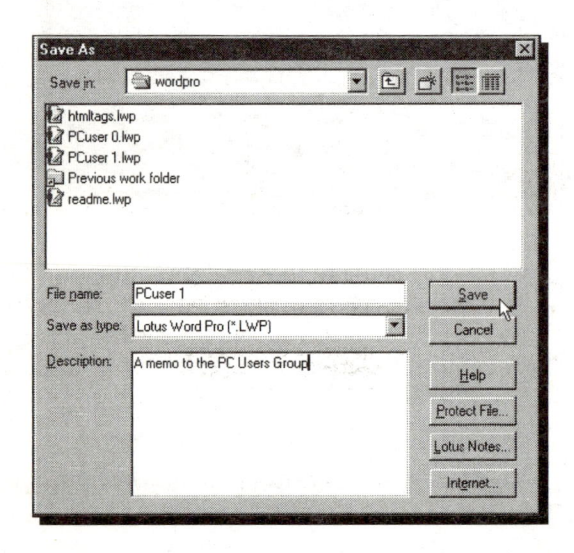

Type a name, such as **PCuser 1** in the **File name** box, and an optional description in the **Description** box, and press the **Save** button.

Filenames cannot include any of the following keyboard characters: /, \, >, <, *, ?, ", |, :, or ;. Word Pro adds the file extension **.lwp** automatically and uses it to identify its documents.

You can select a drive other than the default one, by clicking the down arrow against the **Save in** box, as shown below.

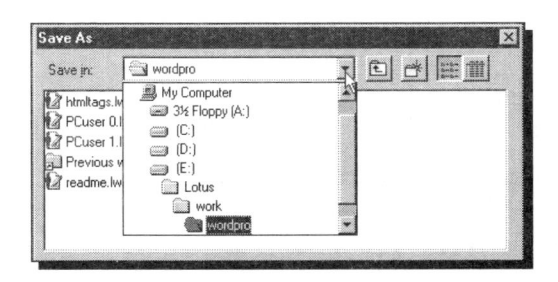

You can also select a folder in which to save your work by clicking the Up One Level button, shown below,

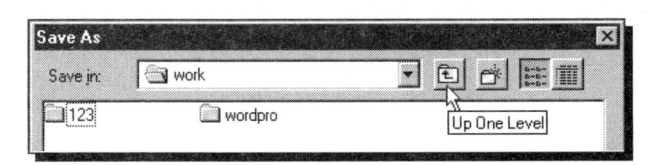

or, if you do not have a suitably named folder, create one using the Create New Folder button, shown below.

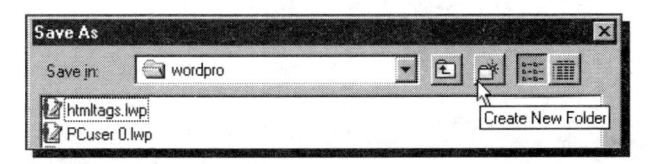

By clicking the **Save as type** button at the bottom of the **Save As** dialogue box, you can save a document in a variety of other formats, including text, rich text, Microsoft Word, WordPerfect, and HTML.

Closing a Document:

There are several ways to close a document in Word Pro. Once you have saved it you can click its 'X' close button, or double-click on the Document Control button at the left end of the menu bar; you would usually use these when you have several files open together.

If you want to close the current document, and then open a new one or a different one, do the following:

- Click its '**x**' close button, or choose **File, Close** to close the current document (remove it from your computer's memory) before using either

- **File, New Document** (or clicking 🗋) to create a new file, or

- **File, Open** (or clicking 📂) to use an existing file.

If the document (or file) has changed since the last time it was saved, you will be given the option to save it before it is removed from memory.

If a document is not closed before a new document is opened, then both documents will be held in memory, but only one will be the current document. To find out which documents are held in memory, use the **Window** command to reveal the following menu:

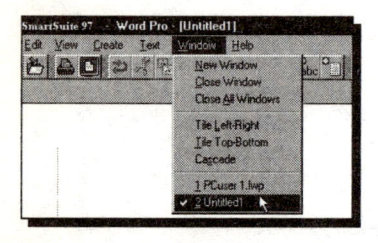

In this case, the second document in the list is the current document, and to make another document the current one, either type the document number, or point at its name and click the left mouse button.

To close a document which is not the current document, use the **Window** command, make it current, and close it with one of the above methods.

3. EDITING WORD PRO DOCUMENTS

It will not be long, when using Word Pro, before you will need to edit your document. One of the first things you should do is to left-click on the Spell Check button on the Status bar, shown here, and click the Show Misspelled Words option.

Next, use the **File, New Document** command (or click 🗋) to create a new file, and type the words 'Computors are fun to usr', exactly as misspelled here.

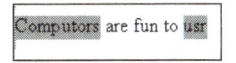

What should appear on your screen is shown here, but with misspelled words appearing highlighted in blue. In addition, whenever the cursor is placed on a misspelled word, the Spell Check button on the Status bar changes from grey to blue. Placing the cursor on the first word and left-clicking the Spell Check button, displays:

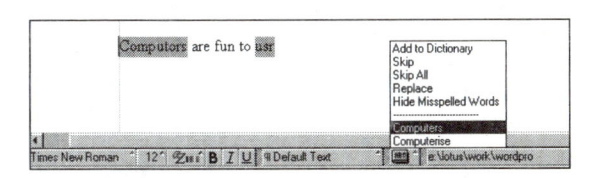

To correct this word, left-click on 'Computers'. Next, place the cursor on 'usr' and click the Spell Check button once more to display:

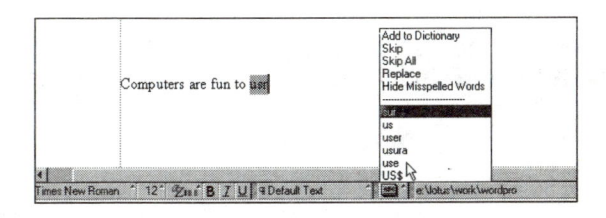

As before, to correct this word, left-click the word 'use'.

This is possibly the most time-saving enhancement in the Spell Checker (to be discussed later).

Other editing options could include deleting unwanted words or adding extra text in the document. All these operations are very easy to carry out. For small deletions, such as letters or words, the easiest method to adopt is the use of the <Del> or <BkSp> keys.

With the <Del> key, position the cursor on the left of the first letter you want to delete and press <Del>; the letter is deleted and the following text moves one space to the left. With the <BkSp> key, position the cursor immediately to the right of the character to be deleted and press <BkSp>; the cursor moves one space to the left pulling the rest of the line with it and overwriting the character to be deleted.

Word processing is usually carried out in the insert mode. Any characters typed will be inserted at the cursor location (insertion point) and the following text will be pushed to the right, and down, to make room. To insert blank lines in your text, place the cursor at the beginning of the line where the blank line is needed and press <Enter>. To remove the blank line, position the cursor on it and press <Del>.

When larger scale editing is needed you have several alternatives. You could first 'select' the text to be altered (to be discussed next), then use the **Cut**, **Copy** and **Paste** operations available in the **Edit** sub-menu, or click on Toolbar button alternatives, shown here.

Another method of copying or moving text is to use the 'drag and drop' facility (also to be discussed shortly).

Selecting Text

The procedure in Word Pro, as with most Windows based applications, is first to select the text to be altered before any operation, such as formatting or editing, can be carried out on it. Selected text is highlighted on the screen. This can be carried out in two main ways:

A. Using the keyboard, to select:

- A block of text.

    Position the cursor on the first character to be selected and hold down the <Shift> key while using the arrow keys to highlight the required text, then release the <Shift> key.

- From the present cursor position to the end of the line.

    Use <Shift+End>.

- From the present cursor position to the beginning of the line.

    Use <Shift+Home>.

- From the present cursor position to the end of a document division.

    Use <Shift+Ctrl+End>.

- From the present cursor position to the beginning of a document division.

    Use <Shift+Ctrl+Home>.

B. With the mouse, to select:

- A block of text.

  Press down the left mouse button at the beginning of the block and while holding it pressed, drag the cursor across the block so that the desired text is highlighted, then release the mouse button.

- A word.

  Double-click within the word, or see below.

To select a word, a sentence, a paragraph, or an entire division of a document, place the cursor on the desired word, sentence, paragraph, or document division and click the right mouse button. This opens up a menu of options, shown to the left. Highlighting **Select**, gives you four further choices, and left-clicking one of these highlights the appropriate block of text.

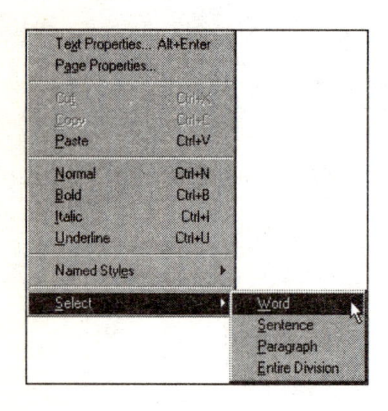

Copying Blocks of Text

Once text has been selected (highlighted) it can be copied to another location in your present document, to another Word Pro document, or to another Windows application, via the clipboard. As with most of the editing and formatting operations there are several alternative ways of doing this, as follows:

- Using the **Edit, Copy** command sequence from the menu, to copy the selected text to the Windows clipboard, moving the cursor to the start of where you want the copied text to be placed, and using the **Edit, Paste** command.

- Using the quick key combinations, <Ctrl+Ins> (or <Ctrl+C>) to copy and <Shift+Ins> (or <Ctrl+V>) to paste.

- Use the 'Copy to clipboard' and 'Paste from clipboard' Toolbar buttons; this method can only be used with a mouse.

  To copy the same text again to another location, or to any open document window or application, move the cursor to the new location and paste it there with any of these methods. It is stored on the clipboard until it is replaced by the next Cut, or Copy operation.

Selected text can be copied by the 'drag and drop' technique. This requires you to:

(a) select the text you want to copy by highlighting it, (b) press the <Ctrl> key and place the mouse pointer over the selected text so that it changes to a small hand, (c) press and hold the left mouse button so that the small hand closes and a plus '+' sign appears to indicate that you are copying, (d) drag the text to the place where you want to copy it, and (e) release the mouse button.

The copied text will insert itself where placed, even if the overstrike mode is in operation. Text copied by this method is not placed on the clipboard, so multiple copies are not possible, as with the other methods.

Moving Blocks of Text

Selected text can be moved to any location in the same document by either of the following:

- Using the **Edit, Cut,** command or <Shift+Del> (or <Ctrl+X>).
- Clicking the 'Cut to clipboard' Toolbar button, shown here.

Next, move the cursor to the required new location and use either of the following procedures:

- The **Edit, Paste** command.
- Any other paste actions as described previously.

The moved text will be placed at the cursor location and will force any existing text to make room for it. This operation can be cancelled by simply pressing <Esc>. Once moved, multiple copies of the same text can be produced by other **Paste** operations.

Selected text can be moved by the 'drag and drop' technique. This requires you to (a) select the text you want to copy by highlighting it, (b) place the mouse pointer over the selected text so that it changes to a small hand, (c) press and hold the left mouse button so that the small hand closes, (d) drag the text to the place where you want to move it, and (e) release the mouse button.

Deleting Blocks of Text

When text is 'cut' it is removed from the document, but placed on the clipboard until further text is either copied or cut. With Word Pro any selected text can be deleted by pressing **Edit**, **Cut**, or clicking the 'Cut to clipboard' Toolbar button, shown here, or by pressing the <Del>, or <BkSp> keys. However, using **Edit, Cut**, allows you to use the **Edit, Paste** command, but using the <Del> or <BkSp> keys, does not.

The Undo Command

As text is lost with the delete command, you should use it with caution, but if you do make a mistake all is not lost as long as you act promptly. The **Edit, Undo** command or <Ctrl+Z> (or <Alt+BkSp>) reverses your most recent editing or formatting commands.

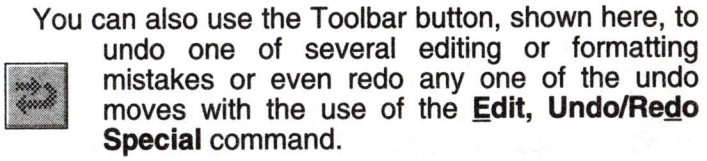

You can also use the Toolbar button, shown here, to undo one of several editing or formatting mistakes or even redo any one of the undo moves with the use of the **Edit, Undo/Redo Special** command.

Undo does not reverse any action once editing changes have been saved to file. Only editing done since the last save can be reversed.

Finding and Changing Text

Word Pro allows you to search for specifically selected text, or character combinations. To do this use the **Find & Replace Text** option (<Ctrl+F>) from the **Edit** command sub-menu which opens the following dialogue box:

Typing a word in the **Fi<u>n</u>d** box only and clicking the **Find** button, will highlight each occurrence of the supplied text in turn so that you can carry out some action on it, such as change its font or appearance. You have the choice of searching for 'Whole words only', 'Words starting with', 'Words ending with', or 'Words containing', as shown to the left.

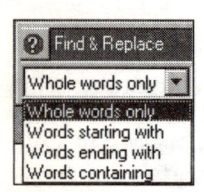

If you type a replacement text in the **Replace <u>w</u>ith** box (in a long article you might, for example, decide to replace every occurrence of the word 'microcomputers' with the word 'PCs'), then you will be given the option to either **Replace A<u>l</u>l** occurrences of the selected word, **Replace** each occurrence of the word as it is found, or skip to the next word without replacing it by clicking the **Find** button once more. Use of the arrow buttons prior to clicking the **Find** button can change the search direction through the document.

Clicking the **O<u>p</u>tions** button on the **Find & Replace** dialogue box, displays the dialogue box shown on the next page. From here, you can choose to **Look in** the 'Entire document' or the 'Current division', select the Find Options and Replace Options, including the ability to select and replace font names, font sizes and text attributes by clicking the character button on the dialogue box shown here.

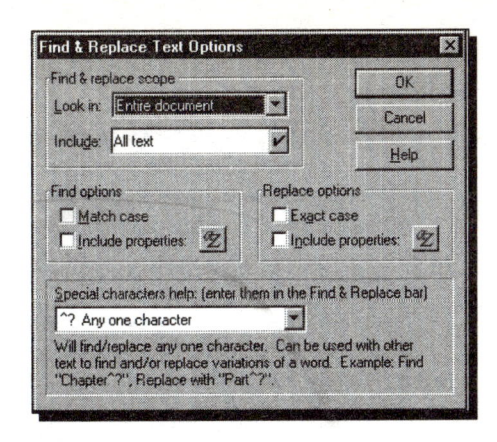

Finally, by clicking the down-arrow against the **Special characters help** box, you can search for, and replace, various specified document marks, tabs, returns, etc., or a combination of both these and text.

Below we list only two of the many key combinations of special characters that could be typed into the **Find** box.

Type	*To find or replace*
^?	Any single character within a pattern. For example, searching for nec^?, when 'Whole words only' is selected, will find neck. If 'Words containing' had been selected, then words such as neck, connect, etc., would be found.
	Any string of characters. For example, searching for c^*r, when 'Whole words only' is selected, will find such words as cellar, chillier, and character. If 'Words containing' had been selected, then words such as cellar, chillier, character, etc., would be found.

45

Page Breaks

The program automatically inserts a 'soft' page break in a document when a page of typed text is full. To force a manual, or hard page break, either type <Ctrl+Enter> or use the **Text, Insert Page Break** command. This places a small image of a new page together with a series of dots across the page to indicate the page break, as shown below.

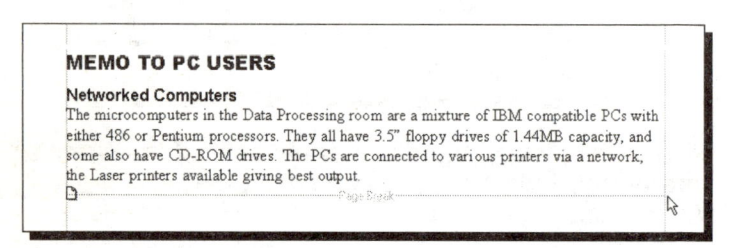

> **MEMO TO PC USERS**
>
> **Networked Computers**
>
> The microcomputers in the Data Processing room are a mixture of IBM compatible PCs with either 486 or Pentium processors. They all have 3.5" floppy drives of 1.44MB capacity, and some also have CD-ROM drives. The PCs are connected to various printers via a network; the Laser printers available giving best output.
> ....Page Break................................

The above page break marks are only shown if the option to display them is set in the **View Preferences** dialogue box shown below. Use the **View, Set View Preferences** command to see and set this and other view preferences.

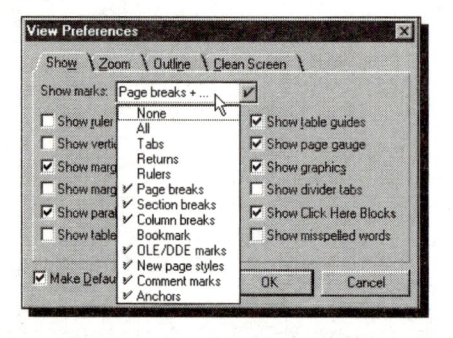

To delete manual page breaks place the cursor just in front of the new page small image and press the <Del> key. Soft page breaks which are automatically entered by the program at the end of pages, cannot be deleted.

Using the Spell Checker

The package has a very comprehensive spell checker which whenever it thinks it has found a misspelled word, highlights it, provided you have activated this facility, as discussed at the beginning of this chapter.

However, the spell checker can also be used in another way. To spell check your document, either click the 'Check spelling' button on the Toolbar, shown here, or use the **Edit, Check Spelling** command (or <Ctrl+F2) to display:

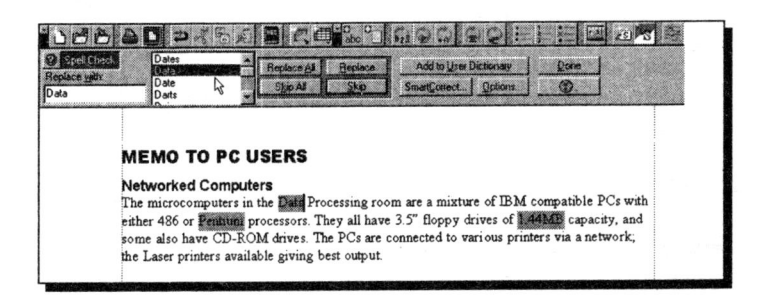

Word Pro starts spell checking from the point of insertion onwards. If you want to spell check the whole document, move the insertion pointer to the beginning of the document before starting. If you want to check a word or paragraph only, highlight it first. Once Word Pro has found a misspelled word, you can either correct it in the document, or select a word from the suggestions list and press the **Replace** button.

The main dictionary cannot be edited. However, the system has the ability to add specialised and personal dictionaries with the facility to customise and edit them. If you are using a personal dictionary and choose **Add to User Dictionary**, the specified word is added to that dictionary. To add an alternative dictionary, or correct a word in the user dictionary, click the **Options** button to display the following dialogue box.

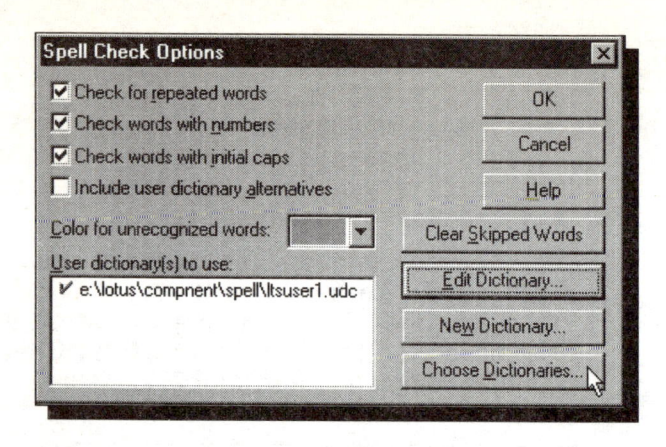

From here, amongst other options, you can add a new dictionary, choose the dictionaries to be used, and change the colour of unrecognised words.

Using the Thesaurus

If you are not sure of the meaning of a word, or you want to use an alternative word in your document, then the thesaurus is an indispensable tool. To use the thesaurus, simply place the cursor on the word you want to look up and select **Edit, Check Thesaurus** command. As long as the word is recognised, the following dialogue box will open.

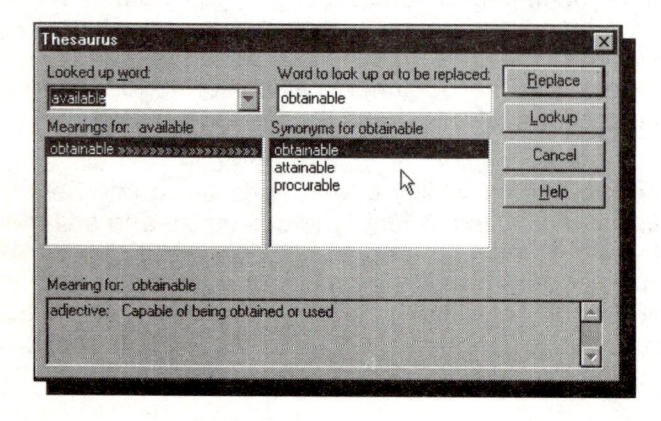

This is a very powerful tool. You can see information about an item in the **Meanings** list, or you can look up a synonym in the **Synonym** list. To change the word in the **Word to look up or to be replaced** text box, select an offered word in either the **Meanings** or the **Synonym** list box, or type a word directly into the **Word to be replace**d text box, and press the **Replace** button.

You can use the thesaurus like a simple dictionary by typing any word into the **Word to be replace**d text box and clicking the **Lookup** button. If the word is recognised, lists of its meaning variations and synonyms will be displayed. Pressing the **Replace** button will place the word into the document.

Printing Documents

When Windows was first installed on your computer the printers you intend to use should have been selected, and the SETUP program should have installed the appropriate printer drivers. Before printing for the first time, you would be wise to ensure that your printer is in fact properly installed. To do this, click on **Start** then select **Settings** and click the **Printers** menu option to open the **Printers** dialogue box shown below.

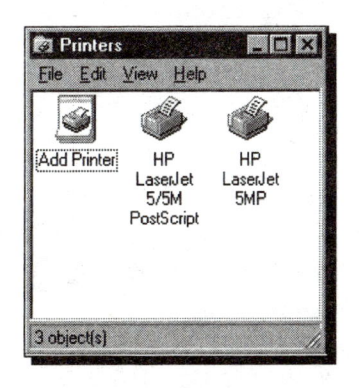

Here, two printer drivers have been installed; an HP LaserJet 5MP as the 'default' printer and an HP LaserJet 5/5M PostScript. In our case these are both configured to output to a printer via the parallel port LPT1. This refers to the socket at the back of your PC which is connected to your printer. LPT1 is short for Line Printer No. 1. Your selections may, obviously, not be the same.

Next, return to or reactivate Word Pro and, if the document you want to print is not in memory, either click the 'Open' button on the Toolbar, or use the **File, Open** command, to display the **Open** dialogue box shown below.

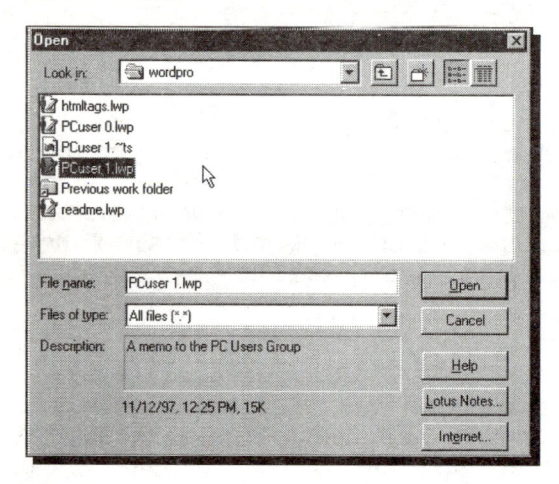

Use this dialogue box to locate the file (document) you want to print, which will be found on the drive and folder (directory) on which you saved it originally. To locate such a folder, it might be necessary to use the 'Up One Level' button on the dialogue box, shown here. Once the folder has been located, select it and click the **Open** button (or double-click its name), to load it into your computer's memory.

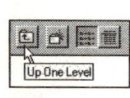

To print your document, do one of the following:

- Click the Print icon on the Toolbar, shown here, which prints the document using the current defaults.

- Use the **File, Print** command which opens the **Print** dialogue box, shown on the next page.

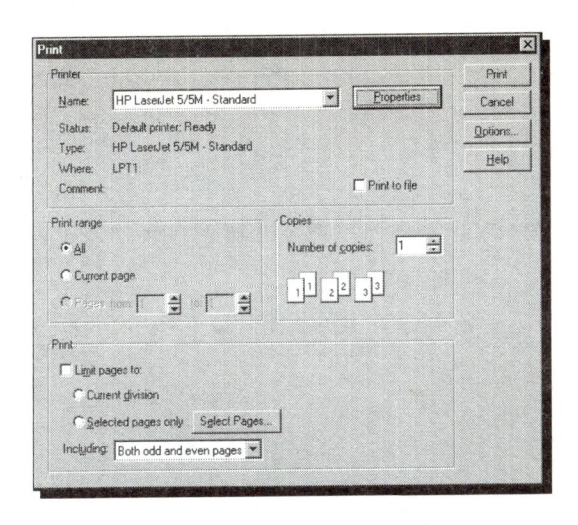

From here you could change the selected printer by clicking the down arrow against the **Name** box which displays the available printers on your system, or print to file. The other settings in the **Print** dialogue box allow you to select the number of copies, and which contiguous pages, you want printed. You can also select to print the current page (the one appearing on your screen at the time), limit the printed pages to the division of the document, or select groups of pages. To achieve the latter, click the **Select Pages** button at the bottom of the screen which displays the following dialogue box:

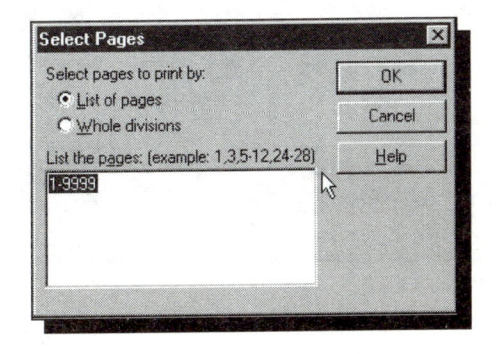

Clicking the **Properties** button at the top of the **Print** dialogue box, displays the **Properties** dialogue box for the selected printer, shown below, which allows you to select the paper size, orientation needed, paper source, etc.

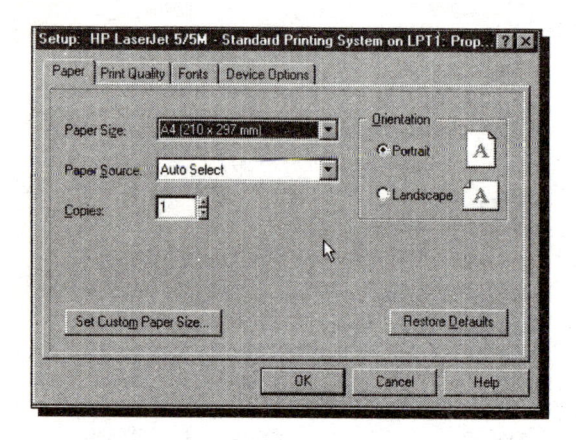

The **Options** button at the top right of the **Print** dialogue box, gives you access to some more advanced print options, shown below, such as printing in reverse order, with crop marks, with pictures, with comments (annotations), on printed forms, or as a booklet.

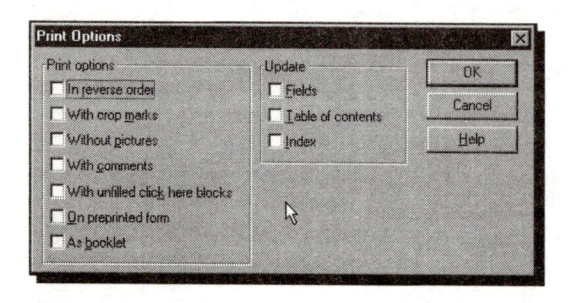

Clicking the **OK** button on these various dialogue boxes, causes Word Pro to accept your selections and return you to the **Print** dialogue box. Selecting **OK** on this dialogue box, sends print output from Word Pro to your selection, either the printer connected to your computer, or to an encoded file on disc. Selecting **Cancel** on any dialogue box, aborts the selections made on that dialogue box.

Do remember that, whenever you change printers, the appearance of your document may change, as Word Pro uses the fonts available with the newly selected printer. This can affect the line lengths, which in turn will affect both the tabulation and pagination of your document.

Before printing to paper, click the 'Zoom to full page' icon on the Toolbar, shown here, or use the **View, Zoom to Full Page** command, to see how much of your document will fit on your selected page size. This depends very much on the chosen font. Thus, this print preview option allows you to see the layout of the final printed page, as shown below, which can save a few trees and equally important to you, a lot of frustration and wear and tear on your printer.

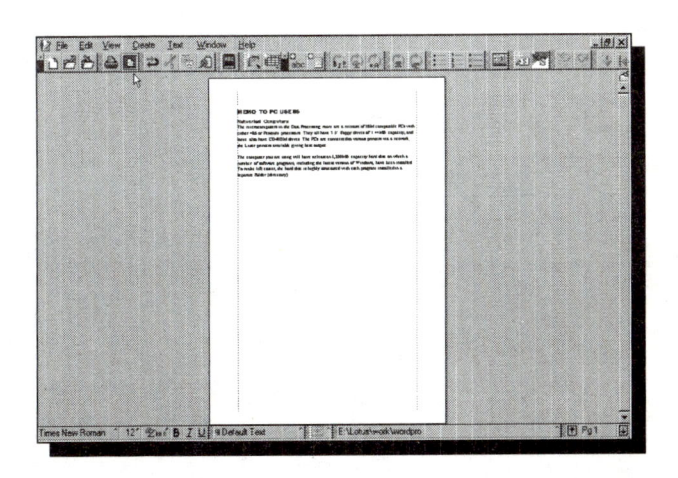

To return to your working document from a print preview display, click the Zoom to full page icon once more, or select the **View, Zoom to 100%** command.

Other enhancements of your document, such as selection of fonts, formatting of text, and pagination, will be discussed in the next chapter.

4. FORMATTING DOCUMENTS

Formatting involves the appearance of individual words or even characters, the line spacing and alignment of paragraphs, and the overall page layout of the entire document. These functions are carried out in Word Pro in several different ways.

Primary text formatting in a document is included in 'Paragraph Styles', while the page layout is included in a document's SmartMaster (template). Within any document, however, you can override paragraph style formats by applying text formatting and enhancements manually to selected text. To immediately cancel manual formatting, select the text and use the

Edit, Undo

command, or (<Ctrl+Z>). The selected text reverts to its original format.

In the long term, you can cancel manual formatting by selecting the text and using the <Ctrl+N> key stroke. The text then reverts to its style format.

Formatting Text

As discussed in Chapter 2 (page 22), formatting information on a specific paragraph of a document appears on the first three boxes of the Status Bar, when the cursor is placed anywhere within that paragraph.

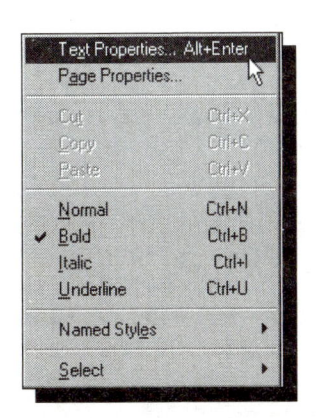

To see more detailed formatting information on specific text, either right-click it and choose the option **Text Properties**, as shown to the left, or select the text and use the **Text, Text Properties** command.

Using either of these commands or clicking the Text properties icon on the Text Toolbar, will display the **Text Info** box, shown below.

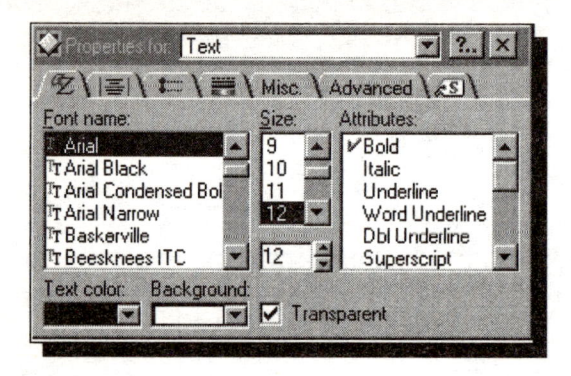

If you use TrueType fonts, which are automatically installed when you set up Windows, Word Pro uses the same font to display text on the screen and to print on paper. The screen fonts provide a very close approximation of printed characters. TrueType font names are preceded by T in the **Font name** box on the **Info** box.

If you use non-TrueType fonts, then use a screen font that matches your printer font. If a matching font is not available, or if your printer driver does not provide screen font information, Windows chooses the screen font that most closely resembles the printer font.

Originally, the title of the **PCuser 1** memo, was typed in 14 point size Arial Black typeface, while the subtitle was typed in 12 point size Arial. The main text was typed in 12 point size Times New Roman.

To change this memo into what appears on the screen dump displayed on the next page, first select the title of the memo and format it to bold, italics, 18 point size Arial and centre it between the margins, then select the subtitle and format it to bold, 14 point size Arial.

All of this formatting can be achieved by using the buttons on the Status Bar, by using the **Info** box, or by using the various options under the **T̲ext** menu option.

MEMO TO PC USERS

Networked Computers

The microcomputers in the Data Processing room are a mixture of IBM compatible PCs with either 486 or Pentium processors. They all have 3.5" floppy drives of 1.44MB capacity, and some also have CD-ROM drives. The PCs are connected to various printers via a network; the Laser printers available giving best output.

The computer you are using will have at least an 1,200MB capacity hard disc on which a number of software programs, including the latest version of Windows, have been installed. To make life easier, the hard disc is highly structured with each program installed in a separate folder (directory).

If you can't access these font styles, it will probably be because your printer does not support them, in which case you will need to select other fonts that are supported.

Save the result under the new filename **PCuser 2**, using the **F̲ile, Save A̲s** command.

In Word Pro all manual formatting, including the selection of font, point size, style, text and background colour attributes (bold, italic, single or double underline, strike-through, super/subscript, hidden and capitals), are carried out by first selecting the text and then executing the formatting command.

The easiest way of activating some of the most common formatting commands is with the SmartIcons, to be found on the Toolbar, and buttons on the Status Bar, shown below. Next comes the **Text Info** box, discussed on the previous page, and last but not least, the choice of an appropriate sub-menu option from the **T̲ext** menu.

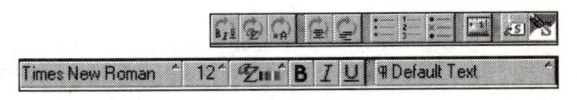

Yet another method is by using quick keys, some of which are listed below:

To Format	*Type*
Bold	Ctrl+B
Italic	Ctrl+I
Underline	Ctrl+U

There are quick keys to do almost anything, but the problem is remembering them! The ones listed here are the most useful and the easiest to remember.

SmartIcons Setup

The default icons appearing on the Toolbar are grouped into two sections, each having a distinctive function. The first grouping (set) is called 'Universal', while the second is called 'Text' and each is preceded by a spacer with a small down-arrow at the top half of it. Moving the mouse pointer on such a spacer, changes it into a small hand, as shown below.

It is, in fact, possible to move individual Toolbar sets to any part of the screen, and also change the SmartIcons contained in each. As an example, we will move the 'Text' set and place it below the 'Universal' set. To do so, move the mouse pointer on to the spacer preceding the set you want to move, and when it changes into a small hand press the left mouse button and drag it below its current position. Releasing the mouse button, fixes the bar into its new position, as shown below.

As you can see, six additional icons have appeared on the 'Text' Toolbar, which previously could not be seen.

Word Pro comes with 20 SmartIcon sets to choose from. After using the program for a while you will know which icons you use most and would best be placed together. To include a new icon on a set, use either the **File, User Setup, SmartIcons Setup** command, or right-click on a displayed set and select **SmartIcon Setup** from the drop-down menu, to display the following dialogue box.

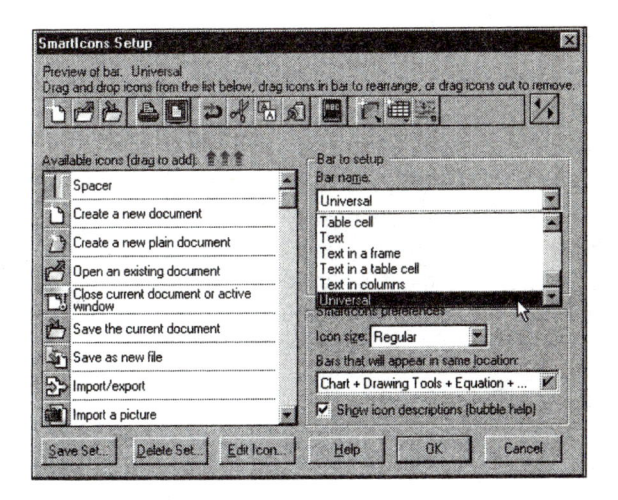

From here, you can select the **Bar name** to select a set which is then displayed at the top of the dialogue box. To add a SmartIcon to your chosen set, simply locate the icon and drag it to the position you want it to appear on the set, then click the **Save Set** button followed by the **OK** button.

As an example, locate the 'Thesaurus' SmartIcon, and add it to the 'Universal' set next to the Check Spelling icon, as follows:

This will make it easier for you to use the thesaurus.

Text Enhancements

Word Pro defines a paragraph as any text which is followed by a paragraph mark, which is created by pressing the <Enter> key. So single line titles, as well as long typed text, can form paragraphs.

The paragraph symbol, shown here, is only visible in your text if you have selected it from the Text Toolbar set. Selecting it once more, removes the symbols signifying tabs and returns from your screen. Such symbols are only displayed to help you and do not appear on printed documents.

Paragraph Alignment:

You can align a paragraph at the left margin (the default), the right margin, centred between both margins, or justified between both margins (as in this book). Like most operations there are several ways to perform alignment in Word Pro. These are:

- Using the 'Cycle through alignment options' button on the Text Toolbar set.
- Using keyboard short cuts, when available.
- Using the **Text**, **Alignment** menu command or the Alignment tab on the **Text Info** box.

The table below describes the buttons on the **Text Info** box and their keystroke shortcuts.

Buttons on Formatting bar	Paragraph Alignment	Keystrokes
	Left	<Ctrl+L>
	Centred	<Ctrl+E>
	Right	<Ctrl+R>
	Justified	<Ctrl+J>

Line and Paragraph Spacing:

The **Text Info** box can also be used to change the displayed (and printed) line and paragraph spacing to a variety of options (single-line, 1½-line, double-line, etc.). To change the line and/or paragraph spacing, do the following:

- Select the paragraph(s) or place the insertion point at the desired location
- Right-click and choose **Te<u>x</u>t Properties** or click the Text Properties icon
- Click the Alignment (2nd) tab to display:

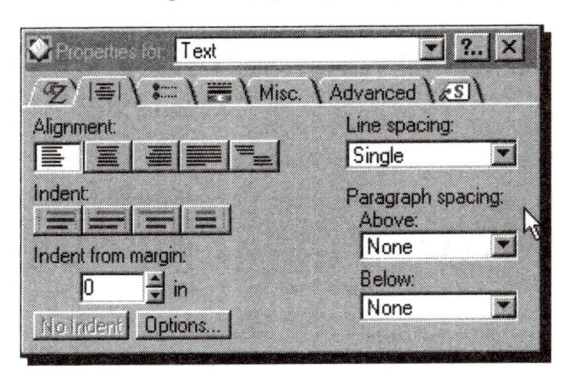

- Select the desired **Line spacing** and/or **Paragraph spacing**

Formatting can take place either before or after the text is entered. If formatting is selected first, then text will type in the chosen format until a further formatting command is given. If, on the other hand, you choose to enter text and then format it afterwards, you must first select the text to be formatted, then carry out the formatting.

Word Pro gives you the choice of 4 types of units to work with, inches, centimetres, points or picas. These can be selected by using the **<u>F</u>ile, <u>U</u>ser Setup, Word Pro <u>P</u>references** command.

Below, we show the **Word Pro Preferences** dialogue box with the General tab selected. Clicking the down arrow against the **Measure in:** box, lists the available units of measurement, as shown.

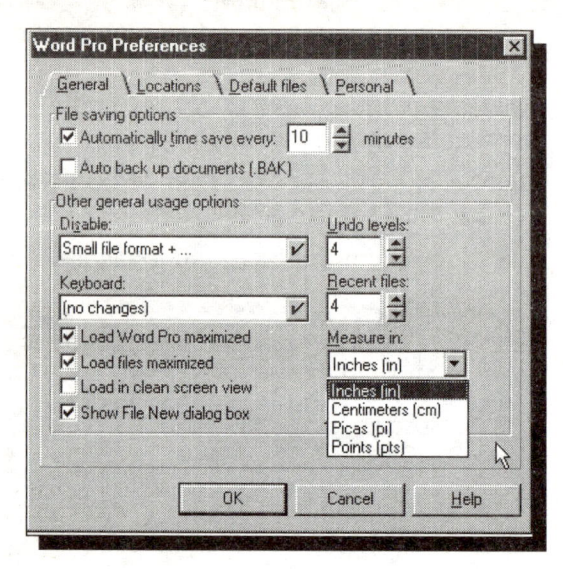

Indenting Text:

Most documents will require some form of paragraph indenting. An indent is the space between the margin and the edge of the text in the paragraph. When an indent is set (on the left or right side of the page), any justification on that side of the page sets at the indent, not the page border.

To illustrate indentation, open the **PCuser 2** file, select the first paragraph by highlighting it, and either click the 'Cycle through indent options' SmartIcon on the Text Toolbar, shown here, or choose the **Text, Alignment, Indent** command (**F7**). As you execute either of these commands in succession, your selected paragraph is indented by different amounts until it cycles through to the beginning.

Hanging Indents:

Different types of indentation can be achieved from the **Text Info** box when the Alignment tab is pressed, as shown below:

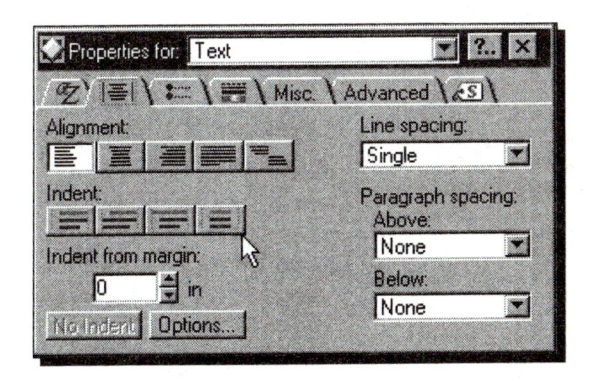

To illustrate the method, use the **PCuser 2** file and add at the end of it the text shown below. After you have typed the text in, save the enlarged memo as **PCuser 3**, before going on with formatting the new information.

In Windows you can work with files in three different ways:

Name Description

My Computer Use the My Computer utility which Microsoft have spent much time and effort making as intuitive as possible.

Explorer Use the Windows Explorer, a much-improved version of the older File Manager.

MS-DOS Use an MS-DOS Prompt window if you prefer to and are an expert with the DOS commands.

Saving the work at this stage is done as a precaution in case anything goes wrong with the formatting - it is sometimes much easier to reopen a saved file (using the **File, Open** command), than it is to try to unscramble a wrongly formatted document!

Next, highlight the last 4 paragraphs of the newly typed text, activate the **Text Info** box, click the third button under **Indent**, and increase the value under **Indent from margin** to 2 inches. As you carry out these changes in the **Text Info** box, the selected paragraphs format as shown below, but remain highlighted. To remove the highlighting, click the mouse button anywhere on the page.

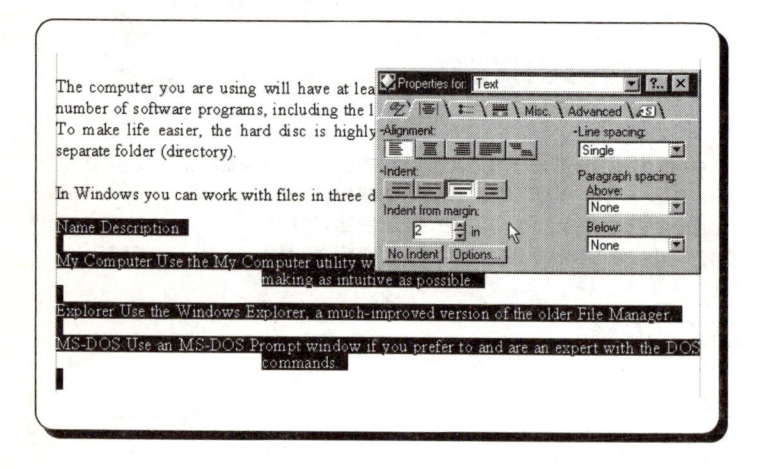

This is still not very inspiring, so to complete the effect we will edit the first lines of each paragraph as follows:

Place the cursor in front of the word 'Description' and press the <Tab> key three times. This places the start of the word in the same column as the indented text of the other paragraphs. To complete the effect place three tabs before the words 'Use' in the next three paragraphs, until your hanging indents are correct, as shown on the next page.

In Windows you can work with files in three different ways:

Name	Description
My Computer	Use the My Computer utility which Microsoft have spent much time and effort making as intuitive as possible.
Explorer	Use the Windows Explorer, a much-improved version of the older File Manager.
MS-DOS	Use an MS-DOS Prompt window if you prefer to and are an expert with the DOS commands.

This may seem like a complicated rigmarole to go through each time you want the hanging indent effect, but with Word Pro you will eventually set up all your indents, etc., as paragraph styles in templates. Then all you do is click in a paragraph to produce them.

When you finish formatting the document, save it under the filename **PCuser 4** using the **File, Save As** command.

Inserting Bullets:

Bullets are small characters you can insert, anywhere you like, in the text of your document to improve visual impact. In Word Pro there are several choices for displaying lists with bullets or numbers. As well as the two buttons on the Text Toolbar set, shown here, others are made available through the **Text Info** box, when the Bullet and number tab is selected. This last choice reveals the following options:

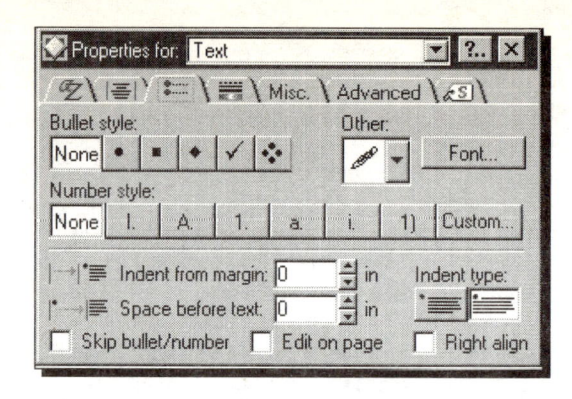

You can select any of the bullets shown here, or click the down-arrow against the **Other** list box to display, as shown here, a variety of other symbols that can be used as bullets. By selecting a different font, with the use of the **Font** button, you can change what is displayed in the **Other** list box.

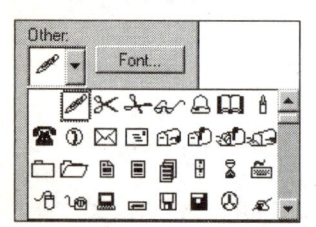

Selecting a **Number style** bullet and then clicking the **Custom** button, displays a further choice of bullets similar to the one selected. For example, selecting A., and pressing the **Custom** button displays the list shown here within the **Custom Numbering** dialogue box. From this dialogue box, you can select an outline numbering sequence to apply to text in your document after which you can specify the outline level position and numbering type for the current paragraph.

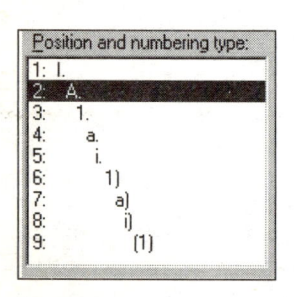

Once inserted, you can copy, move or cut a bulleted line in the same way as any other text. However, you can not delete a bullet with the <BkSp> or <Del> keys.

Inserting Date and Time:

You can insert today's date, the date the current document was created or was last revised, or a date or time that reflects the current system date and time into a document. Therefore, the date can be a date that changes, or a date that always stays the same. In either case, the date is inserted in a date field.

To insert a date field in your document, place the cursor where you want to insert the date, select the **Text**, **Insert Other, Date/Time** command and choose one of the displayed date formats which suits you from the dialogue box shown below.

If you are in the UK, click the **DMY** radio button first, then highlight '21 November 1997' (or whatever date is current), and press **OK**, to insert the date in your document at the chosen position.

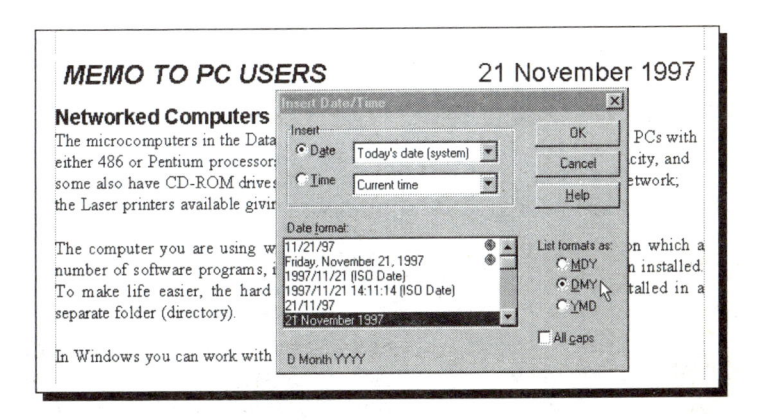

The above screen is a composite of the operation required and the result of that operation.

If you save a document with 'Today's date (static)' in the date field in it and you open it a few days later, the date shown will be the original date the document was created. Should you want to update this date to the current date, select the 'Today's date (system)' before pressing the **OK** button.

Inserting Annotations:

Another powerful feature of Word Pro is the facility to add comments to a document. These act like electronic labels, as shown below.

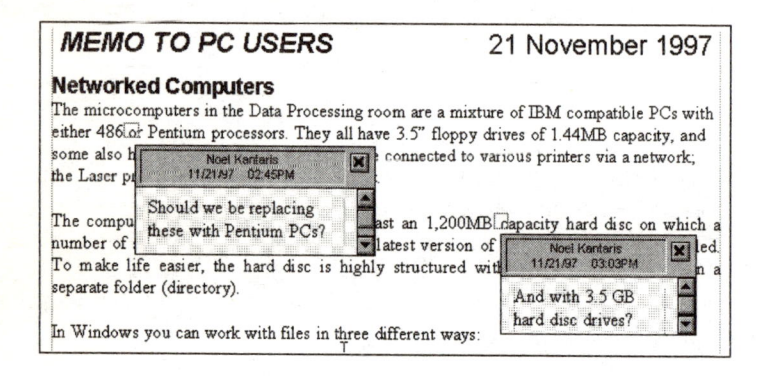

To add comments to a document, place the cursor at the place you want to add a comment, and use the **Create**, **Comment Notes** command. A small banner box opens up for you to type your comment. On closing the box, a small yellow square appears next to the marked word which indicates the existence of a comment.

You can read inserted comments, by simply pointing to the marked word within the document and double-clicking the coloured square. The banner box is then displayed with the actual comment in it. To delete a comment, right-click its marker and select the Delete Note from the displayed quick menu, shown here.

68

Formatting with Page Tabs

You can format text in columns by using tab stops, but first click on the Ruler icon, shown here, to place a ruler at the top of your page. Word Pro has default left tab stops every 0.5 inch from the left margin.

To add a tab in a paragraph or a section of your document, place the insertion pointer within the paragraph, or highlight the section, and right-click the ruler which opens the quick menu shown below. From this menu you can select to create one of the four available tabs (the default being a left tab, shown ticked in the menu). Clicking on a specific position on the ruler, places the selected tab-type on that position.

If, on the other hand, you want more control on setting tabs, select the **Set Tabs** option from the quick menu to open the **Set Tabs on Ruler** dialogue box, also shown below. From here you can choose to have tabular text separated by characters instead of by spaces, by selecting one of the three available characters from the **Leader** box in the dialogue box. The options are none (the default), dotted, dashed, or underline. The Contents and Index pages of this book are set with right tabs and dotted leader characters.

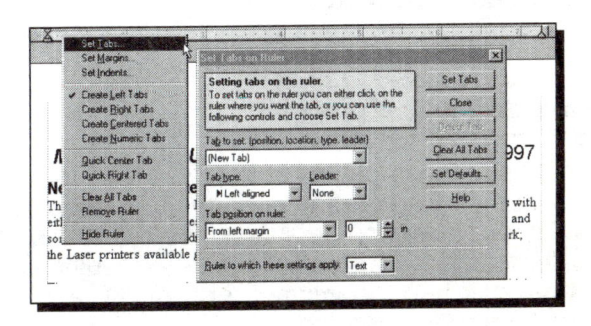

To remove an added tab from the ruler, point to it, click and drag it off the ruler.

69

The tab stop types available have the following function:

Button	Name	Effect
▶	Left	Left aligns text after the tab stop.
↓	Centre	Centres text on tab stop.
◀	Right	Right aligns text after the tab stop.
▶.	Decimal	Aligns decimal point with tab stop.

To clear the ruler of tab settings press the **Clear All Tabs** button in the **Set Tabs on Ruler** dialogue box. When you set a tab stop on the ruler, all default tab stops to the left of the one you are setting are removed.

Note: As all paragraph formatting, such as tab stops, is placed at the end of a paragraph, if you want to carry the formatting of the current paragraph to the next, press <Enter>. If you don't want formatting to carry on, press the down arrow key instead.

Formatting with Styles

We saw earlier on page 26, how you can format your work using 'Paragraph Styles', but we confined ourselves to using the default style only. In this section we will get to grips with how to create, modify, use, and manage styles. As mentioned previously, a Style is a set of formatting instructions which you save so that you can use it repeatedly within a document or in different documents.

You can create a Style for any Word Pro object (character, paragraph, page, frame, table, and table cell). Word Pro creates all styles 'by example' which means that you must first format an object (character, paragraph, frame, and so on), then select it, and finally create the style based on the sample object you have selected. Further, should you decide to change a Style, all the objects associated with that Style reformat automatically.

Finally, if you want to provide a pattern for shaping a final document, then you use what is known as a Template in which you place a collection of Styles. A Template could be appropriate for, say, all your memos, so it can be used to preserve uniformity. It maintains consistency and saves time by not having to format individually each object within the document. All documents which have not been assigned a document template, use the **default.mwp** SmartMaster template, by default.

Paragraph Styles:

Paragraph Styles contain paragraph and character formats and a name can be attached to these formatting instructions. From then on, applying the style name is the same as formatting that paragraph with the same instructions.

Creating Paragraph Styles by Example: Previously, we spent some time manually creating some hanging indents in the last few paragraphs of the **PCuser 4** document. To create a style from this previous work, place the insertion pointer in one of these paragraphs, say, the last one and carry out the following moves:

- Click the right mouse button.
- Choose Text Properties on the displayed quick menu.
- Click the Style tab on the **Text Info** box, as shown on the next page.

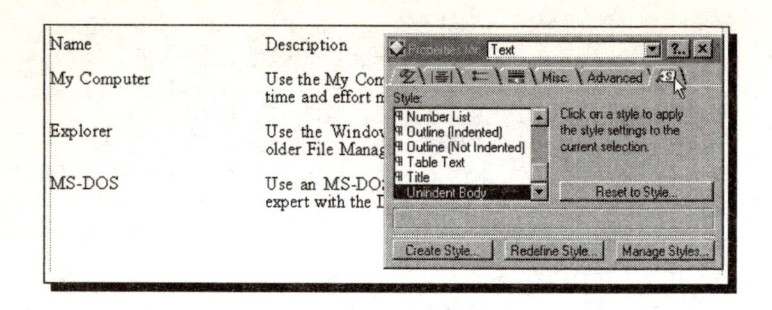

- Click Create Style and type in the **Style name** box 'Hanging Indent' and press **OK**.

Next, highlight the other paragraphs with hanging indents and change their style to the new 'Hanging Indent', by selecting the appropriate style from the displayed **Style** pop-up list, as shown below.

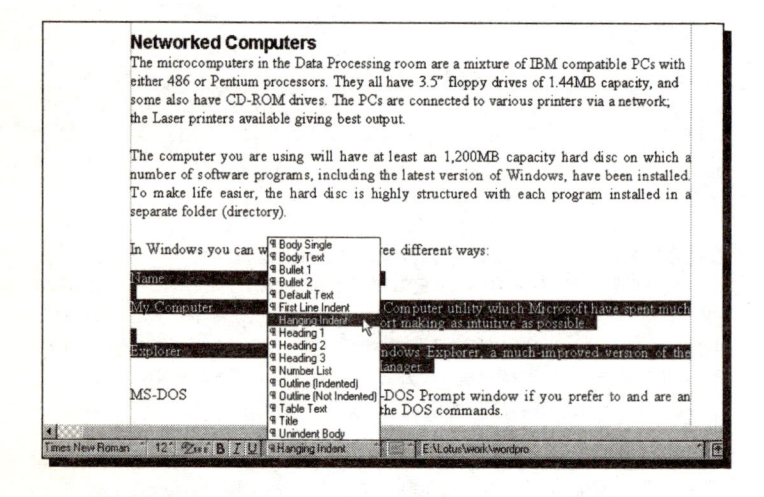

Finally, save the result under the filename **PCuser 5**.

Document SmartMaster Template

A document SmartMaster template provides the overall pattern of your final document. It can include customised styles, contents, and scripts which are defined as follows:

- Styles - consistent formatting information including character, paragraph, frame, table and page layout.
- Contents - text, graphics, OLE objects, tables, frames, and 'Click Here Blocks' (place-holders with instructions on what to type or insert).
- Scripts - automated tasks stored in a SmartMaster template document.

Styles can be created or copied from other documents. Document contents and/or scripts can also be added or deleted from another SmartMaster template. If you don't assign a SmartMaster to a document, then the **default.mwp** template is used by Word Pro. To create a new SmartMaster template, you either modify an existing one, create one from scratch, or create one based on the formatting of an existing document.

Creating a SmartMaster Template:

To illustrate the last point above, we will create a simple document template, which we will call **PCuser**, based on the formatting of the **PCuser 5** document. But first, make sure you have defined the 'Hanging Indent' style as explained earlier.

To create a SmartMaster template based on an existing document do the following:

- Open the existing document.
- Select the **File, Save As** command which displays the **Save As** dialogue box, shown overleaf.

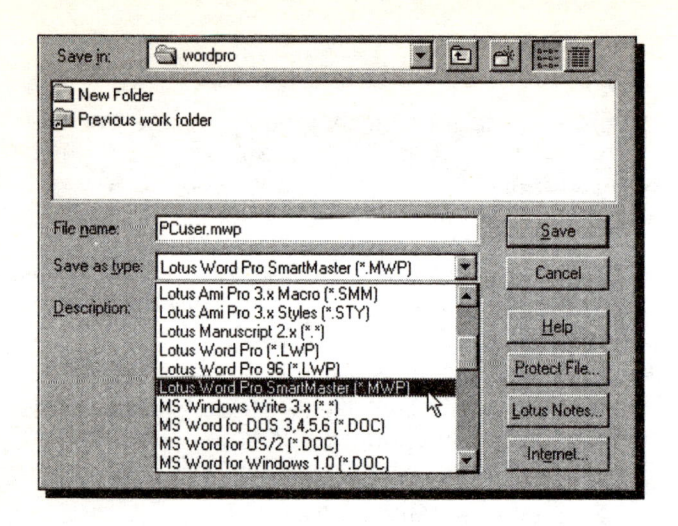

- In the **Save as type** box, select Lotus Word Pro SmartMaster.

- In the **Save in** box, use the folder in which you want to save your SmartMaster template.

- In the **File name** box, type the name of the new SmartMaster (PCuser in our example).

- Press the **Save** button, which opens the template file **PCuser.mwp** in the Word Pro working area.

- Add the text and graphics you want to appear in all new documents that you base on this template, and *delete* any items (including text) you do not want to appear. In our example, we deleted everything in the document, bar the heading, and added the 'Created by Lotus Word Pro' picture using the **File, Import Picture** command and selecting the **_wpdon.gif** file from the **graphics** folder. Our modified SmartMaster is shown on the next page.

MEMO TO PC USERS

To use the new SmartMaster, do the following:

- Use the **File**, **New Document** command which causes the **New Document** dialogue box to be displayed, as shown below.

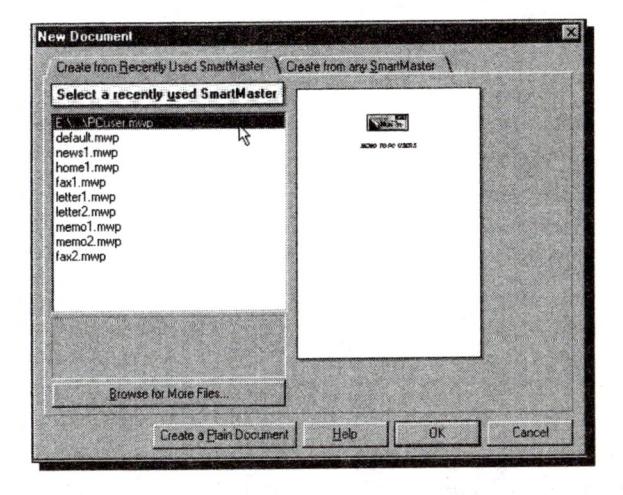

- Click the Create from Recently Used SmartMaster tab and select the name of the template you want to use from the displayed list.

Word Pro has a series of built-in templates to suit every occasion. These can be found, as seen in the above dialogue box, under the tab of Create from any SmartMaster. Try them.

Special Formatting Features

Word Pro has several special formatting features which force text to override style and template formatting. In what follows, we discuss the most important amongst these.

Inserting Drop Capitals:

You can insert a drop cap into your document to emphasise the beginning of a paragraph, as follows:

- Place the insertion pointer anywhere within the paragraph

- Use the **Create, Drop Cap** command to reveal the dialogue box shown below. Select one of the three choices on the drop cap placement and press **OK**.

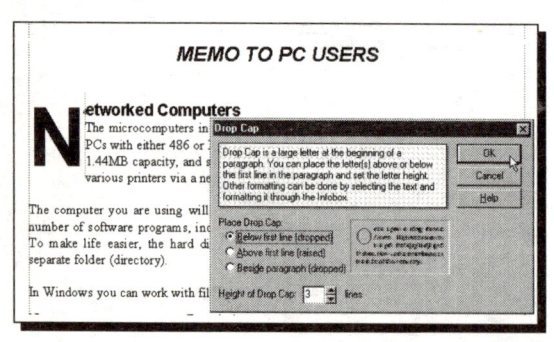

On pressing the **OK** button, the first letter of the appropriate paragraph is enlarged as shown on the above composite screen dump.

To remove a drop cap, simply click the Undo icon on the Toolbar, shown here. If you have carried out other formatting or editing commands and their number exceeds the pre-set undo level, then click on the drop cap so that a frame appears around it and use the **Frame, Delete Frame** command, then replace the deleted letter.

Inserting Special Characters and Symbols:

Word Pro has a collection of Symbol fonts, such as the characters produced by the Symbol, Webdings, and Wingdings character sets, from which you can select characters and insert them into your document using the **Text, Ins_e_rt Other, _S_ymbol** command.

When this command is executed, Word Pro displays the following dialogue box:

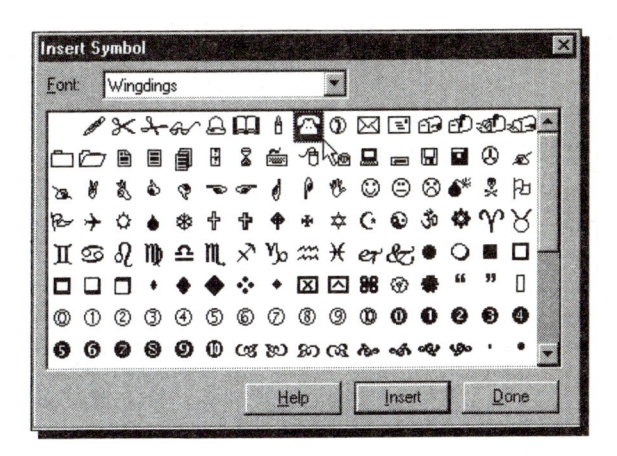

Pressing the down-arrow button next to the **Font** box, reveals the other available character sets. The set showing above is the Wingdings set. If you point and click the left mouse button at a character within the set, it selects it. If you double-click the left mouse button, or press the **Insert** button, it transfers the selected character to your document at the insertion point.

After inserting a symbol, use the <Ctrl+N> key combination to revert to the pre-defined character set, so that you can continue typing with your normal font and point size for that paragraph. To delete a symbol, simply highlight it and press <Del>, or place the insertion pointer just after it and press the <BkSp> key.

Inserting Other Formatting Characters:

You can include other formatting characters in a document, such as

Optional hyphens — To switch optional hyphenation on, use the **File, Document Properties, Document** command and click the Options tab. In the displayed dialogue box, click the **Auto Hyphenation** box and reduce the **Minimum number of characters** to 3 (before) and 2 (after). Hyphens remain invisible until they are needed to hyphenate a word at the end of a line.

Non-breaking hyphens — To prevent unwanted hyphenation, highlight the hyphenated word to select it, click the right-mouse button and choose the **Text Properties** menu option. In the **Text Info** box, click the Font tab and select 'No Hyphenation' in the **Attributes** box to turn off hyphenation. To resume hyphenation, deselect the **No Hyphenation** box.

Non-breaking spaces — To prevent two words from splitting at the end of a line, type the first word, then use the <Ctrl+Spacebar> key combination, then type the second word.

5. DOCUMENT ENHANCEMENTS

In this section we discuss features that enhance a document's appearance, such as page numbering, use of headers and footers, use of footnotes, how to create a document with multiple columns, how to incorporate text boxes, and how to import pictures into frames.

Page Numbering

If you need to number the pages of a document, place the insertion pointer where you would like the page number to appear, then use the **Text, Insert Page Number** command, which displays the following dialogue box:

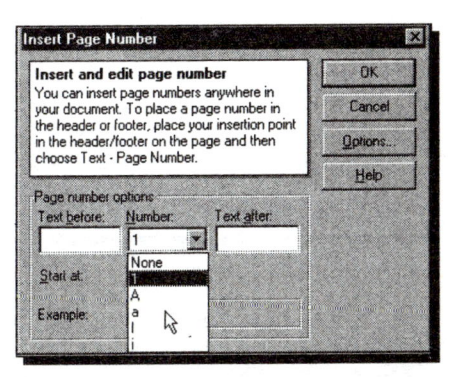

Use this box to select the format of page numbering ('1, A, a, I, or i'), then click the **Options** button to display the dialogue box below. From here you can choose to continue numbering from a previous section or division, begin numbering on a specified page, and include a section or division name in the numbering style.

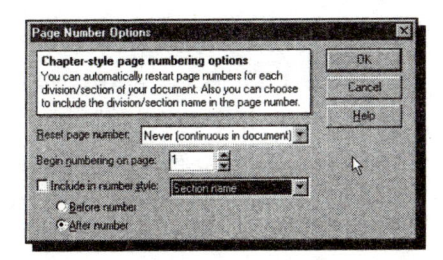

To illustrate page numbering, open the **PCuser 5** document, place the insertion pointer within the footer section of the page, and use the **Text, Insert Page Number** command. Clicking the **OK** button on the displayed dialogue box, inserts a number '1' in the footer. Next, highlight the number 1 to select it then right-click it and choose **Text Properties** option from the quick menu. Click the Alignment tab and centre the page number on the page, as shown below.

```
In Windows you can work with files in three different ways:
Name              Description
My Computer       Use the My Computer utility which Microsoft have spent much
                  time and effort making as intuitive as possible.
Explorer          Use the Windows Explorer, a much-improved version of the
                  older File Manager.
MS-DOS            Use an MS-DOS Prompt window if you prefer to and are an
                  expert with the DOS commands.


                              1
```

To display the above screen as shown, we had to reduce the page length of the memo. To do this, we placed the insertion pointer at the beginning of the memo, then clicked the right mouse button and selected the **Page Properties** option from the displayed quick menu (you could have clicked the Page Properties icon on the Toolbar, shown here, instead). We then selected a custom page size, such as to be able to reduce the page length sufficiently for the text and page number to be displayed close to each other, as shown above.

Finally, if you have followed our page formatting activity, re-set the page size back to A4, before saving the current document as **PCuser 6**.

Using Headers and Footers

Simple headers and footers in Word Pro can consist of text placed in the top or bottom margin area of a page, respectively, with a page number included which can be automatically produced in the same position of every page in the document. More complicated headers and footers can also contain graphics images.

Word Pro allows you to have one header/footer for the first page of a whole document, division or section of a document, and a different one for the rest of the document. It also allows you to select a different header or footer for odd or even pages.

To insert a header or footer in a document, left-click the header or footer area of a page to display an appropriate quick menu, shown below for the case of a header in a composite screen dump. From this menu you can select the **Header Properties** (or **Footer Properties**, if you are working with a footer), to display the relevant **Properties Info** box, also shown below.

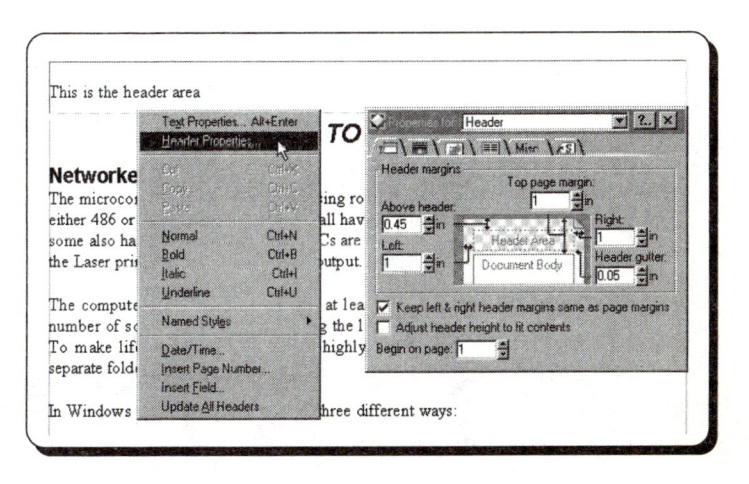

As you can see, the **Header (and Footer) Info** box looks similar to the **Text/Page Info** box.

From here you can adjust margins, select a colour, pattern or line style, place a watermark, adjust the number of columns, set tabs, grids and text alignment, and select, create or manage styles.

In the example below, we chose to insert the system date, a watermark and time of creation on the header area.

---

25 November 1997　　　File Copy　　　11:28 AM

MEMO TO PC USERS

Networked Computers
The microcomputers in the Data Processing room are a mixture of IBM compatible PCs with either 486 or Pentium processors. They all have 3.5" floppy drives of 1.44MB capacity, and some also have CD-ROM drives. The PCs are connected to various printers via a network; the Laser printers available giving best output.

To do this, for yourself, carry out the following steps:

- Place the insertion pointer on the header.
- Use the **Header Info** box to change the **Top page margin** to 1.2 inches and the header margin **Above header** to 0.15 inches.
- Press the <Enter> key twice.
- Right-click the header and select **Date/Time** from the displayed quick menu. Choose the appropriate date format.
- Press the <Tab> key twice.
- Right-click the header and select **Date/Time** from the displayed quick menu. Choose the appropriate time format.
- Press the Watermark tab on the **Header Info** box and select the **filecpy.wmf** file, custom scale it, and place it in the centre of the header.

Using Footnotes

If your document requires footnotes at the end of each page, or endnotes at the end of each section or division, they are very easy to add and later, if necessary, to edit. Place the cursor at the position you want the reference point to be in the document and select **Create, Footnote/Endnote**, which opens the first dialogue box, shown below. Accepting the default place for the footnote marks the text with a numeral and jumps to the bottom of the page where you can type a short explanation.

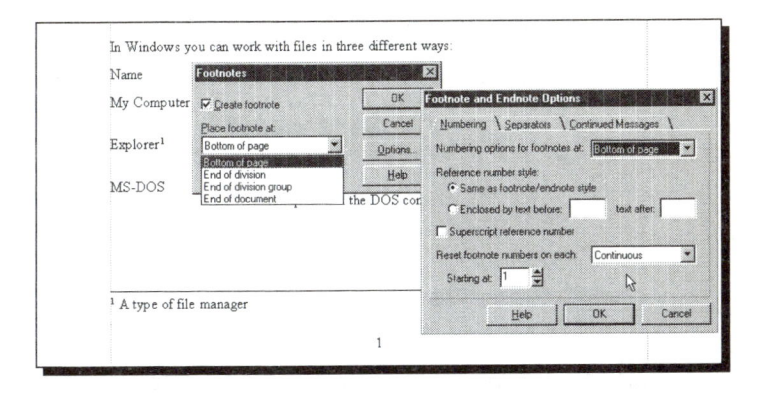

The second dialogue box shown on the composite screen dump above opens when you press the **Options** button of the first, and is to be used before you type your explanatory message at the bottom of the page.

As you can see from the **Footnote and Endnote Options** dialogue box you can use its three tabs to gain access to the formatting of your numbering system, the separation and extent of your footnotes/ endnotes, and the continuation of such notes to the next page, if necessary.

Once you have decided on your selection, save the resultant work under the current filename, **PCuser 6**.

Using Multiple Columns on a Page

You can quickly modify the number of displayed columns on a page by activating the **Page Info** box, clicking the Newspaper Columns tab (the fourth one along), and increase the **Number of newspaper Columns** from 1 to the required number. However, if you want more control over how the columns are displayed, then use the **Create, Parallel Columns** command.

Below, we have placed the insertion pointer in front of the sub-title of the **PCuser 6** memo and then used the **Create, Parallel Columns** command to display:

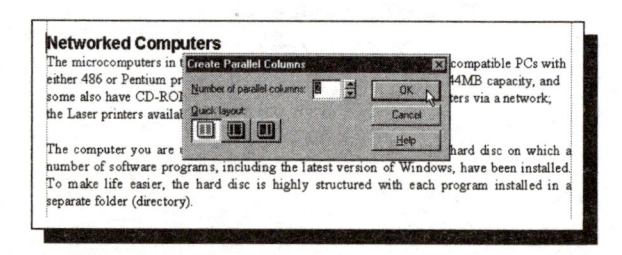

Pressing the **OK** button inserts 2 equal width columns above the sub-title of the memo. Next, select the sub-title and first paragraph of the memo and drag it into the left column box, as shown below:

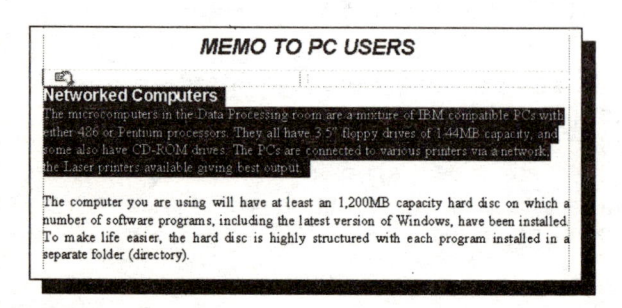

Next select the second paragraph and drag it into the right hand column box, as shown below.

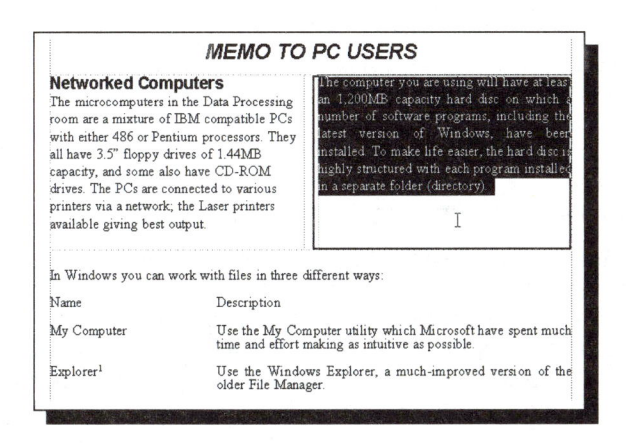

Then, right-click inside the right hand column box and select the **Column Block Properties** option from the Quick menu which displays the **Column Info** box, shown below. Finally, increase the **Top** column margin so that both paragraphs start at the same horizontal line on the page, as shown below.

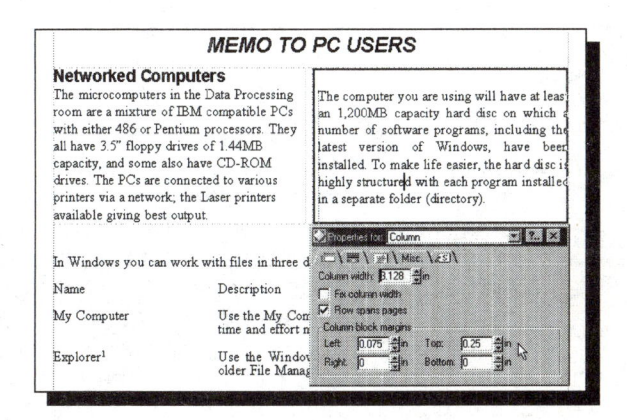

Save the resultant work under the filename **PCuser 7**.

Frames and Drawing

A frame in Word Pro is like a 'mini-document' within the main document that allows you to create multiple layouts on the same page. A frame can contain text, or a picture, and is not affected by the formatting of the main document. You can make document text wrap beside, flow behind, or flow above and below a frame. A page can contain multiple frames, which can overlap, have lines around them or have a shadow effect.

The main reasons for using frames in your documents are to hold graphics, or drawings, to let you place text outside the normal page layout area (in an indention area or margin, for instance), or to allow you to create a heading to span a page formatted with newspaper-type columns.

Frames can be moved, or copied, around your document using the same **Edit** commands as ordinary text. The text included in a frame can be formatted manually, or with paragraph styles, as in the main document.

Creating a Frame:

There are two main ways to create a new frame. Either with the **Create, Frame** command and filling in a dialogue box, or interactively with the mouse. We will assume that you are happy using a mouse and will concentrate on this last method.

Start by opening the **PCuser 6** file, then click your mouse on the 'Create frame manually' SmartIcon, shown here, then position the cross hairs of the frame mouse pointer at the end of the second sentence, hold the left mouse button down and drag the dotted frame until it forms an approximate square with about 1.5 inch sides, as shown on the next page. Releasing the mouse button, fixes the frame on the page at the position of placement.

> ### *MEMO TO PC USERS*
>
> **Networked Computers**
> The microcomputers in the Data Processing room are a mixture of IBM compatible PCs with either 486 or Pentium processors. They all have 3.5" floppy drives of 1.44MB capacity, and some also have CD-ROM drives. The PCs are connected to various printers via a network; the Laser printers available giving best output.
>
> The computer you are using will have at least an 1,200MB capacity hard disc on which a number of software programs, including the latest version of Windows, have been installed. To make life easier, the hard disc is highly structured with each program installed in a separate folder (directory).
>
> In Windows you can work with files in three different ways:

At the moment the frame is 'selected', and looks like the top one in the box alongside. The grey squares are 'handles', which are used to enlarge the frame, provided the mouse pointer changes to a double-headed arrow when placed on them. Changes can only be made if a frame is selected. If the mouse is clicked outside the frame it will lose its frame looks and handles, and revert to its normal shape, as shown here on the bottom box alongside. The positioning and looks of the frame are easily changeable, as we shall see in the following section.

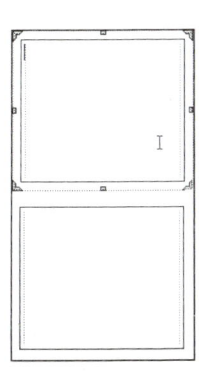

To size a frame, select it so that the square selection handles appear around the frame, then move the mouse pointer over one of the selection handles until it turns to the two-headed sizing arrow. Drag the sizing arrow to change the frame to the required size, then release the mouse button.

Dragging one of the corner handles will drag the two attached frame sides with the pointer, but dragging a centre line handle will only move that side. Try these actions until you are happy with the resultant frame size.

Moving a Frame:

A frame can be moved around your document by first selecting it, then dragging it with the mouse (move the mouse pointer over the edge of the frame until it turns to an open small hand, as shown here, then click and drag to the desired position). The outline of the frame shows the position in which it will be placed once you let go of the left mouse button, as shown below.

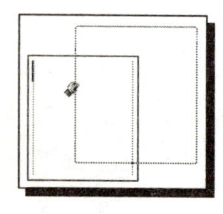

Another way of manipulating a frame is by either right-clicking a selected frame and choosing the **Frame Properties** option from the displayed Quick menu, or using the **Frame, Frame Properties** command. Either of these displays the **Frame Properties Info** box. To see the available positioning of frames, click the Placement tab, to display what is shown below.

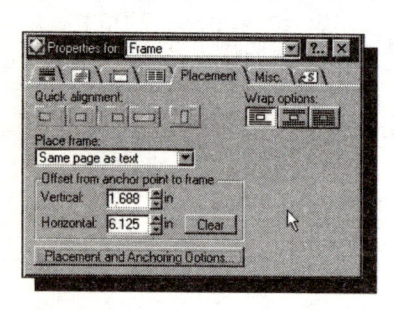

To move a frame up or down from its anchor point (the point in the text on which you placed the insertion pointer before starting to create a frame), specify a value in the **Vertical** box. To move the frame left or right from its anchor point, specify a value in the **Horizontal** box.

From the same **Info** box tab option, you can choose the **Wrap options** for the document text with respect to the frame. There are three wrap options available:

- Wrap around one side of the frame
- Flow above and below the frame
- Flow behind a frame

If you want to wrap text around both sides of the frame, then you must use a page layout with newspaper columns behind the frame and, most importantly, select to anchor the frame either 'On current page', or 'Same page as text' on the **Place frame** box of the **Frame Info** box, as shown below.

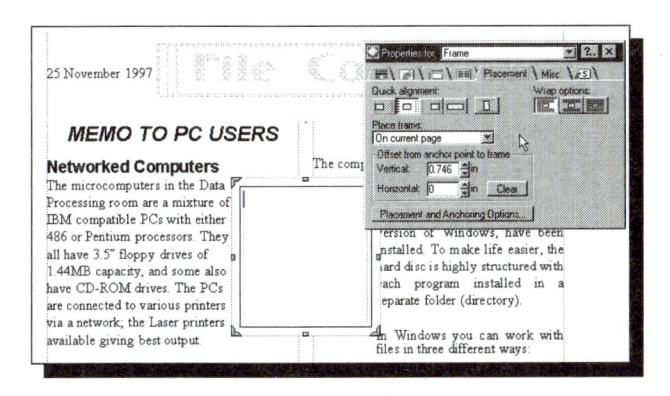

Where you choose to anchor a frame, is extremely important. The options available and what you can do with the resultant frame, are tabulated below.

Anchor Frame	Effect
On all pages	Frame appears where placed, but on all pages. You control all anchor points. The frame does not move if the text around it moves.
On left/right pages	Frame appears where placed, but on either all left pages or all right pages, depending on where the frame was created. You control all anchor points. The frame does not move if the text around it moves.

In text	Frame anchors to a character in the text and moves with it when editing. You cannot change the anchor point. Frame cannot be grouped.
With paragraph above	Frame anchors to the paragraph above it. You can change the frame's horizontal position, but not its vertical. Frame cannot be grouped.
Same page as text	This is the default option for frame placement. The frame appears always on the same page as the anchor point and you can specify both its vertical and horizontal position, relative to the text.
On current page	Frame appears where placed, but only on current page and does not move if the text around it moves. You can change the anchor point.
In text - Vertical	Frame anchors to a specific character in the text and moves vertically with it when editing, but not horizontally. You can adjust anchor points relative to the text anchor point. Frame cannot be grouped.
In frame	This option only applies if the frame is completely inside another frame. The inside frame anchors to the frame around it and moves with it. Frame cannot be grouped.

Placing Text in a Frame:

Once you have your frame where you want it on the page, it is only of any use if you do something with it. So, click the mouse pointer inside the frame, which displays the sizing handles and places the cursor inside the frame, and type in some text (see screen display below). In our example, we also chose to rotate the text using the **Text direction** button on the **Frame Info** box, as shown.

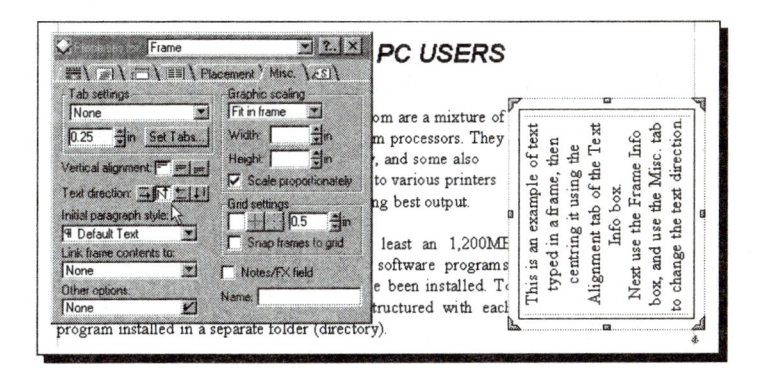

Next, click the mouse button outside the frame, which will cancel the frame selection and save this as **PCuser 8**.

Moving the mouse pointer over the sides of the frame, turns it into a small open hand, allowing you to move the frame to a new position when you click and drag, provided your choice of anchoring that particular frame allows you to do so. You can select the frame by single clicking which will let you re-size it, and if you clicked anywhere on the text within the frame, will also allow you to edit that text.

In our example above, as you move the mouse pointer over the main document text, you will see that the insertion pointer is vertical. However, as you move the mouse pointer over the framed text, the insertion pointer is also rotated in the same direction.

Importing a Graphic

To illustrate the ability of importing a graphic into Word Pro, open the **PCuser 8** file, select all the text in the frame and delete it. Then change the direction of text to its normal upright position, and type the words 'This is an apple'. Next, either click the 'Import a Picture' icon on the Toolbar, shown here, or use the **File, Import Picture** command. Either of these options will display the **Import Picture** dialogue box shown below.

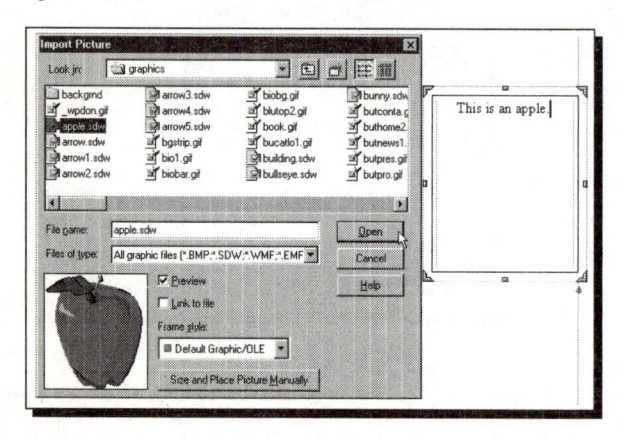

The display above shows the preview of the **apple.sdw** picture file from Word Pro's **graphics** folder. Pressing the **Open** button, places the selected picture in a frame, within the existing text frame. To see what is displayed alongside, you might have to move the picture frame. Note that the picture frame is anchored to the end of the word 'apple', while the text frame is anchored to the page.

Save this document as **PCuser 9**.

The Drawing Tools

As long as you have a mouse, you can use Word Pro's Drawing tools. To use the Drawing tools, either click the 'Create drawing' icon on the Toolbar, shown here (which is only active immediately after a new frame has been created), or double-click inside an already created frame (one that is either empty, or contains a graphic and/or a drawing).

The Drawing tools can also be activated by using the **Create, Drawing** command which creates a drawing frame at the insertion point in your document. You can use the Drawing tools to create, or edit, a graphic consisting of lines, arcs, ellipses, rectangles, and even text boxes. These can either exist in their own right, or be additions to a picture or object.

The various buttons on the Drawing toolbar have the following functions:

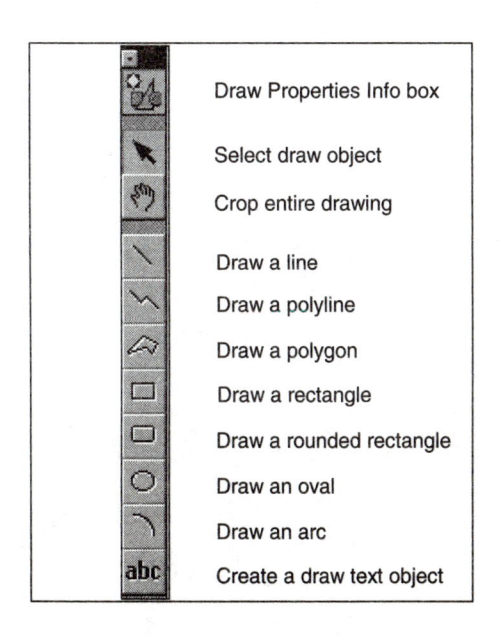

Icon	Function
	Draw Properties Info box
	Select draw object
	Crop entire drawing
	Draw a line
	Draw a polyline
	Draw a polygon
	Draw a rectangle
	Draw a rounded rectangle
	Draw an oval
	Draw an arc
abc	Create a draw text object

Creating a Drawing:

The effects of the drawing tools can be superimposed either on the document area or on top of a graphic. The result is that you can annotate drawings and pictures to your total satisfaction.

To create an object, click on the required Drawing button, such as the **Rectangle**, the **Rounded Rectangle** or the **Oval**, position the mouse pointer where you want to create the object on the screen, and then drag the mouse to draw the object. Hold the <Shift> key while you drag the mouse to create a perfect square, rounded square, or circle. If you do not hold <Shift>, Word Pro creates a rectangle, a rounded rectangle, or an oval.

Editing a Drawing:

To select an object, click on it. Word Pro displays black handles around the object selected.

You can move an object, or multiple objects, within a draw area by selecting them and dragging to the desired position. To copy an object, click at the object, then use the **Edit, Copy** / **Edit, Paste** commands.

To size an object, position the mouse pointer on a black handle and then drag the handle until the object is the desired shape and size.

To delete an object, select it and press the <Del> key. To delete a drawing, hold the <Shift> key down and click each object in turn that makes up the drawing, unless they are grouped or framed, then press <Del>.

To delete a frame with all its contents, right-click it and select the **Delete Frame** option from the displayed Quick menu.

Do try out some of these commands using the **PCuser 9** document file, but do not save the results of your experimentation under the same file name.

Using Layered Drawings:

To illustrate layered drawings, open a new document using the **default.mwp** SmartMaster. Then use the three drawing shapes, oval, rectangle and polygon to draw the three overlapping shapes shown below. Drawings, or pictures, layered on top of each other can create useful visual effects, provided you remember that the top drawing and/or picture can obscure the one below it.

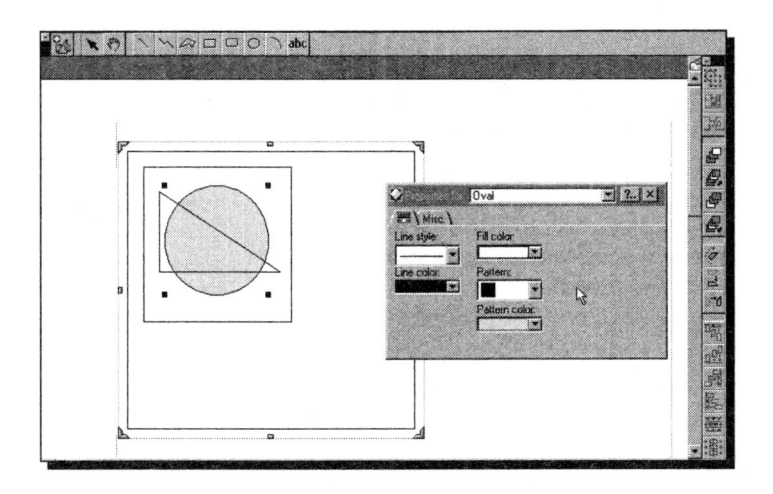

Each shape can be selected in turn by first clicking the 'Select draw object' icon from the Drawing toolbar, shown here, before using the **Properties for Info** box, shown in the screen dump above, to select a solid **Pattern** and **Pattern color**. Note that as each shape is selected, the name on the **Info** box changes to the name of that shape.

The order you draw or manipulate these shapes is not important as you can always select one and use the 'Send object to front' or 'Send object to back' options to rearrange them to your taste.

If you want to move shapes within a frame, but wish to retain their relative position, then it is imperative that you first use the 'Select all objects' icon, shown here at the top, then use the 'Group selected draw objects' icon, shown at the bottom, before attempting to move them.

If you do not want to group all the objects within a frame, then you must select in turn each shape you want to group together, while holding down the <Shift> key, before clicking the 'Group selected draw objects' icon.

Finally, to obtain what is shown below, we grouped all three shapes and pressed the Misc. tab of the **Properties for Info** box, double-clicked the grouped objects to display the rotational handles, and used them to rotate the objects by the amount in degrees and in the direction indicated in the **Info** box. Save your drawing under the filename **Drawing 1**.

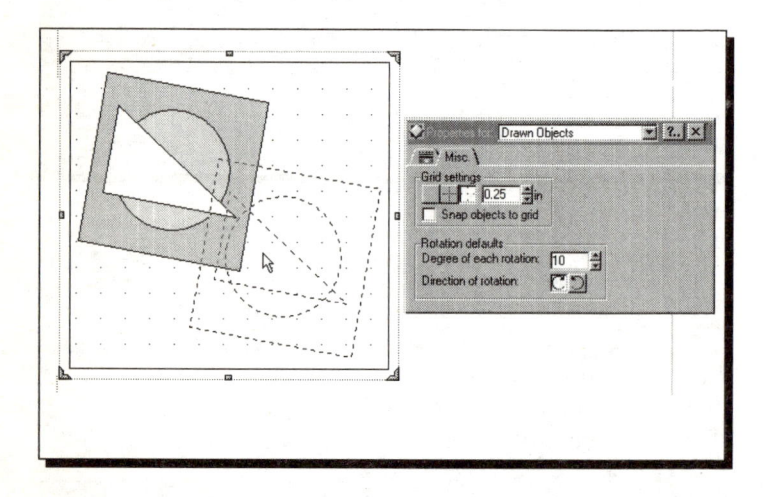

Next, try to move the whole group of objects down and to the right (you can tell they are grouped because attempting to move them, moves the whole group, shown above in a dotted outline).

6. USING TABLES AND GRAPHS

The ability to use 'Tables' is built into most top-range word processors these days. At first glance the process might look complicated and perhaps only a small percentage of users take advantage of the facility, which is a pity because using a 'Table' has many possibilities. If you have worked with a spreadsheet, such as Lotus 1-2-3 (to be discussed in the next chapter) or Excel, then you are familiar with tables.

Tables are used to create adjacent columns of text and numeric data. A table is simply a grid of columns and rows with the intersection of a column and row forming a rectangular box which is referred to as a 'cell'. In Word Pro you can include pictures, charts, notes, footnotes, tabs, and page breaks in your tables. There are several ways to place information into a table:

- Type the desired text, or numeric data.
- Paste text from the main document.
- Link two tables within a document.
- Insert data created in another application.
- Import a picture.
- Create a chart on information held in a table.

The data is placed into individual cells that are organised into columns and rows, similar to a spreadsheet. You can modify the appearance of table data by applying text formatting and enhancements, or by using different paragraph styles.

Creating a Table

Tables can be created either by pressing the 'Create table grid' button on the toolbar, shown here, or by using the **Create, Table** command. Using the latter, displays the dialogue box shown below, which enables you to select a different **Table style**, if you have created one.

As an example we will step through the process of creating the table shown on page 100. Open a 'New Document' file (it could be an existing file, in which case you place the insertion point where you want the table to appear), then click on the 'Create table grid' button and drag down and to the right.

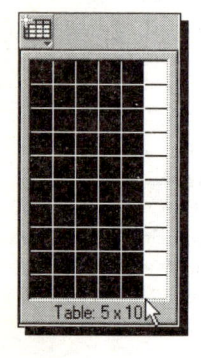

As you drag the mouse, the 'Table' button expands to create the grid of rows and columns. At the bottom of the box there is an automatic display of the number of columns and rows you are selecting by this method. When you release the mouse button, a table is inserted in your document the size of the selected grid.

For our example, we require a 5x10 cell table. Once this appears in position, the cursor is placed in the top left cell awaiting your input. The cells forming the table, are displayed with lines around each cell.

Navigating Around a Table:

To move around in a table, simply click the desired cell, or use one of the keyboard commands listed below.

Press this	*To do this*
Tab	Moves the insertion point right one cell, in the same row, and from the last cell in one row to the first cell in the next row. Once the last cell of the last row has been reached, pressing <Tab>, adds another row at the end of the table.
Shift+Tab	Moves the insertion point left one cell. Once the first cell of the first row has been reached, pressing <Shift+Tab>, adds another row at the beginning of the table.
↑,↓,←, and →	Moves the insertion point within cells, between cells, and between the cells in a table and the main document text.
Home	Moves the insertion point to the beginning of the current line, and pressing it once more to the first cell of that row.
End	Moves the insertion point to the end of the current line within a cell, and pressing it once more to the last cell of the current row.

Now type in the information given on the next page, and format your table using the **Properties Text Info** box to align the contents of the various cells as shown. Do note that right-clicking a table also allows you to access the **Cell Properties Info** box.

Types of Removable Storage Media				
Description	Capacity MB	Price/Unit	No. Bought	Cost
High-density Diskettes	1.44	£0.35	80	
Super Discs 3.5"	120	£10.00	3	
Tape Cartridges	560	£6.00	3	
Write CDs	650	£2.50	5	
Removable Hard Discs	1,200	£140.00	1	
			Total	

To enter the heading as shown, highlight the first cell of the first row, then use the **Table, Connect Row** command to join all the cells of that row into one. Now you can type the heading, centre it, format it in bold, and increase its font size to your liking. To join fewer cells than an entire row, select them and use the **Table, Connect Cells** command.

The line in the cell of the penultimate row and last column was typed by using the underscore '_' character which can be obtained by typing the key combination <Shift+->. Inserting this character repeatedly, gives the impression of a continuous horizontal line.

Changing Column Width and Row Height:

The column width and row height of cells in a table can be changed by clicking the 'Table Cell Properties' icon, and pressing the 'Size and margin' tab of the displayed **Table Cell Info** box. From here you can change all cell dimensions and margins.

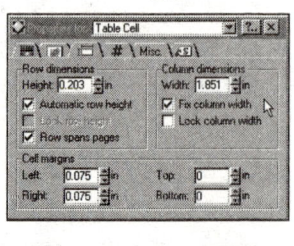

Cell widths can also be changed by dragging a column boundary, provided the **Fix column width** in the **Table Cell Info** box, shown above, is not ticked.

The overall effects of these actions are as follows:

Keys	Effect
No key	as the column to the left changes, all columns to the right change proportionally, but the overall width of the table remains the same.
Ctrl key	only the columns to the left and right are re-sized proportionally with the overall width of the table remaining the same size.

The height of a row depends on its contents. As you type text into a cell, its height increases to accommodate it. You can also insert empty lines before or after the text by pressing the <Enter> key, which also increases the height of a cell. All other cells in that row become the same height as the largest cell.

When you have finished, save your work under the filename **Table 1**. We will use this table to show you how you can insert expressions into cells to make your table behave just like a spreadsheet.

Entering Expressions:

To enter an expression into a table's cell, so that you can carry out spreadsheet type calculations, select the cell and use the **Table, Insert Formula** command which displays the dialogue box shown below.

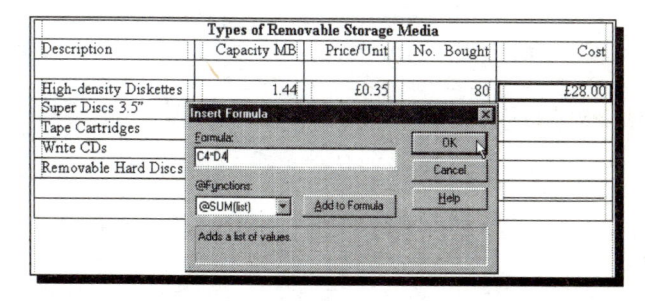

In the previous screen dump, we show both the formula we want Word Pro to evaluate and the result of the calculation once the **OK** button is pressed.

The cost of purchase in cell E4, is calculated as:

```
=C4*D4
```

The '=' sign in an expression such as the above is optional. If you realise that you have made a mistake in typing your formula, after pressing the **OK** button, you can either retype it or click the 'Edit formula in table cell' icon, shown here, which displays the **Insert Formula** dialogue box with the cell formula in it ready for you to edit.

Word Pro performs mathematical calculations on numbers in cells and inserts the result of the calculation as a field in the cell that contains the insertion pointer. Cells are referred to as A1, A2, B1, B2, and so on, with the letter representing a column and the number representing a row. Thus, B3 refers to the hatched cell.

Fill in the rest of column E by copying the formula in E4 to the range E5 to E8 (to do this, first place the cell pointer in E4, then click the Copy SmartIcon, then move the cell pointer to E5, hold the left mouse button down while highlighting the required range, then click the Paste SmartIcon).

To calculate the total cost of purchases in our table, place the insertion pointer in cell E10 and either click the 'Edit formula in table cell' icon or use the **Table, Insert Formula** command. Next, select the function you require (in our case the @SUM( ) function) from the **@Functions** box, press the **Add to Formula** button, and replace the bracketed word 'list' with the required range. In our case, this reads as:

```
@SUM(E4..E8)
```

as shown on the next page.

On pressing **OK**, Word Pro calculates the result and places it in cell E10. The completed table should look as follows:

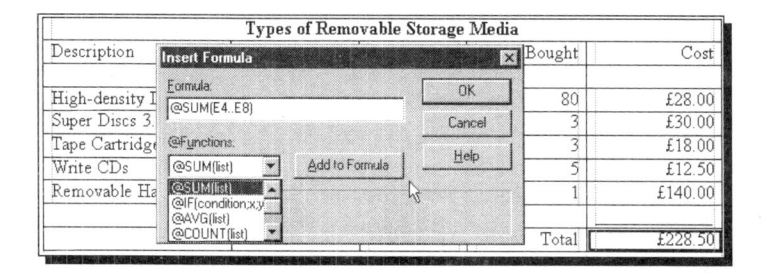

In the above screen dump we show both the result of a calculation and the process you have to go through to get that result. To obtain the £ sign in the columns that contain currency, select the cells within these columns in turn, and click the 'Table Cell Properties' icon, then press the # tab and select the appropriate currency.

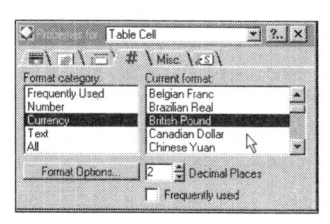

In a formula you can specify any combination of mathematical and logical operators from the following:

Addition	+
Subtraction	–
Multiplication	*
Division	/
Percent	%
Powers and roots	^
Equal to	=
Less than	<
Less than or equal to	<=
Greater than	>
Greater than or equal to	>=
Not equal to	<>

The functions below accept references to table cells:

| AVG( ) | COUNT( ) | IF( ) |
| MAX( ) | MIN( ) | SUM( ) |

The main reason for using formulae in a table, instead of just typing in the numbers, is that formulae will still give the correct final answer even if some of the data is changed.

Editing a Table:

You can edit a table by inserting or deleting columns or rows, or by merging or splitting cells, as follows:

To insert a row or column: Select where you want the new row or column to appear, remembering that the selected row (or column) and all rows below (or columns to its right) will move down (or to the right). To select a row, place the mouse pointer to the left of the desired row, as shown here to the left, and click the left mouse button. To select a column, move the mouse pointer to the top of the desired column, as shown here to the right, and click the left mouse button. Once a row (or column) is selected, use the **Table, Insert, Row** (or **Column**) command, or click the appropriate SmartIcon shown here.

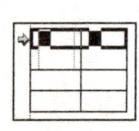

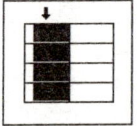

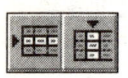

To delete a row or column: Select the row(s) or column(s) you want to delete, then use the **Table, Delete, Row** (or **Column**) command, or click the appropriate SmartIcon shown here.

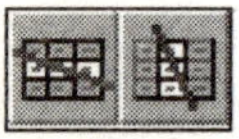

To delete an entire table: Click anywhere within the table you want to delete, then use the **Table, Delete, Entire Table**) command, or click the SmartIcon shown here.

To connect cells: Select the cells you want to connect, then use the **Ta<u>b</u>le, Connect Cell<u>s</u>** command, or click the SmartIcon shown here.

To split cells: Move the insertion pointer to the cell you want to split, then use the **Ta<u>b</u>le, Di<u>s</u>connect Cells** command.

To split a table: To split a table, click the row that you want to be the last row of the first table and select the **Ta<u>b</u>le, S<u>p</u>lit Entire Table** command. Using this command on the first row of our table, displays the following:

Types of Removable Storage Media				
Description	Capacity MB	Price/Unit	No. Bought	Cost
High-density Diskettes	1.44	£0.35	80	£28.00
Super Discs 3.5"	120	£10.00	3	£30.00
Tape Cartridges	560	£6.00	3	£18.00
Write CDs	650	£2.50	5	£12.50
Removable Hard Discs	1,200	£140.00	1	£140.00
			Total	£228.50

The font size of the title in the first table above and the height of its row were increased to look more appropriate as a title to the second table. Be careful with splitting tables, because there does not appear to be a facility of merging them back to one.

Adding designer borders to tables: Finally you can enhance the looks of a table by adding one of the pre-defined designer borders, as shown below.

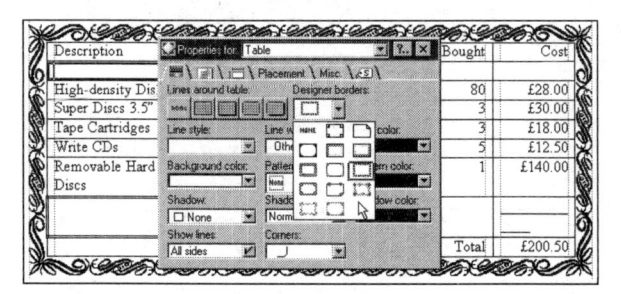

Using the Chart Facility

Word Pro provides a chart facility which can be used to represent data graphically, whether such data has been created locally or imported from another SmartSuite application.

To demonstrate one of the ways in which you can chart data, we will use the information held in **Table 3**. First open the file, then use your editing skills to transform the table to what is displayed below.

Description	Capacity MB	Price/Unit	No. Bought	Cost
High-density Diskettes	1.44	£0.35	80	£28.00
Super Discs 3.5"	120	£10.00	3	£30.00
Tape Cartridges	560	£6.00	3	£18.00
Write CDs	650	£2.50	5	£12.50
Removable Hard Discs	1,200	£140.00	1	£140.00

Note that we have deleted the row immediately below the word 'Description', as well as the last two rows of the table. This is essential, because to chart data you must have contiguous information, without any empty rows or columns in between.

Save the resultant work as **Table 4**. Then select the table, as shown below, by either highlighting it, or using the **Ta_b_le, Selec_t_, Entire _T_able** command.

Description	Capacity MB	Price/Unit	No. Bought	Cost
High-density Diskettes	1.44	£0.35	80	£28.00
Super Discs 3.5"	120	£10.00	3	£30.00
Tape Cartridges	560	£6.00	3	£18.00
Write CDs	650	£2.50	5	£12.50
Removable Hard Discs	1,200	£140.00	1	£140.00

Next, and while the table is selected, copy it to the Clipboard, then move the insertion pointer to where you would like the chart to appear (in our case below the table), and use the **Create, Chart** command. This displays the following dialogue box.

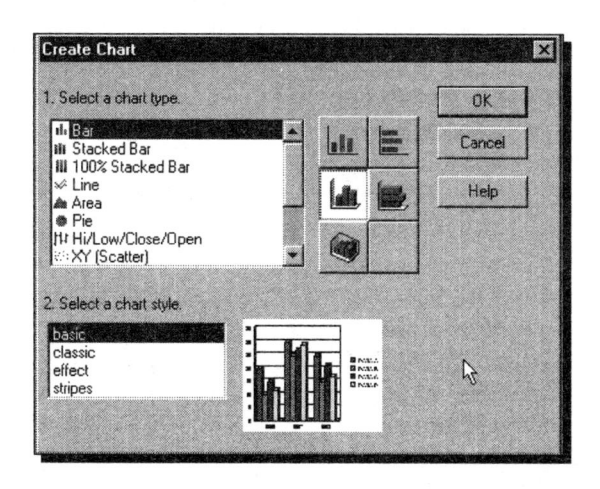

In this dialogue box you can choose the chart type best suited to your data. In our case, we have chosen to represent our data in a 3-D Bar chart. Pressing the **OK** button displays the **Edit Data** dialogue box, shown below.

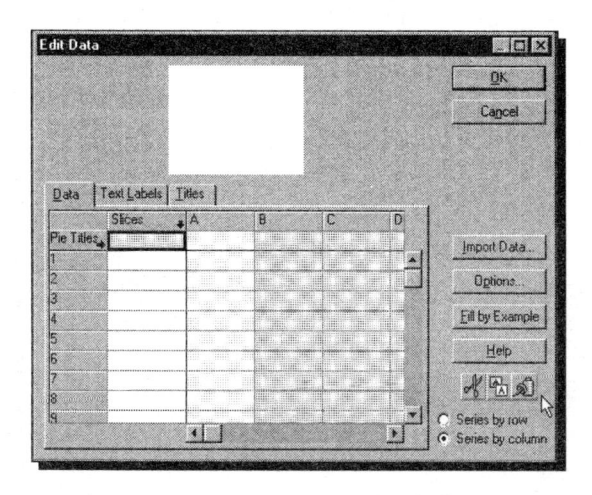

Now move the insertion pointer to the extreme top left position, and press the Paste icon pointed to above.

This has the effect of pasting the data held on the Clipboard into the **Edit Data** dialogue box, as shown below.

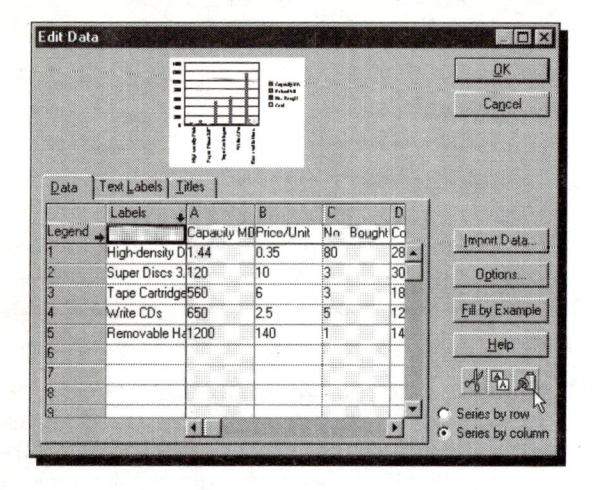

Now pressing the **OK** button charts your data at the insertion point within a frame, as shown below.

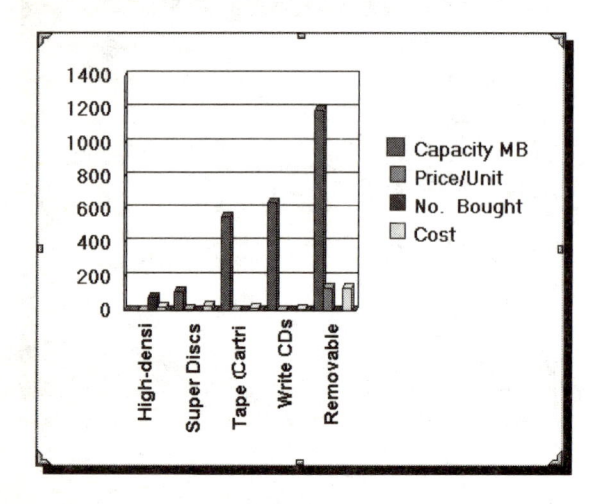

Pre-defined Chart Types:

To select a different type of chart, use the **Chart, Chart Type** command, or double-click within the chart area, which opens the **Chart Properties Info** box shown below.

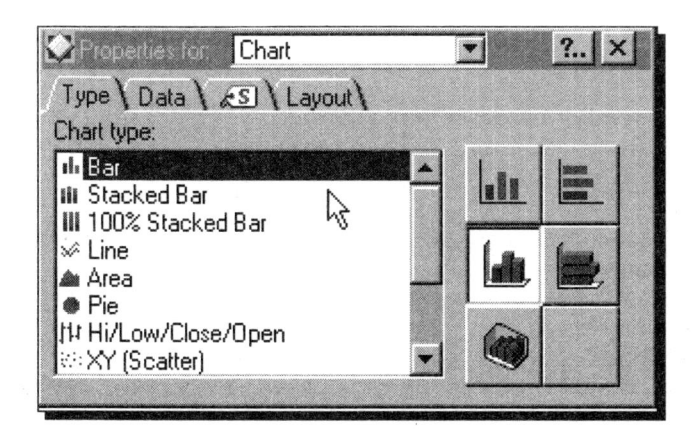

From here you can select a different chart **Type**, **Data** series, **Style**, and **Layout**, by using the appropriate tab of the **Info** box.

The Chart Type option lists 12 different charts. These chart-types are normally used to describe the following relationships between data:

Bar	for comparing differences in data by depicting changes in vertical or horizontal bars.
Stacked Bar	for comparing cumulative data.
100% Stacked Bar	for comparing cumulative data as a percentage of the whole.
Line	for showing continuous changes in data with time.

Area for showing a volume relationship between two series, such as production or sales, over a given length of time.

Pie for comparing parts with the whole. You can use this type of chart when you want to compare the percentage of an item from a single series of data with the whole series.

Hi/Low/Close/Open for showing high-low-close type of data variation to illustrate stock market prices or temperature changes.

XY Scatter for showing scatter relationships between X and Y. Scatter charts are used to depict items which are not related over time.

Radar for plotting one series of data as angle values defined in radians, against one or more series defined in terms of a radius.

Mixed for combining different chart types into one chart. Mixed charts can include area, bar, or lines.

Number Grid for representing your data in a grid form.

Doughnut for comparing parts with the whole. Similar to pie charts, but can depict more than one series of data.

You can change the type of chart by selecting one of the twelve alternate types from the **Chart Properties Info** box, provided your data fits the selection.

Improving a Chart:

A Word Pro Chart can be improved by giving it a title, and x- and y-axis titles. One way of doing this, is to use the **Chart Properties Info** box and click the down-arrow to the right of the **Chart** box, as shown below.

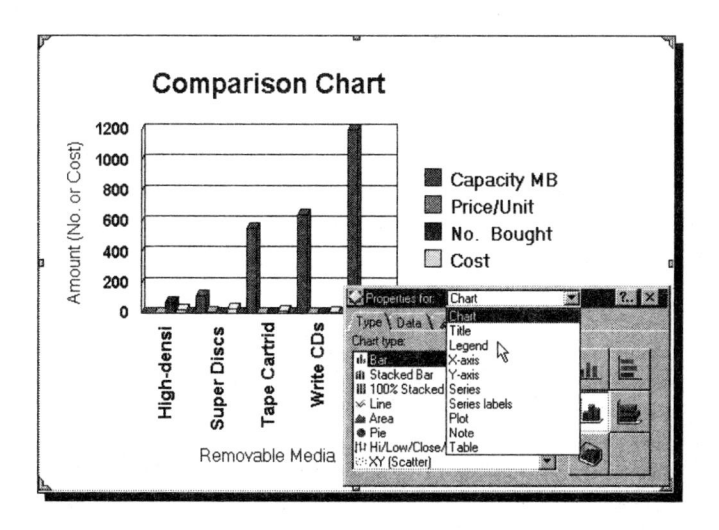

This allows you to reach the listed properties for Title, Legend, etc. As an example, we used this facility to give our chart the title 'Comparison Chart', and the x- and y-axis descriptions as 'Amount (No. or Cost)' and 'Removable Media', respectively.

When you have carried out all the required changes to your chart, save the Word Pro document as **Table 5**.

As you practise with Word Pro's Table and Chart components, you will notice that they are a bit limited in their functionality. For example, you can only use a small number of functions within a table, and you can only place Legends in pre-determined positions around a chart with the additional limitation on the length of the x-axis labels, as shown overleaf.

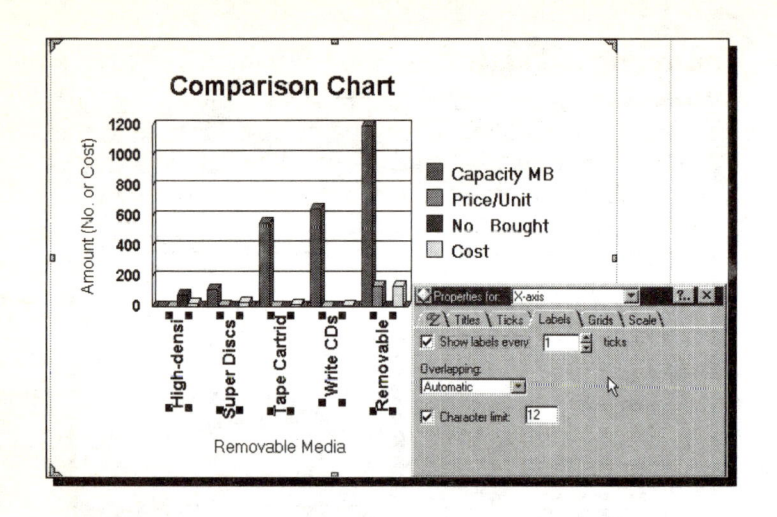

If your work demands greater functionality and flexibility than that which is offered within Word Pro's Table and Chart facilities, then may we suggest you use Lotus 1-2-3, the subject of the next few chapters, which is the more appropriate SmartSuite 97 application for dealing with such topics. Once a table or a chart has been set up within Lotus 1-2-3, then it is an easy enough operation to link them into a Word Pro document, as we shall see later.

7. THE LOTUS 1-2-3 SPREADSHEET

Lotus 1-2-3 is a powerful and versatile software package which, over the years, has proved its usefulness, not only in the business world, but with scientific and engineering users as well.

The program's power lies in its ability to emulate everything that can be done by the use of pencil, paper and a calculator. Thus, it is an 'electronic spreadsheet' or simply a 'spreadsheet'. Its power is derived from the power of the computer it is running on, and the flexibility and accuracy with which it can deal with the solution of the various applications it is programmed to manage. These can vary from simple listings to budgeting and forecasting, or to the solution of complex scientific and engineering problems.

Starting the Lotus 1-2-3 Program

Lotus 1-2-3 is started in Windows either by clicking the **Start** button then selecting **Programs, Lotus SmartSuite** and clicking on the 'Lotus 1-2-3 97' option on the cascade menu, or by clicking the Lotus 123 icon on the Task Bar, shown here.

In either case, the Lotus 1-2-3 program starts to load and after the opening screen, it displays the **Welcome to Lotus 1-2-3** dialogue box shown at the top of the next page.

As you can see, Lotus 1-2-3 gives you the option to either open an existing workbook (if they do exist, they will be listed for you to choose one), browse for more workbooks, or create a blank workbook by pressing one of the similarly named buttons at the bottom of the dialogue box.

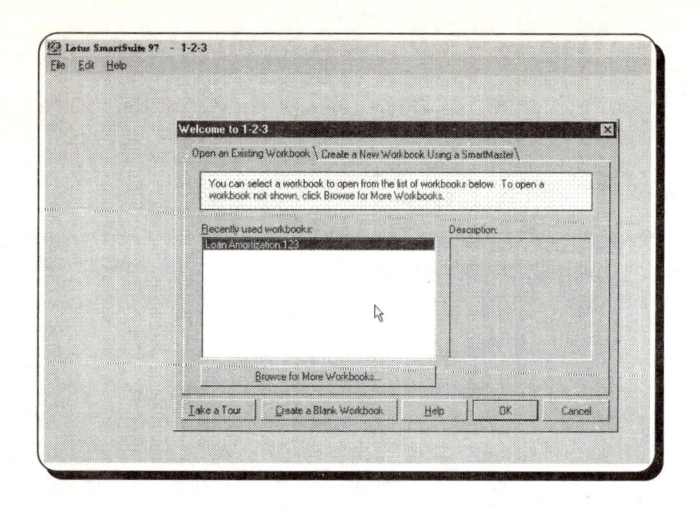

Pressing the 'Create a New Workbook Using a SmartMaster' tab on the above dialogue box, displays the available SmartMaster workbooks, as shown below.

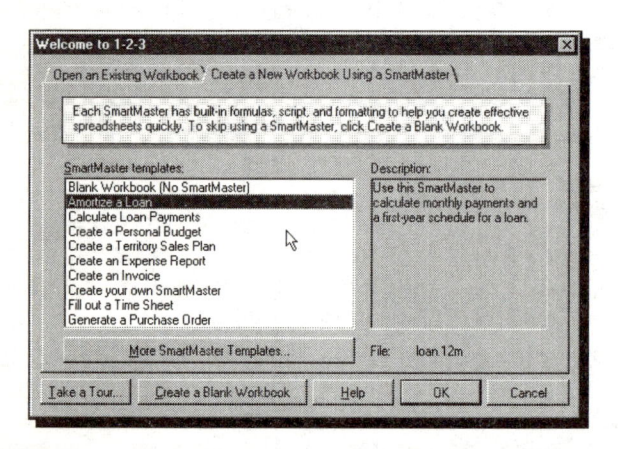

As you highlight each listed SmartMaster template, an explanation of its function is given in the **Description** box to the right of the templates list.

The Lotus 1-2-3 Screen

Opening a Lotus 1-2-3 blank workbook, displays with a similar Title bar, Menu bar, Toolbar and Status bar to those of Word Pro. Obviously there are some differences, but that is to be expected as the two programs serve different purposes.

The opening screen of 1-2-3 is shown below. It is perhaps worth looking at the various parts that make up this screen, or window, if only to see how similar it is to that of Word Pro. 1-2-3 follows the usual Windows conventions with which you should be familiar by now.

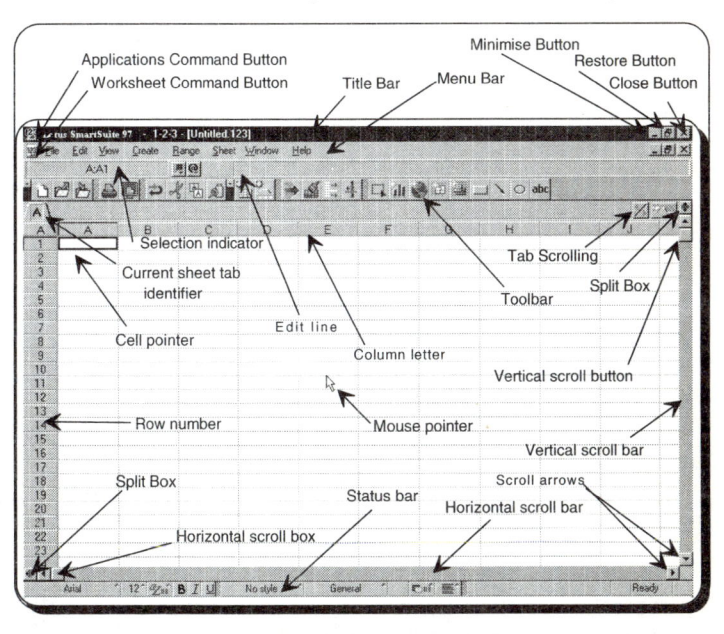

The window as shown above takes up the full screen area. If you click on the application restore button, the top one of the two restore buttons at the top right of the screen, you can make 1-2-3 show in a smaller window. This can be useful when you are running several applications at the same time and you want to transfer between them with the mouse.

Note that the 1-2-3 window, which in this case displays an empty and untitled (Untitled.123) workbook, has some areas which have identical functions to those of Word Pro (see page 19), and other areas which have different functions. Below, we describe only the areas that are exclusive to 1-2-3.

Area	*Function*
Selection indicator	Contains the cell co-ordinates, a named range of cells, a chart item, or a drawing object.
Edit line	Contains the navigator (which allows you to go to named ranges), and the function button that allows you to list the most currently used, or all the 1-2-3 functions. The rest of the edit line box can display a number, a label, or the formula behind a result that you have entered.
Cell pointer	Marks the current cell.
Column letter	The letter that identifies each column.
Row number	The number that identifies each row.
Tab scrolling	Clicking on these buttons, scrolls sheet tabs right or left, when there are more tabs than can be displayed at once.
Current sheet	Shows the current sheet of a number of sheets in a file. These are named A, B, C, etc., by default, but can be changed to, say, North, South, East, and West. Clicking on a sheet tab, moves you to that sheet.
Split Boxes	Allow you to split the screen.

Workbook Navigation

When you first enter 1-2-3, the program sets up a series of huge electronic pages, or worksheets, in your computer's memory, many times larger than the small part shown on the screen. Individual cells are identified by column and row location (in that order), with present size extending to 256 columns and 8,192 rows. The columns are labelled from A to Z, followed by AA to AZ, BA to BZ, and so on, to IV, while the rows are numbered from 1 to 8,192.

A worksheet can be thought of as a two-dimensional table made up of rows and columns. The point where a row and column intersect is called a cell, while the reference points of a cell are known as the cell address. The active cell (A1 when you first enter the program) is boxed. A workbook is made up of several worksheets.

Navigation around the worksheet is achieved by using either the mouse or the keyboard. To move the active cell with a mouse, do the following:

- Point to the cell you want to move to and click the left mouse button. If the cell is not visible, move the window by clicking on the scroll bar arrowhead that points in the direction you want to move,

- To move a page at a time, click in the scroll bar.

- For larger moves, drag the box in the scroll bar, but the distances moved will depend on the size of the worksheet.

To move the active cell with the keyboard, use one of the following keys or key combinations:

- Pressing one of the four arrow keys ($\rightarrow \downarrow \leftarrow \uparrow$) moves the active cell one position right, down, left or up, respectively.

- Pressing the <PgDn> or <PgUp> keys moves the active cell down or up one visible page.

- Pressing the <Ctrl+→> or <Ctrl+←> key combinations moves the active cell one visible screen to the right or one visible screen to the left, respectively.
- Pressing the <Ctrl+Home> key combination, moves the active cell to the A:A1 position of the current workbook.
- Pressing the <End Ctrl+Home> key combination, moves the cell pointer to the bottom right corner of the active area in the last non-blank sheet in the current workbook.
- Pressing the **F5** function key will display the **Go To** dialogue box shown below.

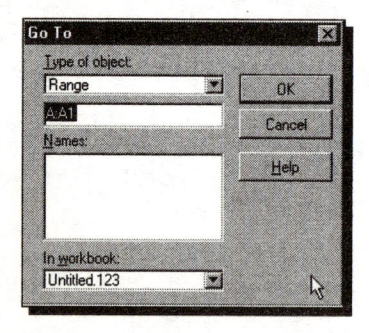

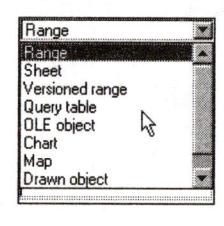

In the **Type of object** box you can either select a range (such as A:C5 which sends the cell pointer to Sheet A, cell C5), or select from a list of named objects in the active workbook (to be discussed shortly) by clicking the down-arrow to the right of the box, which displays the list shown in the top right screen dump.

When you have finished navigating around the worksheet, press the <Ctrl+Home> key combination which will move the active cell to the A:A1 position (provided you have not fixed titles in any rows or columns or have no hidden rows or columns - more about these later).

Note that the area within which you can move the active cell is referred to as the working area of the worksheet, while the letters and numbers in the border at the top and left of the working area give the 'co-ordinates' of the cells in a worksheet.

The location of the active cell is constantly monitored by the 'selection indicator'. As the active cell is moved, this indicator displays its address, as shown below.

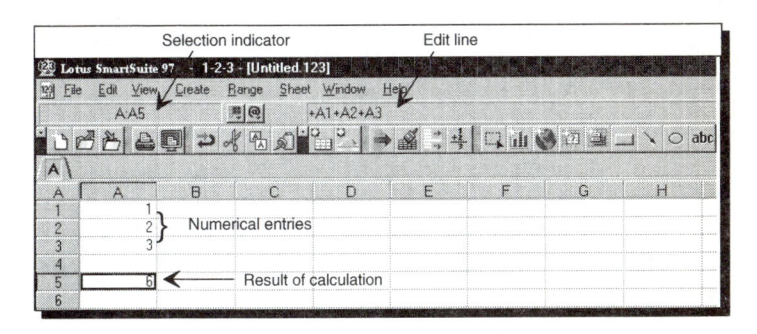

![Screenshot showing Selection indicator and Edit line in Lotus SmartSuite 97 1-2-3, with numerical entries 1, 2, 3 in cells and result of calculation 6]

The contents of a cell are displayed above the Toolbar within what is known as the 'Edit line'. If you type text in the active cell, what you type appears in both the 'Edit line' and the cell itself.

Typing a formula which is preceded by either the plus (+), or equal (=) sign to, say, add the contents of three cells, causes the actual formula to appear in the 'Edit line', while the result of the actual calculation appears in the active cell after pressing <Enter>.

Moving Between Sheets:

Before you can move between sheets of a workbook, you need to create a few more than the one displayed when you create a blank workbook. To create additional sheets (or worksheets), either click the 'Create New Sheet' button, shown here and situated to the right of the Tab Scrolling buttons, or use the **Create, Sheet** command.

Below, we have created two additional sheets which were given their default names B and C by the program. Adding sheets with the Create New Sheet button, adds each one after the sheet that is current at the time.

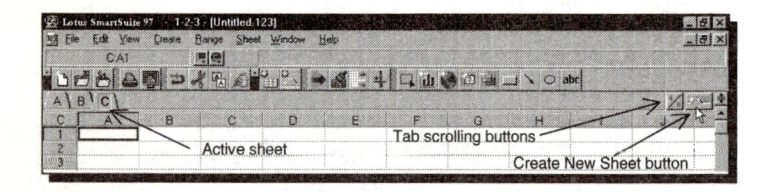

You can move between sheets by simply clicking the tab of the one you want to use, or if you have too many sheets in a workbook and the one you want to use is not visible, then click one of the Tab Scrolling buttons to bring it into view before making it current by clicking its tab.

With the keyboard, you can scroll to the right one sheet at a time, and make it active at the same time, by using the <Ctrl+PgUp> key combination. Using <Ctrl+PgDn> scrolls in the reverse direction.

Renaming Sheets:

Renaming a sheet is very easy. Simply double-click on the tab of the sheet you want to rename and type a new name, as shown below.

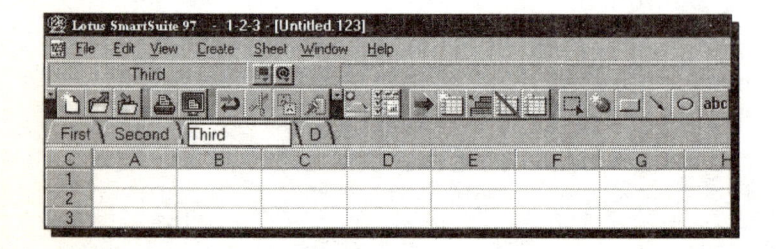

Grouping Sheets:

Grouping contiguous sheets together is useful when you need to apply styles, formats, and other settings of one sheet to other sheets in the group so they are more consistent. To select adjacent sheets, click the first sheet tab, hold down the <Shift> key and then click the last sheet tab in the group. Selecting sheets in the above manner, causes the selected sheets to be shown in white. To cancel the selection, click at the tab of any sheet which is not part of the selected group, or press the <Esc> key.

Once selected, sheets can be grouped together by using the **Sheet, Group Sheets** command which displays the **Group Sheets** dialogue box, allowing to specify from which sheet to copy the various styles. Grouped sheets are displayed with their names in italics, as shown below.

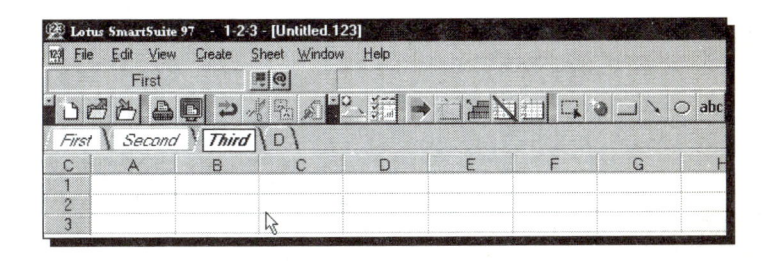

Be careful not to lose data when deleting columns or rows on a worksheet which is part of a group, because when you delete a column or row in one sheet, you also delete it in all other sheets in the group.

To un-group sheets, select one sheet from within the group and use the **Sheet, Clear Sheet Group** command. You will know that the sheets have been cleared of their grouping because their names will not appear in italics anymore.

Selecting a Range of Cells:

To select a range of cells, say, A3:C3, point to cell A3, then

- press the left mouse button, and while holding it pressed, drag the mouse to the right.

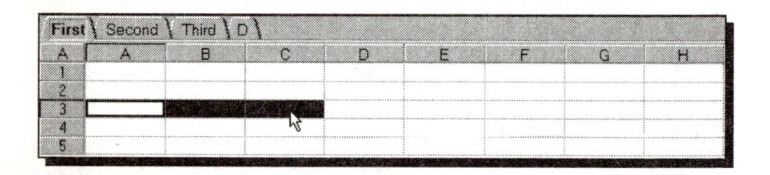

To select a range from the keyboard, first make active the first cell in the range, then

- hold down the <Shift> key and use the right arrow key (→) to highlight the required range.

Shortcut Menus:

While a range of cells in a sheet is selected, or a group of sheets is active, you can access a shortcut menu of relevant commands by pressing the right mouse button. This produces a shortcut menu, as shown here, of the most common commands relevant to what you are doing at the time. Non-accessible commands on a shortcut menu are greyed out.

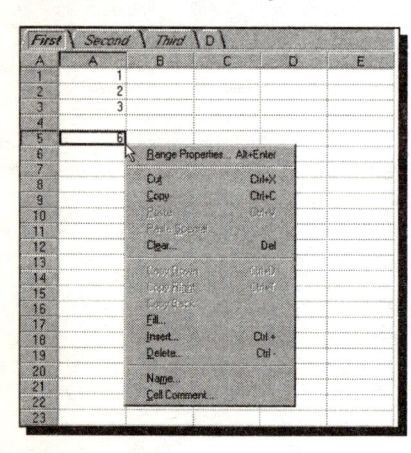

Viewing Multiple Workbook Sheets

To see more clearly what you are doing when working with multiple workbook sheets, type the text '1st' in location A1 of sheet 'First', the text '2nd' in sheet 'Second', and so on. Then use the **Window, New Window** command to add three extra windows to your worksheet. Next, use the **Window, Tile Left-Right** command to display the four sheets as shown below.

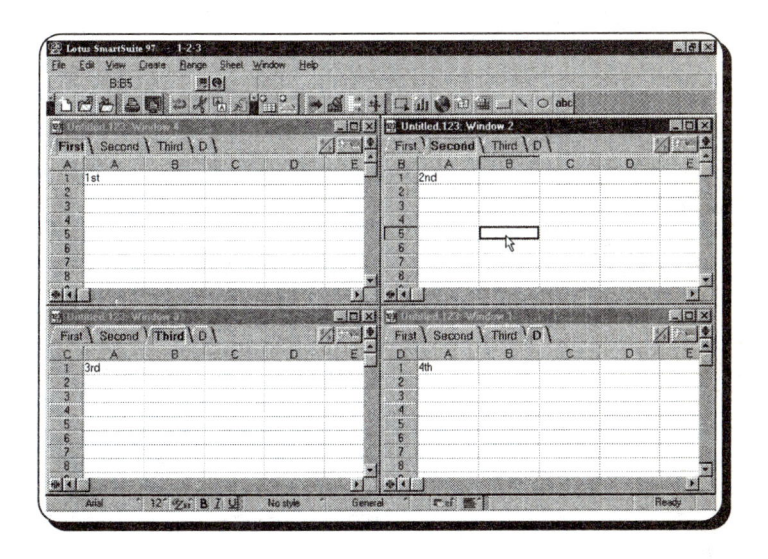

In the above screen, we have pressed the sheet tabs 'First', 'Second', 'Third', and 'D', in a clockwise direction to reveal the contents of these sheets.

To move from one window to another, simply point with the mouse to the cell of the window you want to go to and click the left mouse button. To display a different sheet in each window, go to a window and click the sheet's tab.

To return to single-window view mode from a tiled or cascade mode, click the maximise button of the active window.

123

Entering Information

We will now investigate how information can be entered into a worksheet. But first, make sure you are in sheet 'First', then return to the Home (A1) position, by pressing the <Ctrl+Home> key combination, then type the words:

```
PROJECT ANALYSIS
```

As you type, the characters appear in the active cell. If you make a mistake, press the <BkSp> key to erase the previous letter or the <Esc> key to start again. When you have finished, press <Enter> which displays what you have typed in the 'Edit line'.

Note that what you have just typed in has been entered in cell A1, even though the whole of the word ANALYSIS appears to be in cell B1. If you use the right arrow key to move the active cell to B1 you will see that the cell is indeed empty (the 'Edit line' is empty).

Typing any letter at the beginning of an entry into a cell results in a 'text' entry being formed automatically, otherwise known as a 'label' and is preceded by an apostrophe in the 'Edit line'. If the length of the text is longer than the width of a cell, it will continue into the next cell to the right of the current active cell, provided that cell is empty, otherwise the displayed information will be truncated.

To edit information already in a cell, either

- double-click the cell in question, or
- make that cell the active cell and press the **F2** function key.

The cursor keys, the <Home> and <End> keys, as well as the <Ins> and <Del> keys can be used to move the cursor and/or edit information as required.

You can also 'undo' the last action carried out since the program was last in the **Ready** mode, by clicking the Undo button, shown here.

Next, move the active cell to B3 and type

```
Jan
```

Pressing the right arrow key (→) will automatically enter the typed information into the cell and also move the active cell one cell to the right, in this case to C3. Now type

```
Feb
```

and press <Enter>.

The looks of a worksheet can be enhanced somewhat by using different types of borders around specific cells. To do this, first select the range of cells (A3..C3 in our example), then click the 'Change range properties' icon on the Toolbar, shown here, which displays the **Properties Info** box shown below.

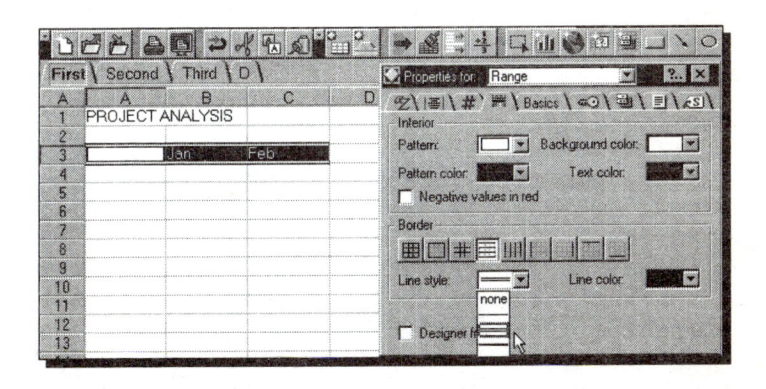

In our example, we have selected first the cell range A3:C3, then the 4th **Border** from the displayed buttons on the **Range Info** box, and finally the double line from the **Line style** drop-down list.

Next, move to cell A4 and type the label Income, then enter the numbers 14000 and 15000 in cells B4 and C4, respectively, as shown overleaf, but note that by default the labels 'Jan' and 'Feb' are left justified, while the numbers are right justified.

Changing Text Alignment and Fonts:

One way of improving the looks of this worksheet is to also right justify the text 'Jan' and 'Feb' within their respective cells. To do this, move the active cell to B3 and select the range B3 to C3 by dragging the mouse, then either click the Alignment button on the Status bar and select the 'Right Align' icon, shown below, or click the Alignment tab of the **Range Info** box and select the appropriate option.

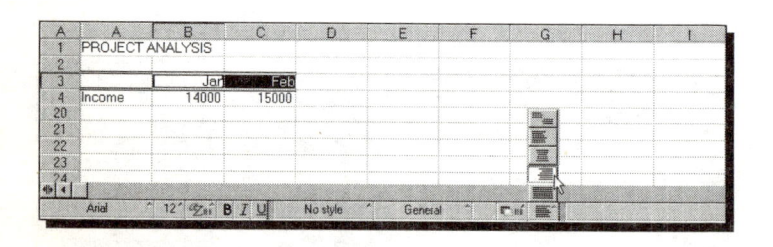

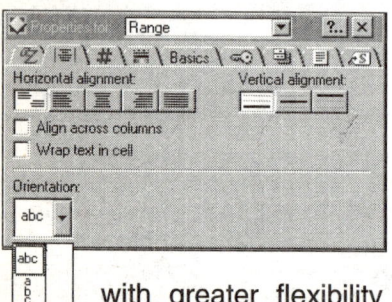

No matter which method you choose, the text should now appear right justified within their cells, as shown above. Using the **Range Info** box is slightly lengthier, but it provides you with greater flexibility in displaying text. For example, you have several options in terms of **Horizontal alignment**, **Vertical alignment** and **Orientation**, as shown here.

We could further improve the looks of our worksheet by choosing a different font for the heading 'Project Analysis'. To achieve this, select cell A1, then click either the 'Font Size' button on the Status bar, or the Font tab on the **Range Info** box to reveal the available point sizes for the selected font. From either of these, choose 14, then embolden and italicise the heading.

Finally, since the numbers in cells B4 to C4 represent money, it would be better if these were prefixed with the £ sign. To do this, select the cell range B4..C4, then click either the 'Number Style' button on the Status bar, or the Number tab on the **Range Info** box, shown here, and select the appropriate currency. The numbers within the chosen range will now be displayed in currency form.

If a cell is not wide enough to accommodate all the digits of a large number, it will appear as shown under the 'Feb' entry. To see the actual number, we must increase the width of column C to more characters than the default 9 characters shown in the pop-up text box when the mouse pointer is placed in between the column letters on the dividing line and the left mouse button is pressed. To change the column width, drag the pointer to the right.

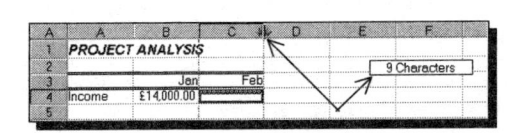

Saving a Workbook

Now, let us assume that we would like to stop at this point, but would also like to save the work entered so far before leaving the program. First, return to the Home position by pressing <Ctrl+Home>. This is good practice because when a workbook is opened later, the position of the cell pointer appears on the screen at the very same spot as when you saved the worksheet, which might cause confusion if above and to the left of it there are no entries - you might think that you have opened an empty worksheet.

Next, choose the **File, Save As** command to reveal the **Save As** dialogue box shown below.

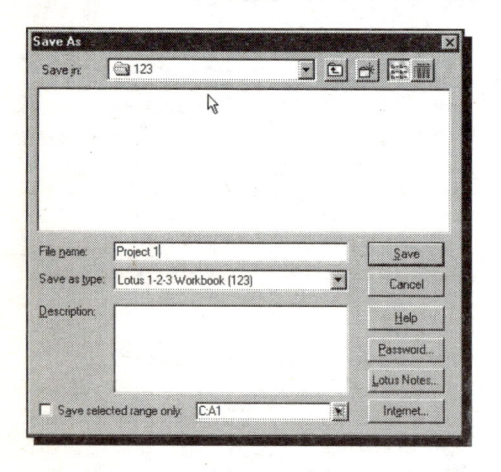

You could select to save your work in the default folder, another folder or a different drive - the choice is yours. Next, type the new name of the file, say, **Project 1** in the **File name** box. The file will be saved in the default file type *Lotus 1-2-3 Workbook (123)*, as displayed in the **Save as type** box. The program adds the file extension **.123** automatically and uses it to identify it later.

If you want to provide protection to your workbook, click the **Password** button and type a password. However, make sure that you remember this password later, otherwise 1-2-3 will refuse you access. Finally, you could type an optional description in the **Description** box, before pressing the **Save** button, to save your work to disc in the chosen folder.

Opening a Workbook

An already saved workbook, or file, can be opened by either clicking at the 'Open' icon, shown here, or selecting the **File, Open** command which both display the **Open** dialogue box. Do not forget to change to the drive where you saved your work. Lotus 1-2-3 asks for a filename to open, with the default *Lotus 1-2-3 Workbook (123;WK*)* being displayed in the **Files of type** box, as shown below. If the file was saved in the folder displayed in the **Look in** box, it will appear in the list box. If this is the case, select it by clicking its name, then click the **Open** button.

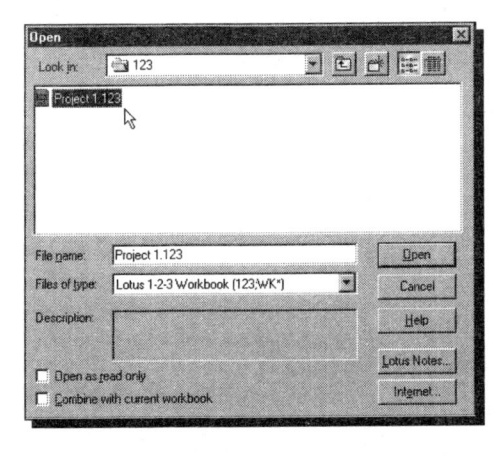

If you haven't saved **Project 1**, don't worry as you could just as easily start afresh.

If you want to change the logged drive, click the down-arrow against the **Look in** box, and select the appropriate drive from the drop-down list. If you need to change the logged folder, click the Up One Level button, shown here, on the **Open** dialogue box and move through the various levels of folders, until you find the one which contains your workbook.

Exiting Lotus 1-2-3

To exit 1-2-3, close any displayed dialogue boxes by clicking the **Cancel** button, and make sure that the word **Ready** is displayed on the status bar (press the <Esc> key until it does), and either

- choose the **File, Exit 1-2-3** command,
- use the <Alt+F4> key combination, or
- click the Close button.

No matter which command you choose, if you have changed any opened workbook, 1-2-3 will warn you and will ask for confirmation before exiting the program.

8. FILLING IN A WORKSHEET

We will use, as an example of how a worksheet can be built up, the few entries on 'Project Analysis' from the previous chapter. If you have saved **Project 1**, then either click the Open button, or use the **File, Open** command, then highlight its filename in the **Open** dialogue box, and click the **Open** button. If you haven't saved it, don't worry as you could just as easily start afresh.

Next, either double-click the contents of a cell to edit existing entries, or simply retype the contents of cells, so that your worksheet looks as near as possible to the one below. For formatting details, see next page.

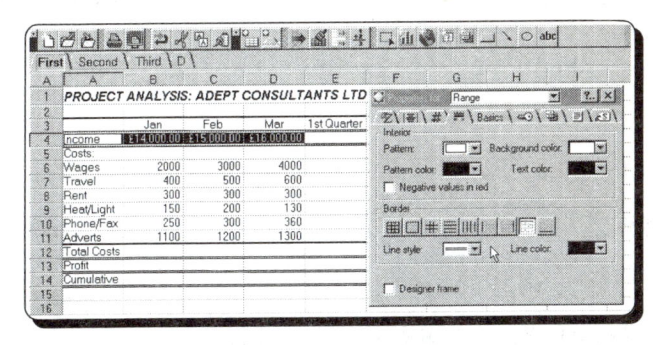

For quick formatting or reformatting of cell ranges, select a cell whose format you want to copy (a blank cell for removing previously applied formats), then click the 'brush' button on the Toolbar, shown here, which changes the mouse pointer to a brush.

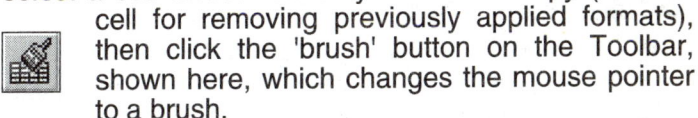

Next, select the range to which you want to copy the chosen format, as shown overleaf. The instant the mouse button is released, the copied format is transfered to the highlighted range. The mouse pointer remains in the shape of a brush, indicating that you can continue to format other ranges, until you click the 'brush' button on the Toolbar once more to return to normal entry mode.

Formatting Entries

The information in cell A1 (PROJECT ANALYSIS: ADEPT CONSULTANTS LTD) was entered left justified and formatted by clicking on the 'Font Size' button on the Status bar, and selecting 14 point font size from the band of available font sizes, then clicking in succession the 'Bold' and 'Italic' icons.

The double line at top and bottom of range A3..C3 of **Project 1** were first removed by copying a blank unformatted cell to the range, then the range A3..E3 was formatted with a single line at the top of the range by clicking the 'Color, pattern and line style' tab of the **Range Info** box, and selecting the appropriate border and line style. The latter formatting was then copied to range A12..E12.

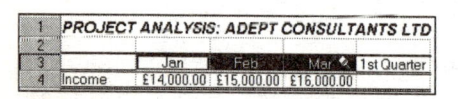

The lines, like the double line at top and bottom of the cell range A4..E4, were entered by using the appropriate border and line style from the **Range Info** box. This formatting was then copied to ranges A13..E13, and A14..E14.

Text entries in the cell block B3..E3 were centred within their respective cells by first selecting the range and then using the appropriate option from the Alignment button on the Status bar.

The numbers within the cell block B4:E4 were formatted by first selecting the range, then clicking either the 'Number Style' button on the Status bar, or the Number tab on the **Range Info** box and selecting the appropriate currency, so that the numbers appeared with two digits after the decimal point and prefixed with the £ sign.

All the text appearing in column A (apart from that in cell A1) was just typed in (left justified), as shown in the screen dump on the previous page.

Filling a Range by Example:

To fill a range by example, select the range, point at the bottom right corner of the selected range and when two sets of directional arrows appear against the mouse pointer, drag the mouse in the required direction, as shown in the screen dump here, where both the action required and the result of that action are shown.

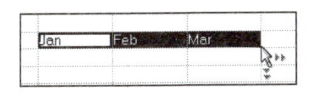

In the above case, we typed 'Jan' in one cell, then dragged the modified cell pointer to the right. On releasing the mouse button, Lotus 1-2-3 filled the next two cells with the text 'Feb' and 'Mar' (1-2-3 anticipates that you want to fill cells by example with the abbreviations for months, and does it for you).

Fill by example, also works with numbers. For example, in what is shown on the left, we started by typing the numeral 1 in one cell, then dragging the modified cell pointer down and to the right to highlight a rectangle. On releasing the mouse button, 1-2-3 fills the selected range by the number sequence shown here.

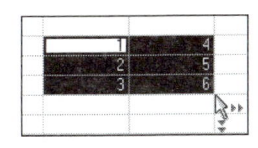

If you want to fill a range by anything other than by example, then use the **Range, Fill** command. This displays the **Fill** dialogue box, shown to the left, which can be used to control both the start, stop, increment and range we wish to fill. Note also the other available options listed in the **Fill using** box.

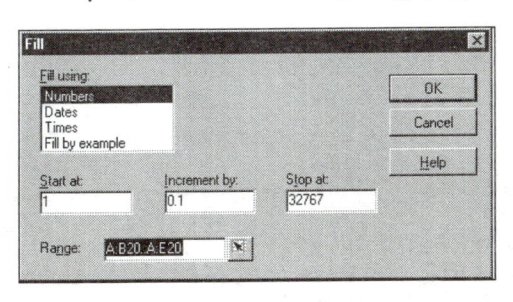

133

Entering Text, Numbers and Formulae:

Lotus 1-2-3 allows you to format both text (labels) and numbers in any way you choose. For example, you can have numbers centre justified in their cells.

When text, a number, a formula, or a Lotus 1-2-3 function is entered into a cell, or reference is made to the contents of a cell by the cell address, then the content at the extreme right of the status bar changes from **Ready** to **Label** (when entering text), **Enter** (when entering a number, a formula, or a function), and **Point** (when reference is made to the contents of a cell). This status can be changed back to **Ready** by either completing an entry and pressing <Enter> or one of the arrow keys, or by pressing <Esc>.

We can find the 1st quarter total income from consultancy, by activating cell E4, typing

```
=B4+C4+D4
```

and pressing <Enter>. The total first quarter income is added, using the above formula, and the result is placed in cell E4. Should you look at the formula in cell E4, you will see that Lotus 1-2-3 has changed your entry to

```
+B4+C4+D4
```

replacing the typed equal (=) sign with a plus (+) sign. Lotus 1-2-3 accepts both starting signs, but reverts to the latter automatically.

Now complete the insertion into the spreadsheet of the various amounts under 'Costs' and then choose the

File, Save As

command to save the resultant worksheet under the filename **Project 2**, before going on any further. Remember that saving your work on disc often is a good thing to get used to, as even the shortest power cut can cause the loss of hours of hard work!

Using Functions

In our example, writing a formula that adds the contents of three columns is not too difficult or lengthy a task. But imagine having to add 20 columns! For this reason 1-2-3 has an in-built summation function which can be used to add any number of columns (or rows).

To illustrate how this and other functions can be used, activate cell E4 and press the Function button shown here. If the function you require appears on the displayed list, choose it, otherwise select the **List all** option to list all the available functions within a dialogue box. From here, you can choose to look at either all the functions, or only those within an appropriate class, as shown to the right, listed in alphabetical order.

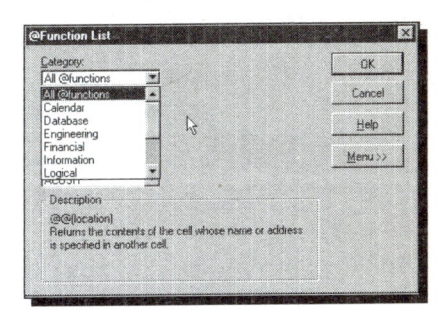

Choosing the **SUM** function from the drop-down list which appears when you press the Function button, inserts the entry @SUM(list) in the cell, as shown to the left. Note the modified cell pointer which indicates that the program is waiting for you to specify a range for the function. Now, place the modified cell pointer on cell B4, press the left mouse button and drag the pointer to the right onto cell D4. On releasing the mouse button, 1-2-3 completes the formula in E4 as @SUM(B4..D4) and pressing <Enter> evaluates the result.

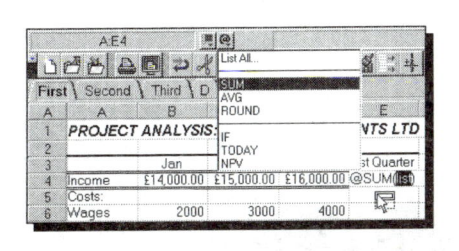

135

Using the AutoSum Icon:

With addition, there is a better and quicker way of letting 1-2-3 work out the desired result. To illustrate this, select the cell range B6:E12, which contains the 'Costs' we would like to add up. To add these in both the horizontal and vertical direction, we include in the selected range an empty column to the right of the numbers and an empty row below the numbers, as shown below.

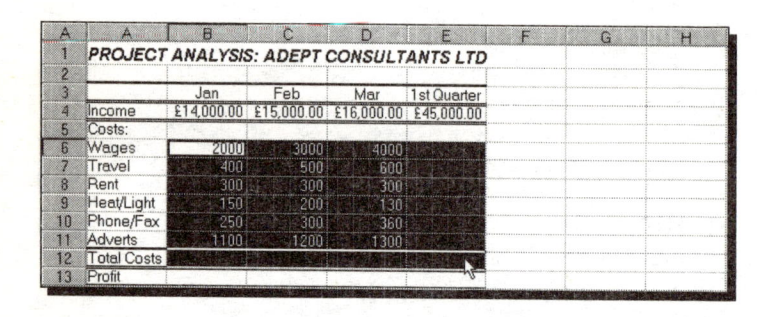

A	A	B	C	D	E	F	G	H
1	PROJECT ANALYSIS: ADEPT CONSULTANTS LTD							
2								
3		Jan	Feb	Mar	1st Quarter			
4	Income	£14,000.00	£15,000.00	£16,000.00	£45,000.00			
5	Costs:							
6	Wages	2000	3000	4000				
7	Travel	400	500	600				
8	Rent	300	300	300				
9	Heat/Light	150	200	130				
10	Phone/Fax	250	300	360				
11	Adverts	1100	1200	1300				
12	Total Costs							
13	Profit							

Pressing the 'AutoSum' icon, shown here, inserts the result of the summations in the empty column and row, as shown below. The selected range remains selected so that any other formatting can be applied by simply pressing the appropriate formatting button.

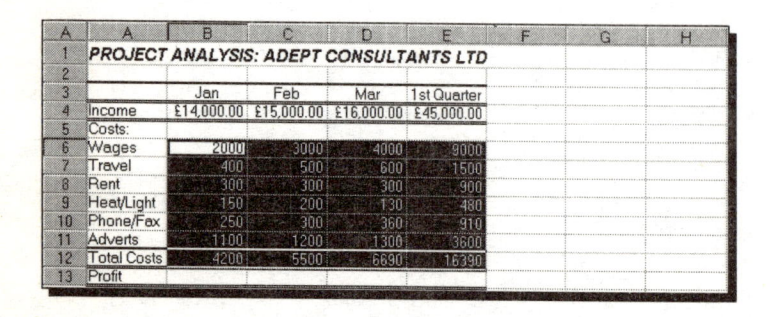

A	A	B	C	D	E	F	G	H
1	PROJECT ANALYSIS: ADEPT CONSULTANTS LTD							
2								
3		Jan	Feb	Mar	1st Quarter			
4	Income	£14,000.00	£15,000.00	£16,000.00	£45,000.00			
5	Costs:							
6	Wages	2000	3000	4000	9000			
7	Travel	400	500	600	1500			
8	Rent	300	300	300	900			
9	Heat/Light	150	200	130	480			
10	Phone/Fax	250	300	360	910			
11	Adverts	1100	1200	1300	3600			
12	Total Costs	4200	5500	6690	16390			
13	Profit							

Now complete the insertion of formulae in the rest of the worksheet, noting that 'Profit', in B13, is the difference between 'Income' and 'Total Cost', calculated by the formula =**B4-B12**. To complete the entry, this formula should be copied using the 'fill by example' method into the three cells to its right.

The 'Cumulative' entry in cell B14 should be a simple reference to cell B13, that is =**B13**, while in cell C14 it should be =**B14+C13**. Similarly, the latter formula is copied into cell D14 using the 'fill by example' method.

Next, format the entire range B6:E12 by selecting the range and clicking the Number (#) tab of the **Range Info** box and selecting the Currency, British Pound options. If you make any mistakes and copy formats or other data into cells you did not mean to, use the **Edit, Undo** command or click the Undo button which allows you to undo what you were just doing. To blank the contents within a range of cells, first select the range, then press the <Del> key.

The worksheet, up to this point, should look as follows:

A	A	B	C	D	E	F	G
1	PROJECT ANALYSIS: ADEPT CONSULTANTS LTD						
2							
3		Jan	Feb	Mar	1st Quarter		
4	Income	£14,000.00	£15,000.00	£16,000.00	£45,000.00		
5	Costs:						
6	Wages	£2,000.00	£3,000.00	£4,000.00	£9,000.00		
7	Travel	£400.00	£500.00	£600.00	£1,500.00		
8	Rent	£300.00	£300.00	£300.00	£900.00		
9	Heat/Light	£150.00	£200.00	£130.00	£480.00		
10	Phone/Fax	£250.00	£300.00	£360.00	£910.00		
11	Adverts	£1,100.00	£1,200.00	£1,300.00	£3,600.00		
12	Total Costs	£4,200.00	£5,500.00	£6,690.00	£16,390.00		
13	Profit	£9,800.00	£9,500.00	£9,310.00	£28,610.00		
14	Cumulative	£9,800.00	£19,300.00	£28,610.00			
15							

Finally, use the **File, Save As** command to save your work under the filename **Project 3**.

Printing a Worksheet

To print a worksheet, make sure that the printer you propose to use was defined when you first installed Windows.

If you have named more than one printer in your original installation of Windows, and want to select a printer other than your original first choice, then select the **File, Print** command, click the down-arrow against the **Print to** box on the displayed **Print** dialogue box and select the required printer, as shown below.

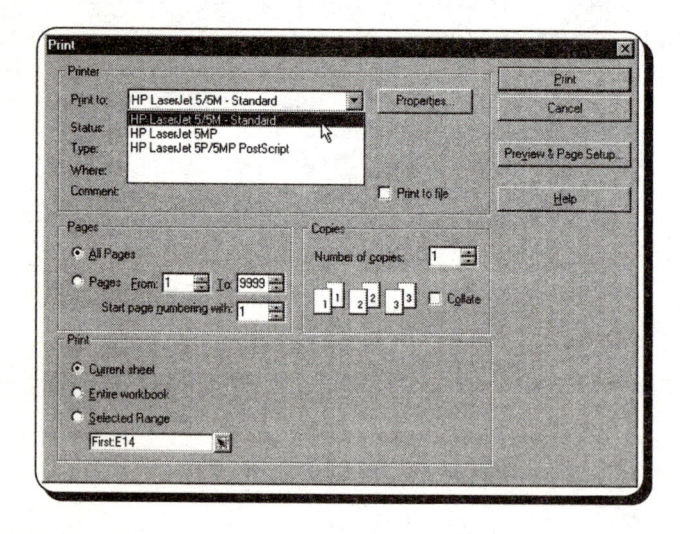

If you want to change the paper size, print orientation or printer resolution, click the **Properties** button on the **Print** dialogue box which causes the **Setup: Print Properties** dialogue box to be displayed, as shown on the next page. These and other changes to the appearance of the printout can also be controlled from the **Preview & Page Setup Info** box which can be displayed by either using the **File, Preview & Page Setup** command, or pressing the **Preview & Page Setup** button on the **Print** dialogue box.

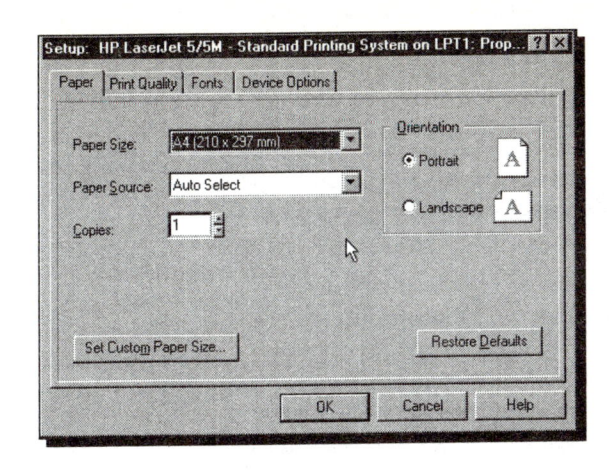

By selecting the appropriate Tab on the above dialogue box, you can change your **Paper** size, **Print Quality**, printer **Fonts** and other **Device Options**.

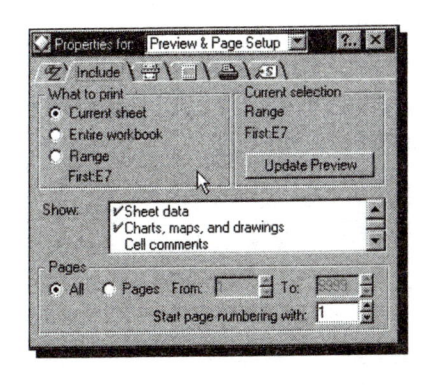

The Include tab of the **Preview & Page Setup Info** box can give you extra control on **What to print**, while the next two tabs control the margins and the headers and footers, respectively. Clicking each tab displays a different dialogue box, appropriate to the function at hand. Try it.

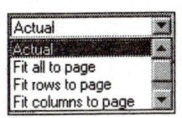

A very useful feature of 1-2-3 is the ability to scale your printout so as to fit it to a page. To activate this facility, click the Margins tab of the **Preview & Page Setup Info** box, click the down-arrow against the **Page fit** box, and select the 'Fit all to page' option.

Page Preview:

As we have already seen, you can preview a worksheet by using the **File, Preview & Page Setup** command, or by clicking the Preview button on the Toolbar, shown here. This not only displays the **Preview & Page Setup Info** box, but also displays a preview of your document so that you can see how it will print on paper.

A very useful option of the preview facility is the ability to select to display the active worksheet, the whole workbook, or a selected range. You can, in addition, choose to look at the formulae embedded in your worksheet as shown below.

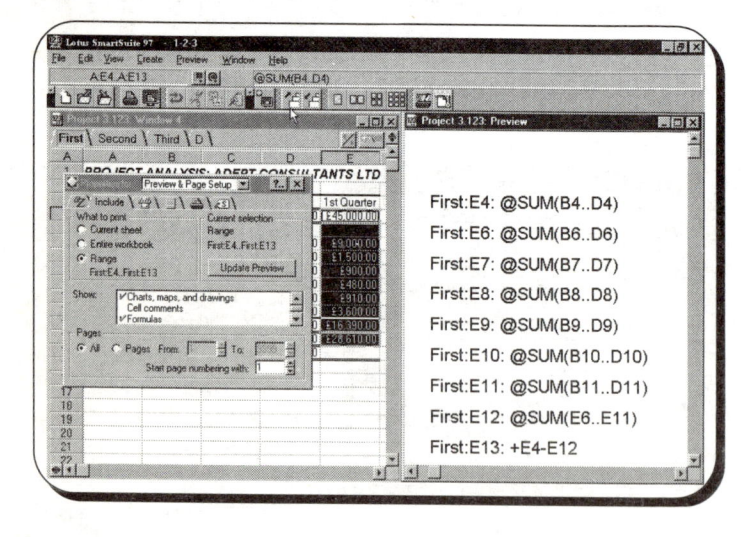

To display the above, first highlight the range E4..E13, of **Project 3**, then click the Preview button on the Toolbar. Next, scroll down the **Show** list and click on 'Formulas', followed by clicking the 'Show Next Page' button on the Toolbar.

The idea of all these preview choices is to make it easy for you to see your work on screen before committing it to paper, thus saving even more trees!

Enhancing a Worksheet

You can make your work look more professional by adopting various enhancements, such as single and double line cell borders, shading certain cells, and adding meaningful headers and footers.

We have already dealt with the single and double line cell borders, so here we will concentrate on shading and adding headers and footers. What we would like to see on our screen is the following:

A	A	B	C	D	E
1	PROJECT ANALYSIS: ADEPT CONSULTANTS LTD				
2					
3		Jan	Feb	Mar	1st Quarter
4	Income	£14,000.00	£15,000.00	£16,000.00	£45,000.00
5	Costs:				
6	Wages	£2,000.00	£3,000.00	£4,000.00	£9,000.00
7	Travel	£400.00	£500.00	£600.00	£1,500.00
8	Rent	£300.00	£300.00	£300.00	£900.00
9	Heat/Light	£150.00	£200.00	£130.00	£480.00
10	Phone/Fax	£250.00	£300.00	£360.00	£910.00
11	Adverts	£1,100.00	£1,200.00	£1,300.00	£3,600.00
12	Total Costs	£4,200.00	£5,500.00	£6,690.00	£16,390.00
13	Profit	£9,800.00	£9,500.00	£9,310.00	£28,610.00
14	Cumulative	£9,800.00	£19,300.00	£28,610.00	

To achieve the above looks, do the following:
- Select range A3..E3
- Click the 'Color, pattern & line style' tab of the **Range Info** box
- Choose **Background color**: plum red, and **Text color**: white
- Select range A4..A14
- Chose **Background color**: 25% grey.

Finally, save the worksheet as **Project 4**, before going on.

Header and Footer Icons and Codes:

With the help of header and footer icons and their codes, shown below, you can position text or automatically insert information at the top or bottom of a report printout.

To add a header and a footer to our printed example, use the **File, Preview & Page Setup** command and click the 'Headers and Footers' tab to display the dialogue box shown below. Next, type in the **Left header** box the words 'Quarterly Profits', and in the **Right header** box the words 'Adept Consultants'. Finally, while the insertion pointer is in the **Left footer** box, click the 'Current system date' button (the first of the **Insert** buttons), and while in the **Right footer** box, click the 'Page number' button (the third of the **Insert** buttons).

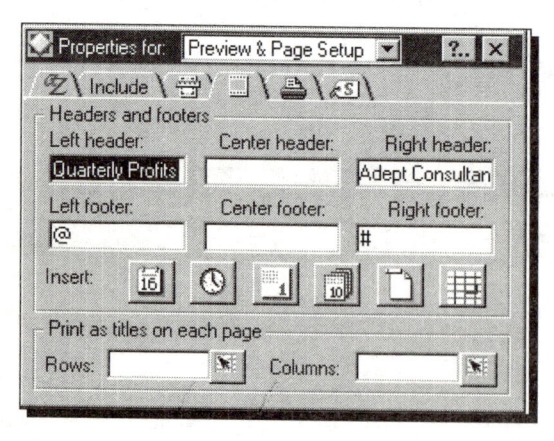

Before printing your worksheet on paper, let us centre it horizontally on the page. To do this, click the 'Margins orientation and placement' tab of the **Preview & Page Setup Info** box, and check the **Left to right** box under the **Center** section, as shown to the left.

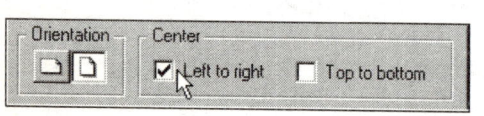

You can now print your worksheet, either by clicking the 'Quick-print the current selection' button on the Toolbar, shown here, which however only appears on the Toolbar if you are in Print Preview mode.

Another way to print your work, is either to use the **File, Print** menu command, or click the Print button on the Toolbar, shown here. In both of these options, the default selection in the **What to print** box of the **Preview & Page Setup** dialogue box (when the Include tab is pressed) is **Current sheet**, unless you have specified otherwise. Finally, printing our worksheet, produces the following page:

Quarterly Profits   Adept Consultants

PROJECT ANALYSIS: ADEPT CONSULTANTS LTD

	Jan	Feb	Mar	1st Quarter
Income	£14,000.00	£15,000.00	£16,000.00	£45,000.00
Costs:				
Wages	£2,000.00	£3,000.00	£4,000.00	£9,000.00
Travel	£400.00	£500.00	£600.00	£1,500.00
Rent	£300.00	£300.00	£300.00	£900.00
Heat/Light	£150.00	£200.00	£130.00	£480.00
Phone/Fax	£250.00	£300.00	£360.00	£910.00
Adverts	£1,100.00	£1,200.00	£1,300.00	£3,600.00
Total Costs	£4,200.00	£5,500.00	£6,690.00	£16,390.00
Profit	£9,800.00	£9,500.00	£9,310.00	£28,610.00
Cumulative	£9,800.00	£19,300.00	£28,610.00	

12/12/97   Page 1

3-Dimensional Worksheets

In Lotus 1-2-3, a Workbook is a 3-dimensional file made up with a series of flat 2-dimensional sheets stacked 'on top of each other'. Each sheet is the same size, and in itself, behaves the same as the more ordinary worksheets. As mentioned previously, each separate sheet in a file has its own Tab identifier at the top of the screen. Ranges can be set to span several different sheets to build up 3-dimensional blocks of data. A cell can reference any other cell in the file, no matter what sheet it is on. The best way to demonstrate a new idea is to work through an example - we will use the worksheet saved under **Project 4**.

Copying Sheets in a Workbook:

We will now fill another three sheets behind the present one, in order to include information about ADEPT Consultants' trading during the other three quarters of the year. The easiest way of doing this is by copying the information in the First sheet, including its formatting and the entered formulae, onto the other three sheets, then editing the numerical information in these appropriately.

First, add three more sheets to your workbook, unless you have already done so, by clicking the Create New Sheet button, then change their names to 'First Quarter', 'Second Quarter', 'Third Quarter' and 'Fourth Quarter, respectively.

To copy information from the first sheet of our example to the new sheets, select the range A1..E14 of the First Quarter by highlighting it, click on the Copy button on the Toolbar to copy it to the clipboard, then click on the Tab of the Second Quarter, place the cell pointer in cell A1, and press the Paste button to make an identical copy of what was held in the First Quarter sheet.

As the information copied to the Clipboard is still intact, to transfer it to Third Quarter sheet, click on its Tab and again press the Paste button, and repeat the process for the Fourth Quarter. The contents of the Second Quarter sheet, after editing, should be as follows:

B	A	B	C	D	E
1	*PROJECT ANALYSIS: Second Quarter*				
2					
3		Jan	Feb	Mar	1st Quarter
4	Income	£15,500.00	£16,000.00	£16,500.00	£48,000.00
5	Costs:				
6	Wages	£3,500.00	£4,000.00	£4,500.00	£12,000.00
7	Travel	£500.00	£550.00	£580.00	£1,630.00
8	Rent	£300.00	£300.00	£300.00	£900.00
9	Heat/Light	£150.00	£120.00	£100.00	£370.00
10	Phone/Fax	£300.00	£350.00	£400.00	£1,050.00
11	Adverts	£1,250.00	£1,300.00	£1,350.00	£3,900.00
12	Total Costs	£6,000.00	£6,620.00	£7,230.00	£19,850.00
13	Profit	£9,500.00	£9,380.00	£9,270.00	£28,150.00
14	Cumulative	£9,500.00	£18,880.00	£28,150.00	

The easiest way to edit the Second Quarter labels is to either use the EDIT key (**F2**), or double-click the cell you want to edit. The numbers held in range B4..D11 are best retyped, while the rest of the cells which hold formulae should be left alone. Be extra careful, from now on, to check the identification Tab at the top of the screen, so as not to get the sheets mixed up. You do not want to spend time editing the wrong worksheet!

After building up the four worksheets (one for each quarter - see below for details on the 3rd and 4th quarters), save the file as **Project 5**.

	Jul	Aug	Sep	Oct	Nov	Dec
Income	17,000	17,500	18,000	18,500	19,000	19,500
Costs:						
Wages	4,000	4,500	5,000	4,500	5,000	5,500
Travel	600	650	680	630	670	700
Rent	300	300	300	300	300	300
Heat/Light	50	80	120	160	200	250
Phone/Fax	350	380	420	400	420	450
Adverts	1,400	1,450	1,500	1,480	1,500	1,530

Linking Worksheets:

A consolidation sheet could be placed in front of our 'stack' of data sheets to show a full year's results. To do so, use the **Create, Sheet** command and choose the **Before current sheet** option on the displayed dialogue box, shown here.

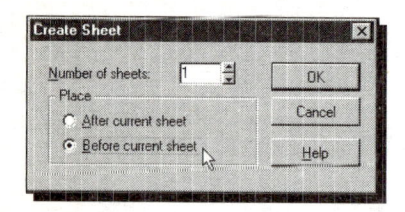

Next, make a copy of the First Quarter sheet and place it in the newly created sheet, delete the entries in columns B to E (by highlighting the range and pressing the <Del> key), then name it 'Consolidation'.

We are now in a position to link the consolidation sheet to the other quarterly data sheets so that the information contained on them is automatically summarised and updated on it. The quarter totals in columns E of sheets First Quarter, Second Quarter, Third Quarter, and Fourth Quarter, can be copied in turn to the clipboard using the **Edit, Copy** command, and then pasted to the appropriate column of the Consolidation sheet with the use of the **Edit, Paste Link** command.

Next, insert appropriate formulae in row 14 to correctly calculate the cumulative values in the Consolidation sheet. The result should be as shown on the next page

Note: Empty cells linked with this method, like those in cells E5 of each quarter, appear as 0 (zero) in the Consolidation sheet. To remove these, highlight the range B5..E5 of the Consolidation sheet, and press the <Del> key.

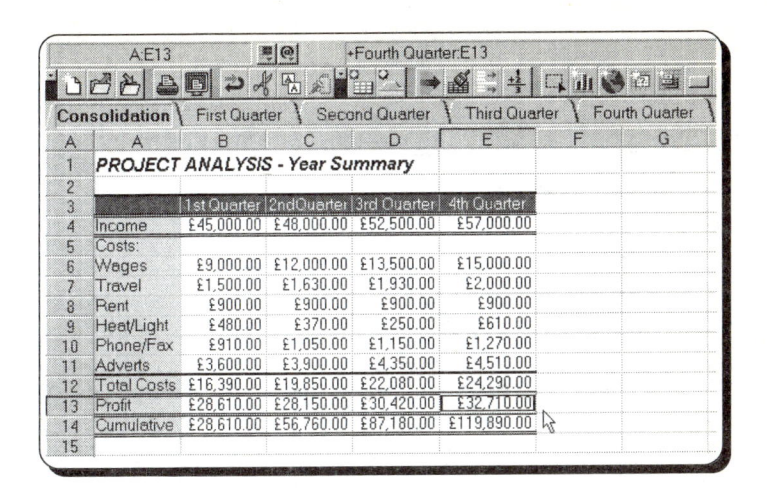

	A	B	C	D	E	F	G
1	PROJECT ANALYSIS - Year Summary						
2							
3		1st Quarter	2nd Quarter	3rd Quarter	4th Quarter		
4	Income	£45,000.00	£48,000.00	£52,500.00	£57,000.00		
5	Costs:						
6	Wages	£9,000.00	£12,000.00	£13,500.00	£15,000.00		
7	Travel	£1,500.00	£1,630.00	£1,930.00	£2,000.00		
8	Rent	£900.00	£900.00	£900.00	£900.00		
9	Heat/Light	£480.00	£370.00	£250.00	£610.00		
10	Phone/Fax	£910.00	£1,050.00	£1,150.00	£1,270.00		
11	Adverts	£3,600.00	£3,900.00	£4,350.00	£4,510.00		
12	Total Costs	£16,390.00	£19,850.00	£22,080.00	£24,290.00		
13	Profit	£28,610.00	£28,150.00	£30,420.00	£32,710.00		
14	Cumulative	£28,610.00	£56,760.00	£87,180.00	£119,890.00		
15							

Finally, save the resultant workbook as **Project 6**.

Relative and Absolute Cell Addresses

Entering a mathematical expression into 1-2-3, such as the formula in cell C14 which was

=B14+C13

causes 1-2-3 to interpret it as 'add the contents of cell one column to the left of the current position, to the contents of cell one row above the current position'. In this way, when the formula was later copied into cell address D14, the contents of the cell relative to the left position of D14 (i.e. C14) and the contents of the cell one row above it (i.e. D13) were used, instead of the original cell addresses entered in C14. This is relative addressing.

To see the effect of relative versus absolute addressing, copy the formula in cell C14 into C16, as shown on the next page.

	A	B	C	D	E	F	G
1	**PROJECT ANALYSIS - Year Summary**						
2							
3		1st Quarter	2ndQuarter	3rd Quarter	4th Quarter		
4	Income	£45,000.00	£48,000.00	£52,500.00	£57,000.00		
5	Costs:						
6	Wages	£9,000.00	£12,000.00	£13,500.00	£15,000.00		
7	Travel	£1,500.00	£1,630.00	£1,930.00	£2,000.00		
8	Rent	£900.00	£900.00	£900.00	£900.00		
9	Heat/Light	£480.00	£370.00	£250.00	£610.00		
10	Phone/Fax	£910.00	£1,050.00	£1,150.00	£1,270.00		
11	Adverts	£3,600.00	£3,900.00	£4,350.00	£4,510.00		
12	Total Costs	£16,390.00	£19,850.00	£22,080.00	£24,290.00		
13	Profit	£28,610.00	£28,150.00	£30,420.00	£32,710.00		
14	Cumulative	£28,610.00	£56,760.00	£87,180.00	£119,890.00		
15							
16			£0.00				

Note that in cell C14 the formula was =B14+C13. However, when copied into cell C17 the formula appears as

=B16+C15

because it has been interpreted as relative addressing. In this case, no value appears in cell C16 because we are attempting to add two blank cells.

Now change the formula in C14 by editing it to

=$B$14+$C$13

which is interpreted as absolute addressing. Copying this formula into cell C16 calculates the correct result. Highlight cell C16 and observe the cell references in its formula; they have not changed from those of cell C14.

In our case, the $ sign must prefix both the column reference and the row reference. Mixed cell addressing is permitted; as for example when a column address reference is needed to be taken as absolute, while a row address reference is needed to be taken as relative. In such a case, only the column letter is prefixed by the $ sign.

When building an absolute cell reference in a formula, it is easier to select the cell with the mouse pointer and keep pressing the **F4** function key until the correct $ prefix is set.

Freezing Panes on Screen

Sometimes there might be too much information on screen and attempting to see a certain part of a sheet might cause the labels associated with that information to scroll off the screen.

To freeze column (or row) labels of a worksheet on screen, move the cell pointer to the right (or below) the column (or row) which you want to freeze, and use the **View, Titles** command, which displays the dialogue box shown below.

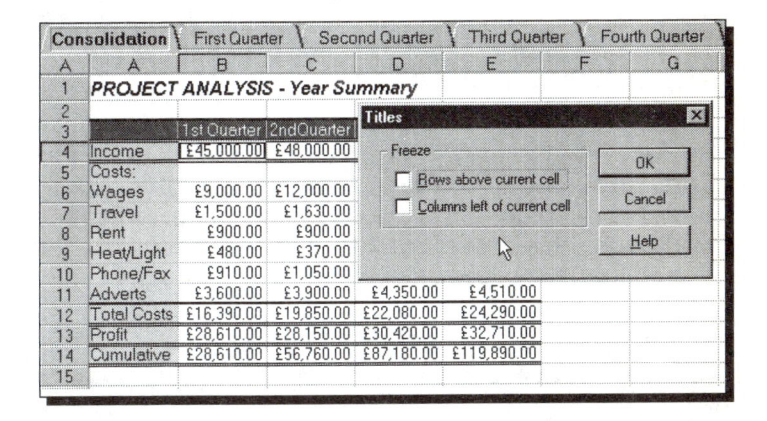

By checking the appropriate squares under the **Freeze** option of the dialogue box, you can freeze on the screen all the rows above the current cell, or all the columns to the left of the current cell, or both. Try it, then see how it works by scrolling information on the screen.

To unfreeze titles, use the **View, Titles** command once more, and unckeck the appropriate boxes under the **Freeze** option.

Linking Files

In the last example (**Project 6**), we built a consolidation report on a separate sheet placed in front of several parallel data sheets. All these sheets were, however, part of the same workbook - saved under the same filename. There may be times, possibly for security reasons, when the consolidation data would be preferable in a completely separate file, which we will use now as an example of how to link files together.

With **Project 6** on the screen, click the 'Create a new workbook' button on the Toolbar to display a Blank Workbook. Then use the **Window, Tile Left-Right** command to display both workbooks on the screen side-by-side.

Next, copy column A from the Consolidation sheet of **Project 6** to the newly created workbook, then use the **Edit, Copy** and **Edit, Paste Link** commands to link the contents of column E of each Quarter sheet to the new workbook. The result, after appropriate formatting, should look as follows:

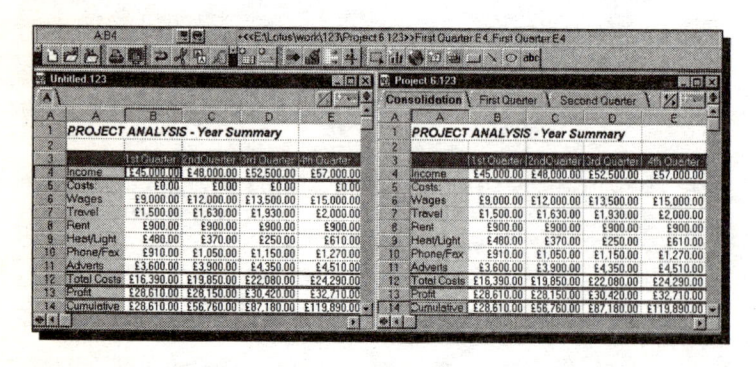

Note the reference in the Edit line when the cell pointer is in B4 of the new workbook. It reads:

    +<<E:\Lotus\work\123\Project 6.123>>First Quarter:E4..First Quarter:E4

Finally, save the new workbook under the filename **Adept 1**.

9. SPREADSHEET CHARTS

Lotus 1-2-3 allows information within a worksheet to be represented in graphical form, which makes data more accessible to non-expert users who might not be familiar with the spreadsheet format. The saying 'a picture is worth a thousand words', applies equally well to charts and figures.

The package allows the use of several chart and graph types, including area, bar, line, pie, XY, hi/low, radar, mixed, and several 3-D options of these charts. In all, 1-2-3 allows twelve different types of charts, with almost 40 pre-defined formats, which can be selected by using the appropriate button on the **Chart Info** box. These are made available to you once you have selected the data you want to chart and clicked on the Chart SmartIcon on the Toolbar. For a list of pre-defined charts and their relationship to data see Chapter 6, page 109.

Charts (you can have several per worksheet) can be displayed on screen at the same time as the worksheet from which they were derived, since they appear in their own 'chart' frame and can be embedded anywhere on a worksheet. Furthermore, they can be sent to an appropriate output device, such as a plotter or printer. Although this charting module is quite extensive, an attempt will be made to present only its basics, in the space available within this book.

Preparing for a Bar Chart

In order to illustrate some of the graphing capabilities of 1-2-3, we will now plot the income of the consulting company we discussed in the **Project 6** file. However, before we can go on, you will need to complete the entries for the all four quarters of trading of the Adept Consultants' example, if you haven't already done so - the data for completing **Project 6** are listed towards the end of previous chapter.

Next, link the quarterly totals to the Consolidation sheet, calculate the year's total, as shown below, and save the resultant workbook as **Project 7**, before going on.

Consolidation	First Quarter	Second Quarter	Third Quarter	Fourth Quarter		
A	A	B	C	D	E	F	G
2							
3			1st Quarter	2ndQuarter	3rd Quarter	4th Quarter	Total
4	Income		£45,000.00	£48,000.00	£52,500.00	£57,000.00	£202,500.00
5	Costs:						
6	Wages		£9,000.00	£12,000.00	£13,500.00	£15,000.00	£49,500.00
7	Travel		£1,500.00	£1,630.00	£1,930.00	£2,000.00	£7,060.00
8	Rent		£900.00	£900.00	£900.00	£900.00	£3,600.00
9	Heat/Light		£480.00	£370.00	£250.00	£610.00	£1,710.00
10	Phone/Fax		£910.00	£1,050.00	£1,150.00	£1,270.00	£4,380.00
11	Adverts		£3,600.00	£3,900.00	£4,350.00	£4,510.00	£16,360.00
12	Total Costs		£16,390.00	£19,850.00	£22,080.00	£24,290.00	£82,610.00
13	Profit		£28,610.00	£28,150.00	£30,420.00	£32,710.00	£119,890.00
14	Cumulative		£28,610.00	£56,760.00	£87,180.00	£119,890.00	
15							

Now we need to select the range of the data we want to graph. The range of data to be graphed in 1-2-3 does not have to be contiguous for each graph, as with most other spreadsheets. With 1-2-3, you select your data from different parts of a sheet with the <Ctrl> key pressed down. This method has the advantage of automatic recalculation should any changes be made to the original data. You could also collect data from different sheets to one 'graphing' sheet by linking them as we did with the consolidation sheet.

If you don't want the chart to be recalculated when you do this, then you must use the **Edit, Copy** and **Edit, Paste Special** commands and check the **Formulas as values** square on the displayed dialogue box, which copies a selected range to a specified target area of the worksheet and converts formulae to values. This is necessary, as cells containing formulae cannot be pasted directly since it would cause the relative cell addresses to adjust to the new locations; each formula would then recalculate a new value for each cell and give wrong results.

The CHART Command:

To obtain a chart of 'Income' versus 'Quarters', select the cell range A3..E4, then either use the **Create, Chart** command or click at the Chart SmartIcon. On doing so, the cursor changes (when in the worksheet area) to a small bar chart, as shown below.

	A	B	C	D	E	F
1	PROJECT ANALYSIS - Year Summary					
2						
3		1st Quarter	2ndQuarter	3rd Quarter	4th Quarter	Total
4	Income	£45,000.00	£48,000.00	£52,500.00	£57,000.00	£202,500.00
5	Costs:					
6	Wages	£9,000.00	£12,000.00	£13,500.00	£15,000.00	£49,500.00
7	Travel	£1,500.00	£1,630.00	£1,930.00	£2,000.00	£7,060.00
8	Rent	£900.00	£900.00	£900.00	£900.00	£3,600.00
9	Heat/Light	£480.00	£370.00	£250.00	£610.00	£1,710.00
10	Phone/Fax	£910.00	£1,050.00	£1,150.00	£1,270.00	£4,380.00
11	Adverts	£3,600.00	£3,900.00	£4,350.00	£4,510.00	£16,360.00
12	Total Costs	£16,390.00	£19,850.00	£22,080.00	£24,290.00	£82,610.00
13	Profit	£28,610.00	£28,150.00	£30,420.00	£32,710.00	£119,890.00
14	Cumulative	£28,610.00	£56,760.00	£87,180.00	£119,890.00	
15						

Now move the mouse pointer to the place you want to position the top-left corner of your chart, press the left mouse button and while keeping it pressed, drag the mouse down and to the right to form a dotted rectangle within which the chart will appear automatically once you release the mouse button. The result could be as follows:

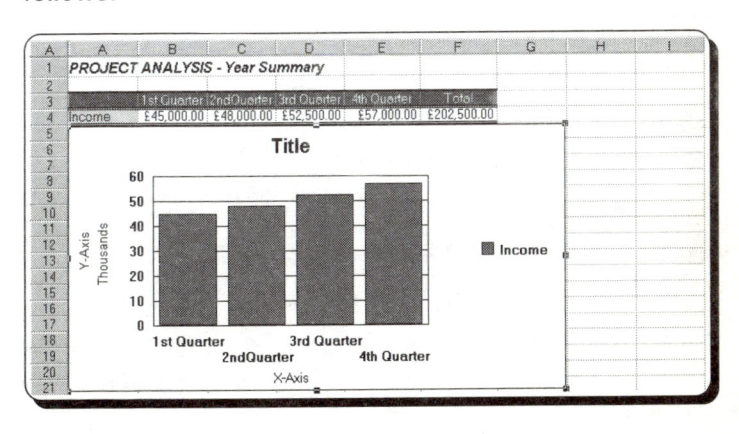

153

Note that while the frame containing a chart is selected (you can tell from the presence of the small black squares around it), the **Range** menu option changes to **Chart**. Also, you can either change the size of a selected chart by dragging the small four-headed arrow pointer (which appears when the mouse pointer is placed at the edges of the frame), move the whole frame to a new position by clicking within it and dragging it to its new position, or change the actual graph type, its colour, border, etc., with the use of the fifteen chart SmartIcons which replace the icons in the second half of the Toolbar when a chart is selected. The function of these SmartIcons is as follows:

- Change chart properties
- Change sheet properties
- Change chart type
- Turn horizontal grid on or off
- Select several objects
- Change to vertical bar chart
- Change to vertical stacked bar chart
- Change to vertical bar with depth chart
- Change to 3D bar chart
- Change to line chart
- Change to area chart
- Change to mixed bar/line chart
- Change to 3D pie chart
- Change to multiple 3D pie chart
- Change to high/low close/open chart

As an example of what you can do with a chart, let us use the 8th Chart SmartIcon to change our chart to a vertical bar with depth, then increase the width of the chart so that the 'Quarter' labels do not appear staggered. Next, double click the title to select its text and type 'ADEPT Consultants', and then change the y-axis text to 'Pounds Sterling' and the x-axis text to 'Year Summary'. Finally, move the title and legend to the positions shown below.

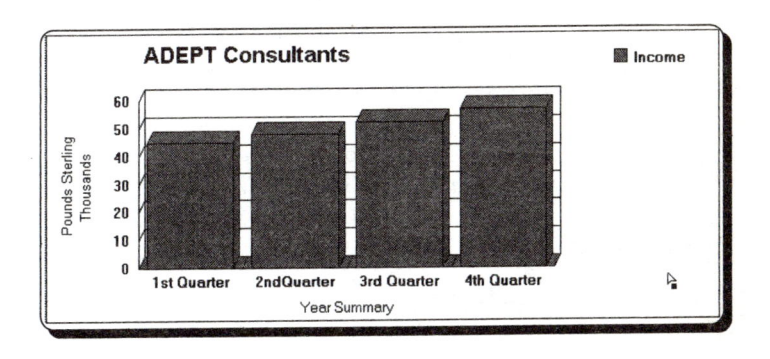

Try it, then change the First Quarter income from £45,000 to £55,000 (by adding £10,000 to, say, the January income) and watch how the change is reflected on the redrawn graph. To revert to the original data entry for the First Quarter's income, use the **Edit, Undo** command, and then save your work under the filename **Project 8**.

When 1-2-3 creates a chart, it plots each row or column of data in the selected range as a 'data series', such as a group of bars, lines, etc. You can have two types of data series; by row, or by column. Lotus 1-2-3 charts data according to the following rules:

1. If the selected range contains more columns than rows of data, or the same number of columns and rows, 1-2-3 plots the data series by rows.

2. If the selected range contains more rows than columns of data, 1-2-3 plots the data series by columns.

The rules relating to data series are illustrated below.

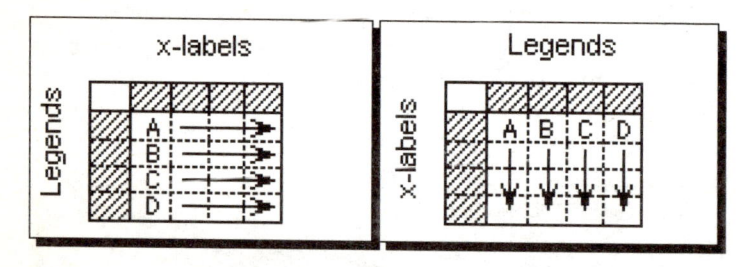

If you select a range to chart which includes column and row headings, and text above or to the left of the numeric data, 1-2-3 uses the text to create the axis labels, legends, title, and subtitle.

Saving and Naming Charts:

When you save a worksheet, the chart or charts you have created are saved with it. Charts are numbered automatically as you create them and are given the default name **Chart #**, where # is a sequential number starting with 1.

If you prefer, you can rename charts so that you can find them easily if you have created a large number of them. To do so, use the **Chart Info** box, click the Basics tab, highlight the existing name and type a new name. As we will be creating quite a number of charts, rename the existing **Chart 1** to **Income Bar**.

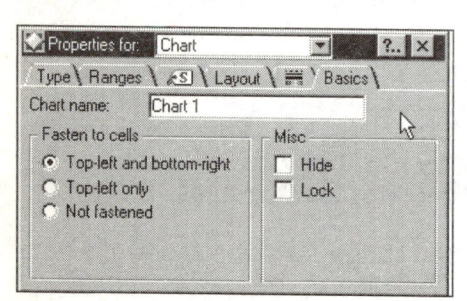

Quick Menus

Clicking the right mouse button brings up a quick menu of commands relevant to the current selection. Below we show the context-sensitive quick menu when a chart is selected.

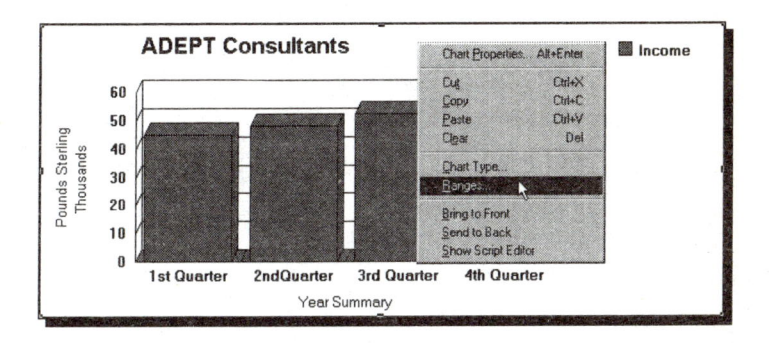

One of the commands in this quick menu is **Ranges** which allows you to specify a chart range that does not conform with the rules mentioned earlier.

On selecting this command, or using the **Chart, Ranges** command from the menu bar, the dialogue box shown to the left is displayed. Here we can choose Data in the **Parts** box, then in the **Subparts** box select Income the **Range** of which is given as B4..E4 of sheet A. This is assigned to the 1st data series, with a total of 30 data series available. Not only can you assign ranges individually, but you can also assign them by row or column, you can plot on a 2nd Y-axis, you can also select mixed types, such as line, area, or bar.

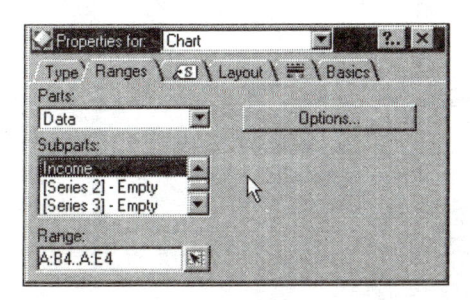

To illustrate these points, select Series 2 in the **Subparts** box of the **Chart Info** box, click the range button to the right of the **Range** box and specify with the modified cell pointer the range A:B13..A:E13, which is the profit row. Next, click on the Type tab of the **Chart Info** box and select Mixed chart which displays immediately the new chart. Below you can see how Profit varies with Income.

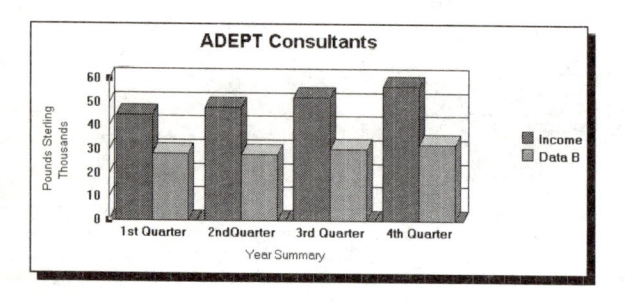

To change the legend name of the new series, shown above as **Data B**, right-click on its identifying square, and select **Series Properties** from the drop-down Quick menu. In the displayed **Series Info** box, shown below, type 'Profit' in the **Legend label** box, check the **Plot against 2nd Y-axis** box, and select Line in the **Mixed type** box.

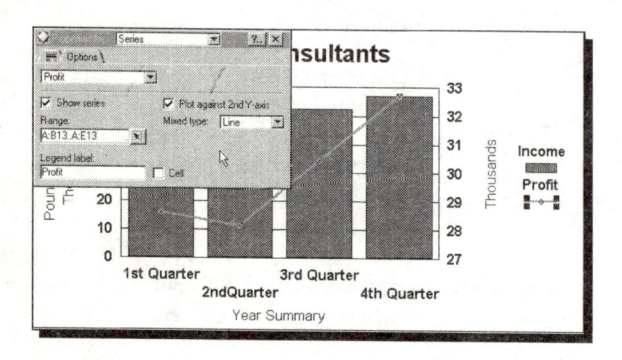

Save this workbook under the filename **Project 9**.

Customising a Chart

We have already seen how to add or change titles, axis labels and legends, and how to select, move and size chart objects. In what follows, we will use new chart examples to emphasise these and introduce other capabilities which will help you to customise a chart.

Drawing a Multiple Bar Chart:

As an exercise, we will consider a new vertical bar-type chart which deals with the quarterly 'Costs' of Adept Consultants. To achieve this, select the cell range B3..E3 then press the <Ctrl> key and while holding it down, select the range A6..E11. On pressing the Chart SmartIcon (or using the **C̲reate, C̲hart** command), and selecting the target area, the vertical bar chart of the 6 different quarterly costs is drawn automatically. The range selection, shown on the composite screen dump below, disappears once the chart is drawn.

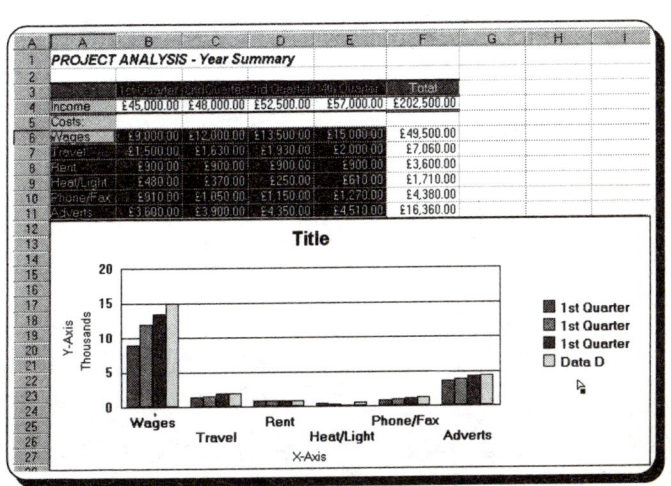

Note: The program has incorrectly labelled the legends, an error which did not exist in the previous version of Lotus 1-2-3!

To corrected this error, first left-click in turn each legend square which has the wrong description against it, so as to select it, then right-click it and choose the **Series Properties** menu option to display the **Series Info** box, as shown below. Next, check the **Cell** box at the bottom of the dialogue box, and then type the appropriate cell reference in the **Legend label** box.

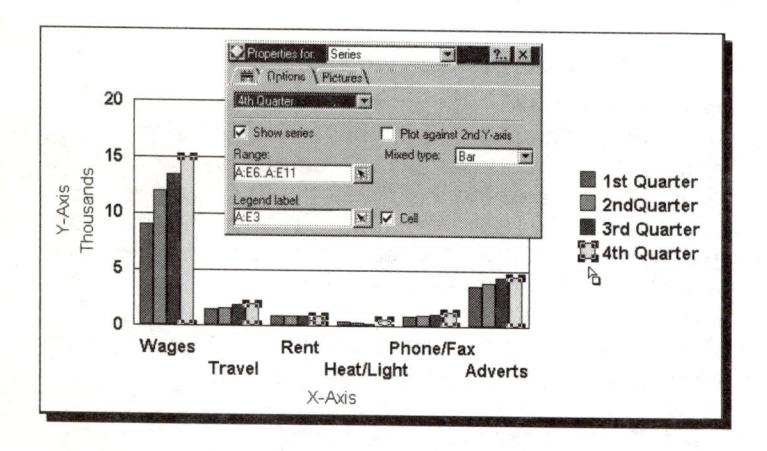

Because the selected range contains more rows than columns of data, 1-2-3 follows the 2nd rule of data series selection.

To have the 'quarters' appearing on the x-axis and the 'costs' as the legends, we need to first make a copy of the chart in question using the **Edit, Copy** and **Edit, Paste** commands, so that we do not lose the original chart. Next, select the copy of the chart to be modified, right-click it and choose the **Chart Properties** menu option to display the **Chart Info** box. Press the **Options** button on this box and under **Assign Ranges** of the displayed **Range Options** dialogue box, select the 'Series by row' option and press the **OK** button. The selected chart will then automatically change to what is shown in the composite screen dump on the next page.

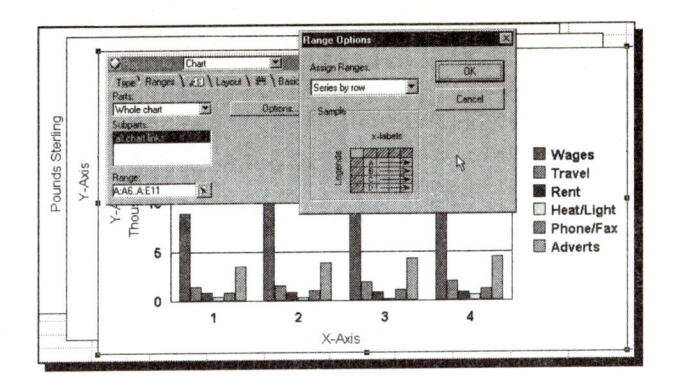

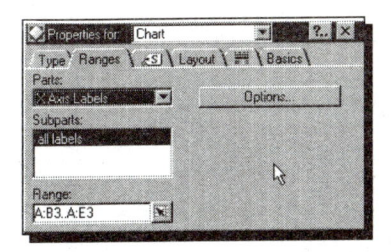

All you have to do now is click the Ranges tab of the **Chart Info** box, select X Axis Labels under **Parts** and specify B3..E3 under **Range**, as shown to the left.

In the above chart screen dump, you will notice that we have intentionally arranged for each chart frame to be on top of the other in cascade form. To display another chart on top, simply right-click on its frame and select the **Bring to Front** option from the drop-down Quick menu. If the chart is completely obscured, right-click the one you can see and select the **Send to Back** option. Repeat this last procedure until the chart you want to see displays on top.

If you make a mistake and you want to start again, make sure the unwanted chart is first selected, then press the <Del> key. Once you are satisfied with your efforts, save the chart under the name **Costs Bar** and your workbook under the filename **Project 9**.

Drawing a Pie Chart:

Let us now draw a chart of the 'Total Costs' versus 'Quarters'. On specifying the ranges B3..E3 and A12..E12, Lotus 1-2-3 draws a bar chart. To change the chart type, simply select the chart, then click the Type tab of the **Chart Info** box and choose Pie from the displayed **Chart Type** list. The chart would be redrawn to the following:

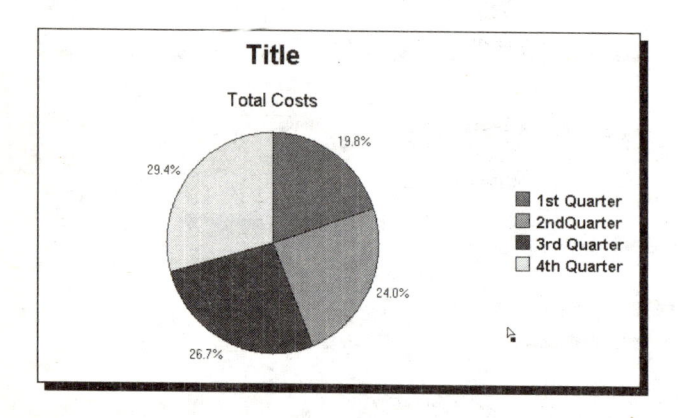

This chart tells us that the costs have been increasing from 19.8% for the 1st quarter to 29.4% for the 4th quarter, in a clockwise direction, but it doesn't tell us much more.

As a last example in chart drawing, we will use the 'Total' values of the costs (to be found under column F) in the Consolidation worksheet of **Project 9** to plot a 3-D pie chart. To achieve this, select range A6..A11, press the <Ctrl> key down and select range F6..F11. Next choose a 3D pie chart from the **Chart Info** box to display a chart with the percentage of each total quarterly expenditure appearing against the various segments, as shown on the next page.

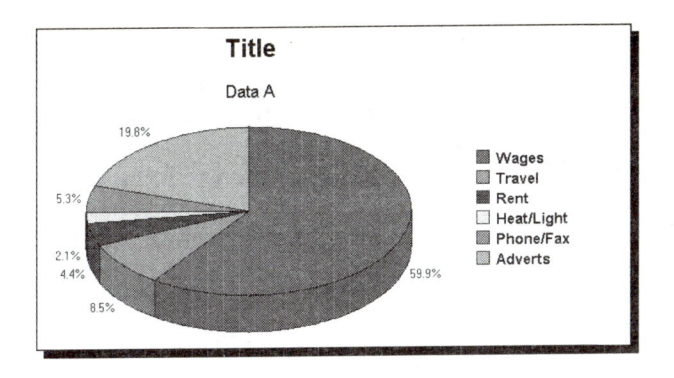

We can now change the 'Title' and 'Sub-title' to 'Project Analysis' and 'Total Yearly Costs', by double-clicking each one of these objects in turn and typing the required text. In the example shown below, the Heat/Light slice is shown in the process of being pulled away from the rest of the chart so as to make it more visible. Being able to 'explode' individual pie slices by dragging, is made possible because each slice is treated as a separate object.

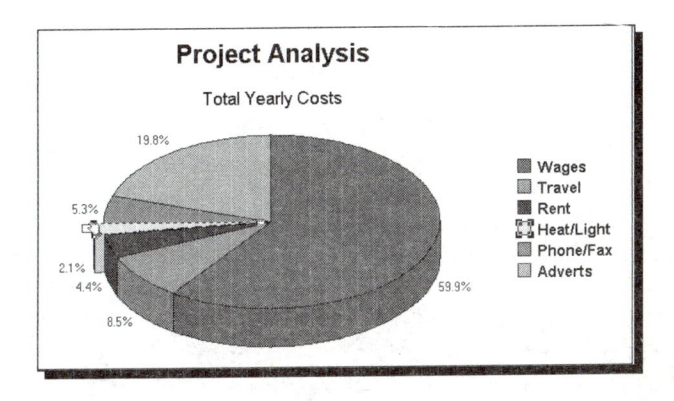

Finally, save the pie chart under the name **Costs Pie** and the workbook under the filename **Project Analysis**.

Annotating a Chart:

As long as you have a mouse, you can use the last three SmartIcons on the Toolbar, shown here, to annotate your chart. Once one of these SmartIcons is used, all the Drawing Tools of SmartSuite 97, as described in Chapter 5 (see page 93) become active. Use your skills acquired earlier to annotate your worksheet and pie chart as shown below.

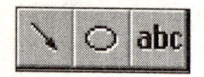

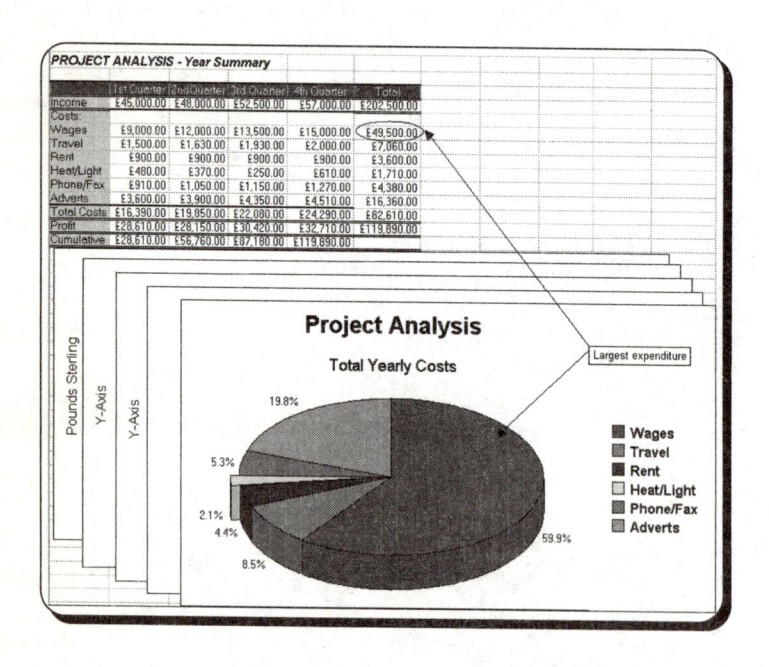

As we have seen earlier, you can use the Drawing tools of SmartSuite to do a lot more than we have shown above. You can, for example, rotate, flip, bring to the front or send to the back, lock, or group selected objects, or even 'Bring a picture into 1-2-3', using the SmartIcon shown here.

10. FREELANCE GRAPHICS

Freelance 97 is a powerful, intuitive and versatile Graphics Presentation package, which is perhaps the easiest to use amongst similar purpose programs.

The key element of Freelance is the creation of presentation pages and the production of ancillary material, such as scripted notes to accompany each page of the presentation, copies of the designed pages, and an outline view of all the information in the presentation. Output can be formatted for 35 mm slides, or electronic presentation on screen. In addition, you can apply the skills you have already gained in using Word Pro and 1-2-3 and use material created in these applications within Freelance.

Starting the Freelance Program

Freelance is started in Windows either by clicking the **Start** button then selecting **Programs, Lotus SmartSuite, Lotus Freelance 97** on the cascade menu, or by double-clicking on the Freelance icon on the Windows Task Bar.

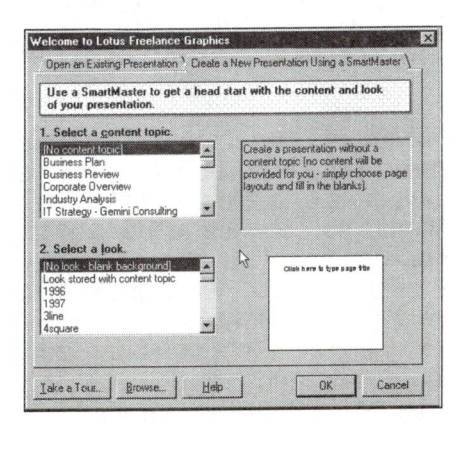

When you start Freelance either for the first time, or if you have not already created a presentation, the program displays the screen shown here, from which you can choose to either create a new presentation, using a SmartMaster, or open an existing presentation.

The Freelance Screen

When Freelance is loaded, and a SmartMaster is chosen (we will use the **Meeting - Team** option from the list of content topics, and **world1** for the look of the presentation), a screen displays, shown below, with similar Title bar, Menu bar, and SmartIcon bar to those of Word Pro and Lotus 1-2-3. Obviously there are differences, but that is to be expected as Freelance serves a different purpose to the other programs.

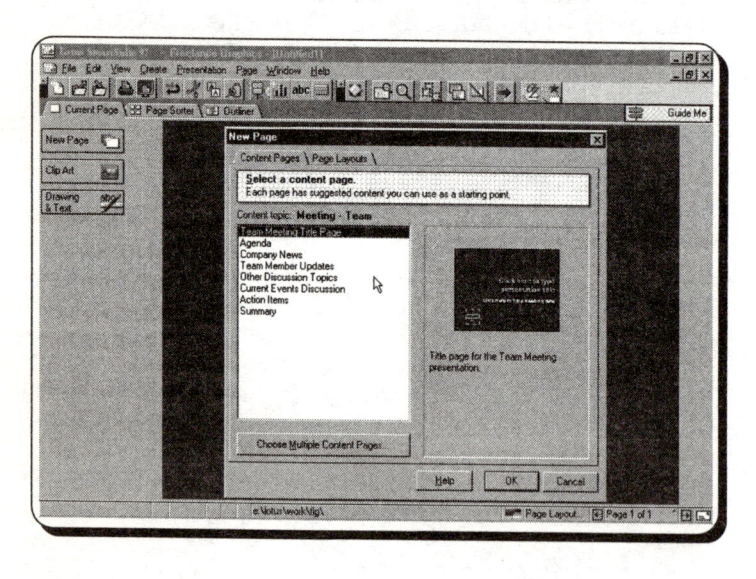

Note the information given on the Status bar at the bottom of the screen. The first button displays information on the default drive and folder in which your work will be saved (should you choose to do so); try clicking on it for other options. The second button allows you to toggle between black and white and colour display. The third button allows you to switch page layout, while the fourth button tells you how many pages this presentation has and allows switching between them. Finally the last button starts TeamMail.

Freelance View Tabs

Having selected the content topic and the look of our presentation template, Freelance displays it and prompts you to type in appropriate information. You could use the **Content Advice** button at this point, or type totally different information, as we have done. We just happened to like the look of this template.

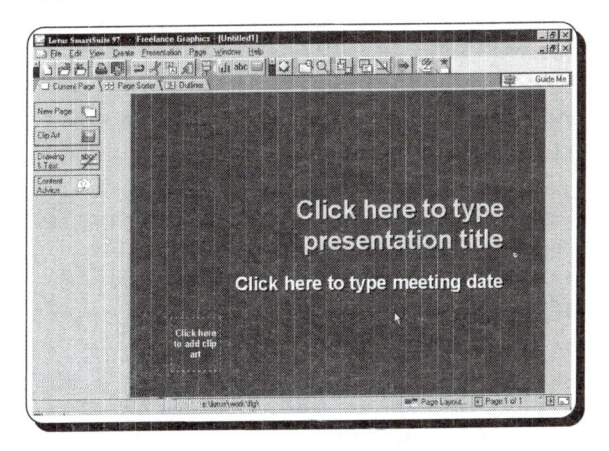

In order to illustrate the various Tab options of Freelance, we have created four pages, as follows:

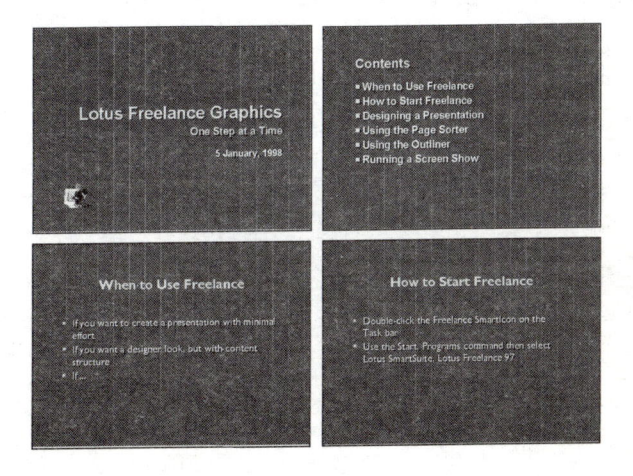

The Current Page Tab:

When you first start designing your presentation, the Current Page tab is active, which allows you to create or edit the current page. If there are more than one page in your presentation, you can make a different page 'current' by using the penultimate button on the Status bar, shown here. Click the left arrow to make the previous page current, or the right arrow to make the next page current.

Note the different SmartIcons that appear on the toolbar when in different views. The following four remain the same irrespective of which view tab you are using.

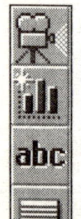

Run screen show from beginning.

Create a chart.

Create a text block.

Add or edit speaker notes.

The following nine SmartIcons appear when in current view, but in display mode (as opposed to edit mode).

Change properties of selected object.

Show whole page.

Drag to 'zoom in' on an area.

Select all objects.

Duplicate pages.

Delete pages.

168

Go to a specific page.

Use one typeface for all text.

Place a logo on every page.

Double-clicking at any text object on the current page, selects the object, which can then be edited. An extra facility allows you to easily change the default title level size, as well as the character size, as shown below.

As soon as you select an object for editing, the nine current page SmartIcons change to the following:

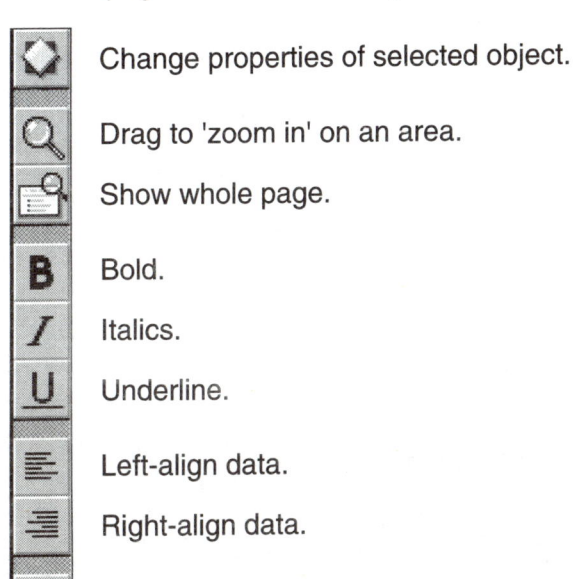

Change properties of selected object.

Drag to 'zoom in' on an area.

Show whole page.

Bold.

Italics.

Underline.

Left-align data.

Right-align data.

Pick-up object attributes.

Apply object attributes.

The Page Sorter Tab:

Clicking the Page Sorter tab, allows you to see more than one page of your presentation, as shown below.

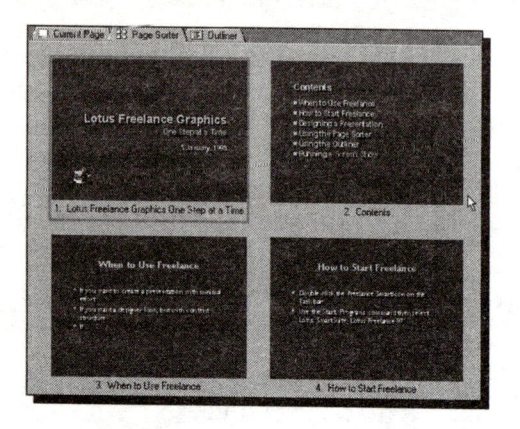

From here you can change the order of the pages of your presentation, by left-clicking a page and dragging it with the mouse to a different position. A selected page is shown with a frame around it, and can be edited by clicking the Current Page tab. When in Page Sorter view, the following icons are displayed.

Change properties of selected object.

Add a new page.

Duplicate pages.

Delete pages.

Copy pages from other presentations.

Move pages.

Begin rehearsing screen show.

Display screen show rehearsal summary.

The Outliner Tab:

Clicking the Outliner tab, allows you to display the page titles and main text in typical outline mode, as shown below.

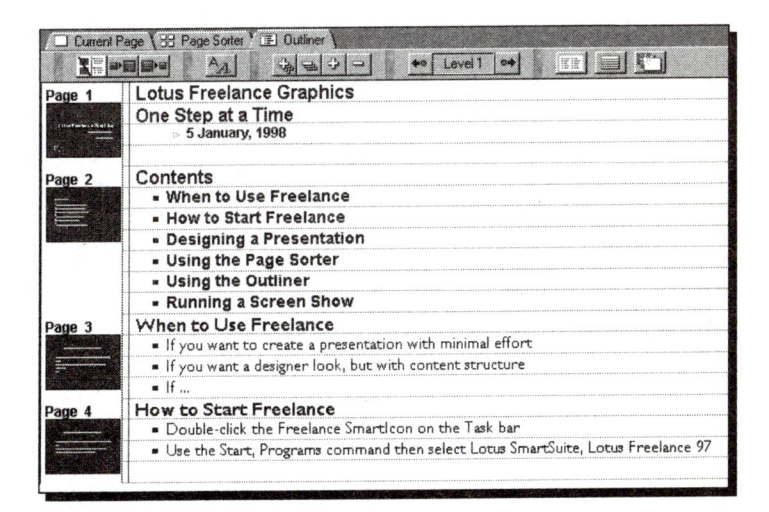

Page 1	**Lotus Freelance Graphics**
	One Step at a Time
	5 January, 1998
Page 2	**Contents**
	• When to Use Freelance
	• How to Start Freelance
	• Designing a Presentation
	• Using the Page Sorter
	• Using the Outliner
	• Running a Screen Show
Page 3	**When to Use Freelance**
	• If you want to create a presentation with minimal effort
	• If you want a designer look, but with content structure
	• If ...
Page 4	**How to Start Freelance**
	• Double-click the Freelance SmartIcon on the Task bar
	• Use the Start, Programs command then select Lotus SmartSuite, Lotus Freelance 97

From this view, it is extremely easy to organise and edit presentation text. For example, you can highlight text and change its font type and size, or you can move text by clicking the small black square to select a whole line of text, then press the left mouse button down to change the pointer to the small hand shown below. A whole line can then be dragged to its new position.

When to Use Freelance
If you want to create a presentation with minimal effort
• If you want a designer look, but with content structure
• If ...

Other icons, which appear at the top of the Outliner page, are self-explanatory. Try using them and see the effect they have.

Notes Pages:

No matter which page view you are in, selecting a page and clicking on the 'Add or edit speaker's notes' icon, shown here, displays the Speaker Note dialogue box shown to the right, This is where you create speaker's notes for any or all of your presentation pages. Clicking the right arrow on the dialogue box takes you to the next page, while clicking the left arrow takes you to the previous page.

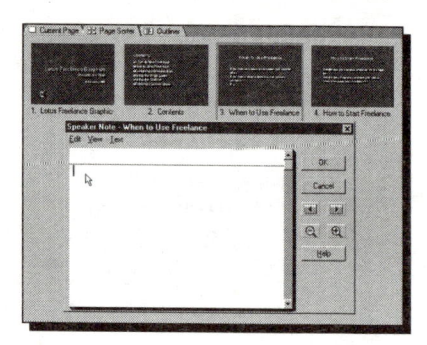

Once you have created speaker's notes for a given page, you can tell that is the case, by the small text image which appears at the bottom of the relevant page.

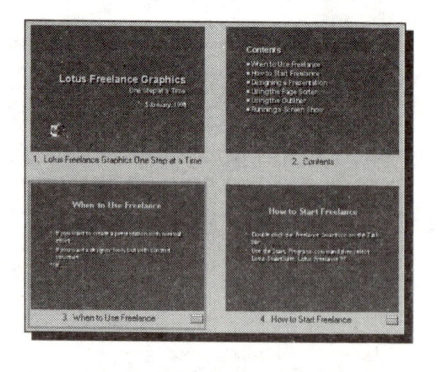

From the screen dump shown to the right you can see that pages 3 and 4 have speaker's notes attached to them. Double-clicking such an image, opens up the Speaker Note dialogue box.

Although you can create speaker notes for each page of your presentation, you only see them when you open the Speaker Note window or when you choose to print speaker's notes with the presentation (either both on the same page or separate with the speaker notes all on one page). A speaker note is not part of the presentation page.

Adding a Clip Art Image or Diagram:

You can add a Clip Art image or a diagram to your presentation by clicking the Clip Art button, shown here, which is displayed at the top left of your screen when the Current Page tab is pressed.

Freelance has a vast number of already drawn images which you can use from the following dialogue box. Clicking the down-arrow against the **Category** box, reveals a list of 27 different categories, each with a variety of pictures, from 1 under 'Roads' to 64 under 'Flags'. There is even one 'Custom' category for you to add your own symbols. Use the right arrow buttons to go forwards through the list and the left arrow button to go backwards.

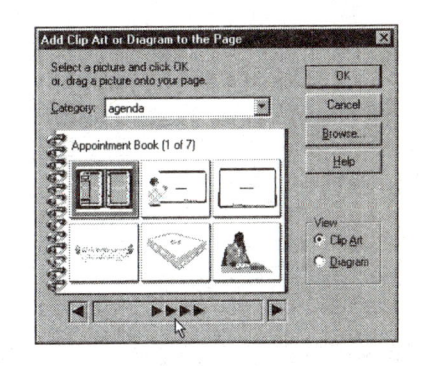

Clicking the **Diagram** radio button at the bottom of the above dialogue box, reveals 12 categories of diagrams, one of which is labelled as 'Custom' for you to add your own diagrams.

If you want to see a screen show of the available Clip Art, or Diagrams, select under **View** which type you wish to see, then click on the 'start' button at the bottom of the dialogue box (the one pointed to above). This starts the show, and flicks through the stored images until you press the 'stop' button pointed to here.

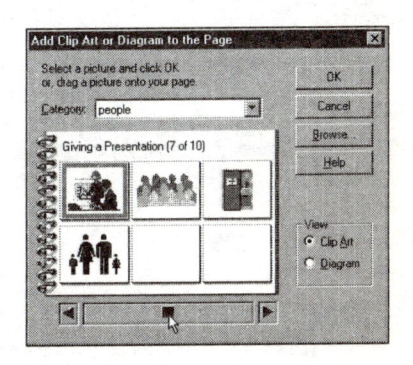

Adding a Drawing and Text:

You can add a drawing and text to your presentation by clicking the Drawing & Text button, shown here, which is displayed below the Clip Art button when the Current Page tab is pressed. Doing so, opens up a Tools box, shown to the left, from which you can choose to insert in to your presentation any number of shapes, similar to those of the Drawing Tools discussed in Chapter 5 (see page 93).

In addition, a number of 'Shapes with text' and 'Connectors' are listed. Those buttons marked with a small down-arrow, when clicked, display further choices, as shown to the right.

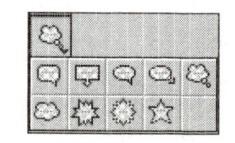

Pressing the **Flowchart** button situated above the 'Connectors' on the Drawing & Text box, reveals a list of symbols, as shown to the left, which can be used to build up a flowchart.

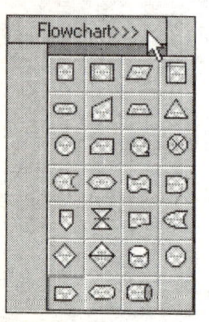

Below right we illustrate some of the capabilities of the Drawing & Text options of Freelance, by adding a speech bubble to the Clip Art on the first page of our presentation. Use the 'Drag to zoom-in on an area' SmartIcon, shown here, to enlarge that section of the page.

When you finish your presentation, save it under the filename **Present 1**.

Screen Show

Clicking the 'Run screen show from beginning' SmartIcon, allows you to see your work as an electronic presentation, with each page filling the screen. To see the next page in full-screen, left-click the mouse anywhere within the displayed page. To return to a previous Freelance view from a full-screen Show, press <Esc> and click the **Quit Screen Show** button on the displayed dialogue box, or click the right mouse button to display the Quick menu, and choose the **End Screen Show** menu option.

You could automate the electronic presentation procedure with the use of the **Presentation, Set Up Screen Show** command, which displays the following dialogue box.

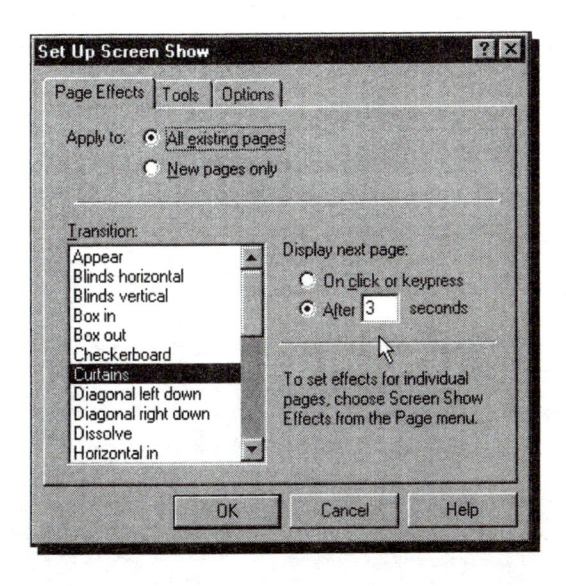

From here you can select a **Transition** and the timing of your display. Try it!

Enhancing a Screen Show:

A screen show can be greatly enhanced by keeping certain uniformity between slides. For example, it is a good idea to have all text using the same font and including a company logo on all pages.

To change typeface globally, click the 'Use one typeface for all text' SmartIcon, pointed to below, which displays the dialogue box to the left. Once you select the typeface and specify the target areas, pressing the **OK** button, displays a warning to the effect that such changes cannot be reversed.

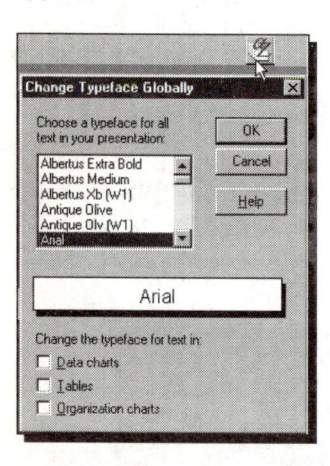

Carry out these cosmetic changes to the text of **Present 1**, then embolden the text on pages 3 and 4. Finally, click the 'Place a logo on every page' SmartIcon, shown to the right, which displays the screen below, in which we have already used the Clip Art facility to import and size an image on the top right hand corner of the screen.

Printing a Presentation

Before you commit your presentation to paper, use the **File, Page Setup** command to provide header and/or footer information, as follows:

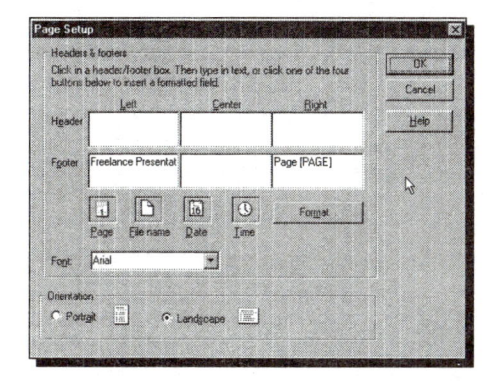

Such information is not displayed on your screen show, but it is included on your printouts.

Next, do have a look at your work so far, using the **File, Print Preview** command, which for the second page of our presentation displays as follows:

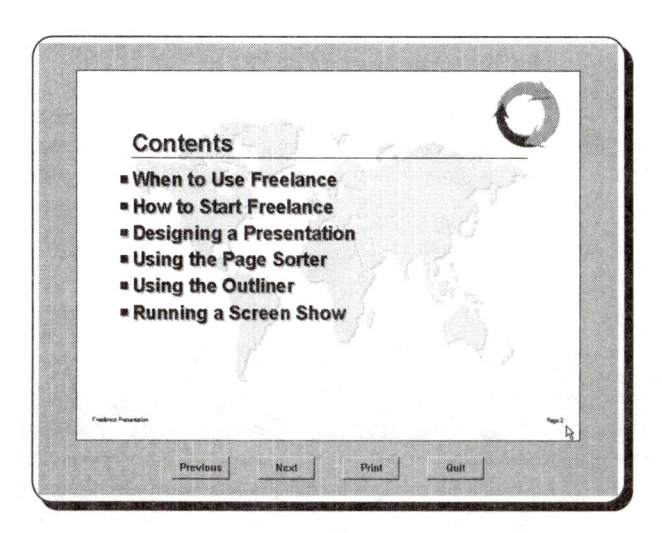

Before going on, save your work under **Present 2**.

Finally, use the **File, Print** command, to display the Print dialogue box, as follows:

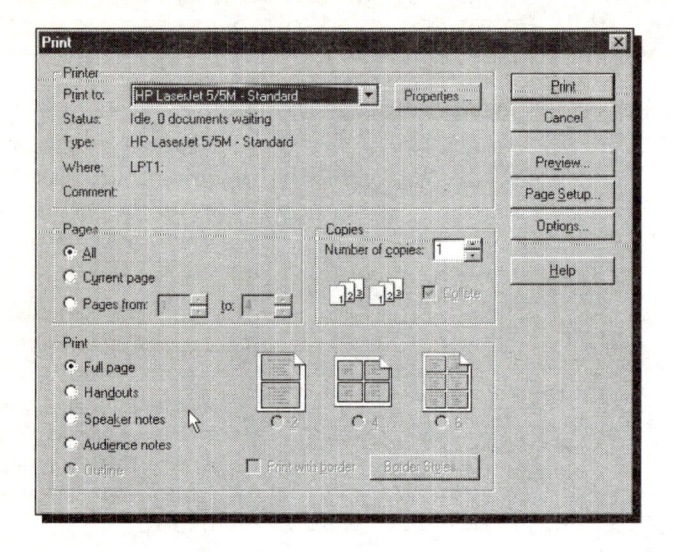

Do note the facilities available to you at the bottom of this dialogue box. Apart from being able to print your presentation on **Full page**, you can also choose to print **Handouts**, **Speaker notes**, or **Audience notes**, in a variety of formats.

* * *

Freelance is obviously capable of a lot more than we have introduced here, but you should now have the confidence to explore more of the package by yourself. Have fun!

* * *

11. THE APPROACH DATABASE

Lotus Approach is a relational database *application* designed to allow users to store, manipulate and retrieve information easily and quickly from created or imported two-dimensional database tables. Approach refers to such tables as databases, and you can create a variety of formats (the default being dBASE IV), which can be joined to bring together data from separate files and use it as if it were all stored in one place; hence the name database application.

The forms, reports, and other views in an Approach application file can use data from any of the databases joined in that file. To make accessing the data easier, each 'record' of data within a database is structured in the same fashion, i.e., each record will have the same number of 'fields'.

We define an Approach application file and its elements as:

Approach file — A collection of forms, reports, and other views, which use data from one or more joined databases.

Database — A collection of records, which are organised for a specific theme.

Record — Information relating to a single entry and comprising one or more fields, such as people's first names, surnames, address, etc.

Field — Information of the same type, such as people's surnames, or date of birth.

The maximum size of a database file created in Approach 97 is 2 gigabytes. You can have up to 30 such files open at the same time (depending on memory), but the number of records in each database is limited to 1 billion (of 4,000 bytes each), while the maximum number of fields in a record is limited to 255.

A good example of a database is the invoicing details kept on clients by a company. These details could include name of client, description of work done, invoice number, and amount charged, as follows:

NAME	Consultancy	Invoice	Value
VORTEX Co. Ltd	Wind Tunnel Tests	9801	120.84
AVON Construction	Adhesive Tests	9802	103.52
BARROWS Associates	Tunnel Design Tests	9803	99.32
STONEAGE Ltd	Carbon Dating Tests	9804	55.98
PARKWAY Gravel	Material Size Tests	9805	180.22
WESTWOOD Ltd	Load Bearing Tests	9806	68.52

Such a database is too limited for the type of information normally held by most companies. If the same client asks for work to be carried out regularly, then the details for that client (which could include address, telephone and fax numbers, contact name, date of invoice, etc.), will have to be entered several times. This can lead to errors, but above all to redundant information being kept on a client - each entry will have to have the name of the client, their address, telephone and fax numbers.

The relational facilities offered by Lotus Approach, overcome the problems of entry errors and duplication of information. The ability to handle multiple databases at any one time allows for the grouping of data into sensible subsets. For example, one database, called client, could hold the names of the clients, their addresses, telephone and fax numbers, while another database, called invoice, could hold information on the work done, invoice number, date of issue, and amount charged. The two databases must have one unique common field, such as a client reference number. The advantage is that details of each client are entered and stored only once, thus reducing the time and effort wasted on entering duplicate information, and also reducing the space required for data storage.

Starting the Approach Program

Approach is started in Windows either by clicking the **Start** button then selecting **Programs** and selecting **Lotus SmartSuite, Lotus Approach 97** on the cascade menu, or clicking the Approach icon on the Task Bar, shown here.

In either case, the Lotus Approach program starts to load and after the opening screen, it displays the **Welcome to Lotus Approach** dialogue box shown below.

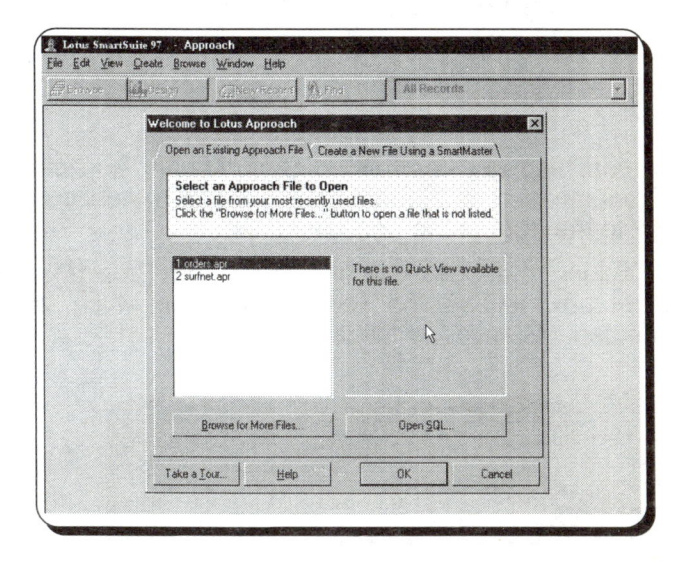

As you can see, Lotus Approach gives you the option to either 'Open an Existing Approach File' (if they do exist, they will be listed for you to choose one), browse for more database files, or create a new file using one of the SmartMaster Applications or Templates, including a blank one of each. To see these, click the tab 'Create a New File Using a SmartMaster' on the dialogue box.

Doing so, reveals the following built-in Applications:

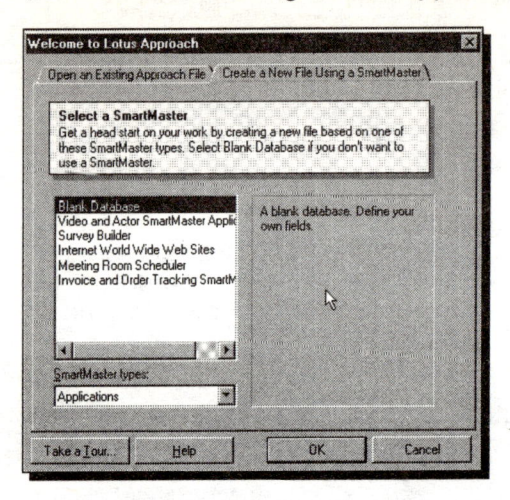

As you highlight each listed SmartMaster application, an explanation of its function is given in the description box to the right of the application list.

Clicking the down-arrow against the **SmartMaster types** box, reveals the Templates option which, when selected, displays the following templates list.

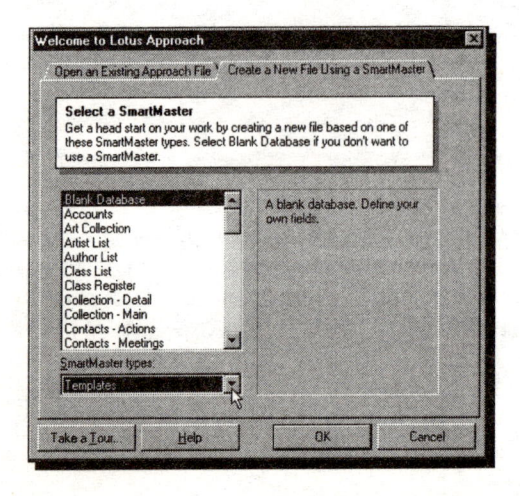

Parts of the Approach Screen

Below we show the Approach screen when a database is open or has been created (otherwise the first Toolbar and the Status bar are not displayed and the second Toolbar remains inactive). For the purpose of demostration we have opened the *surfnet.apr* database, which comes with the package.

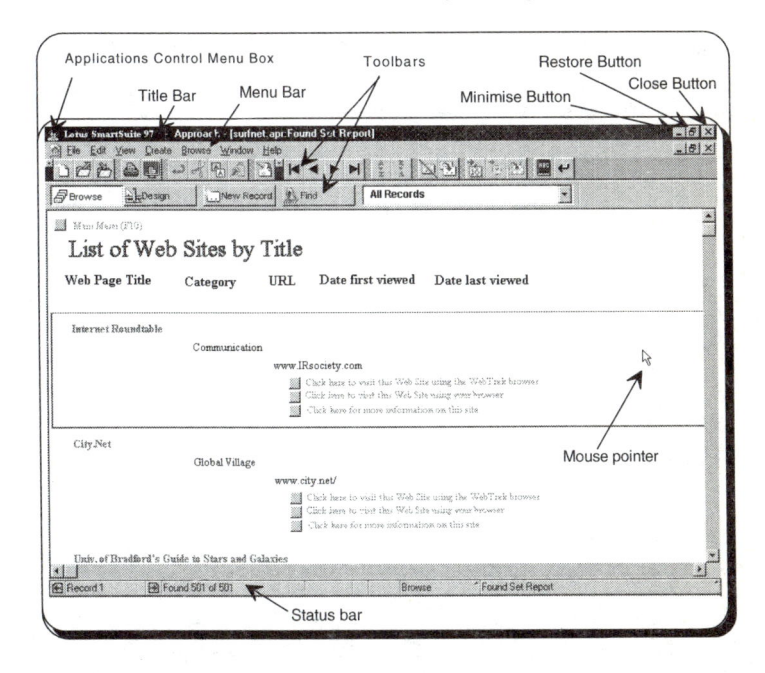

As you can see, these windows have common screen elements with those of other Lotus SmartSuite applications. As usual, depending on what you are doing with Approach, the items on the menu bar can be different from those of the opening screen. For example, clicking the **Design** button on the second Toolbar causes the menu bar to change to the following:

Using Help in Approach

The first time you start Approach, it might be a good idea to look at the help available to you. To do this, cancel the opening dialogue box, then select the **Help, Help Topics** command which causes the following Help screen to be displayed.

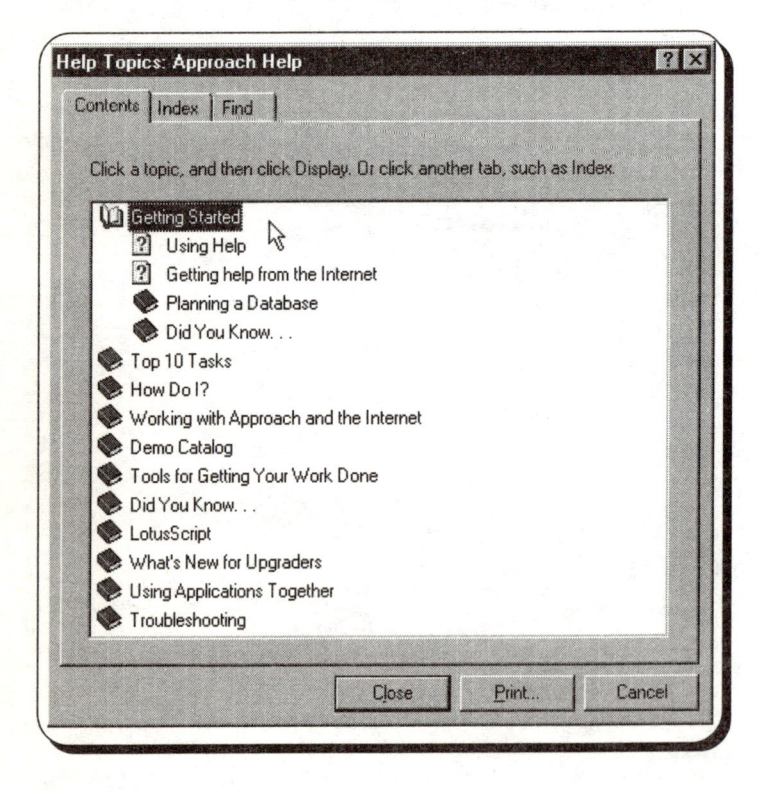

We suggest you spend a little time here browsing through the various help screens, particularly the first three; 'Getting Started', 'Planning a Database', and 'Did You Know'. After doing so, click the Index tab of the **Help Topics** dialogue box, and type the text *database*. The following screen is then displayed.

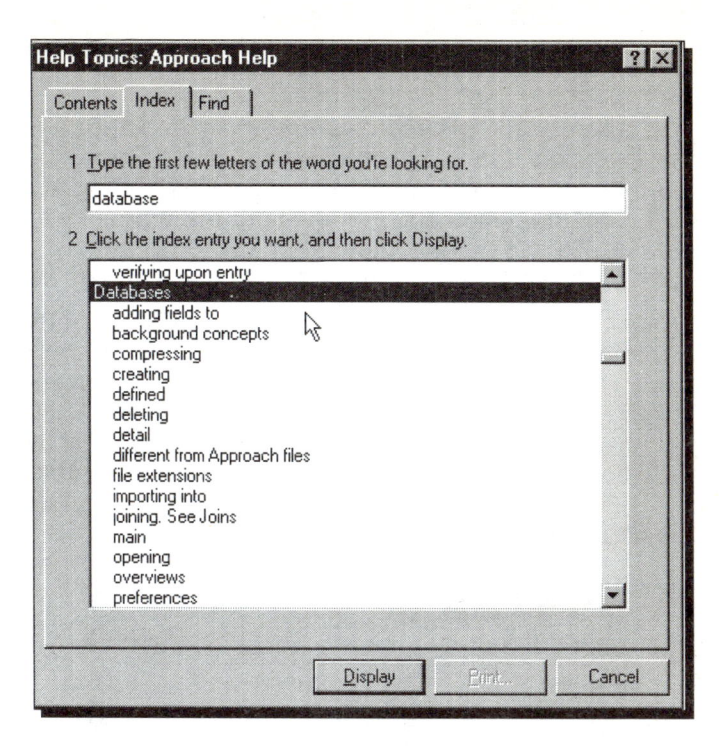

Have a look at the 'creating' topic. On selecting it and clicking the **Display** button, an additional screen opens up, as follows:

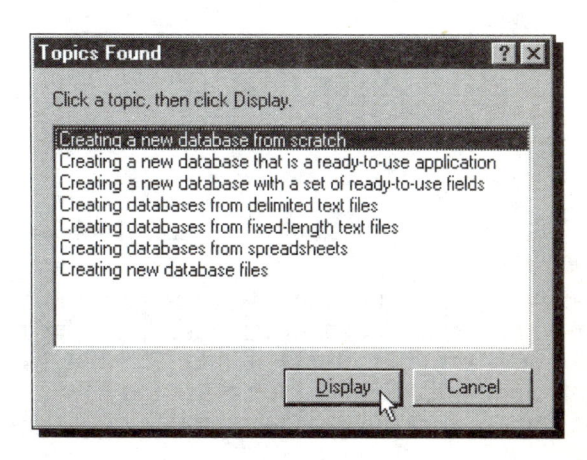

Creating a Database Application

The Approach application we are going to create holds the invoicing details which the firm Adept Consultants keep on their clients. One database will hold the details of the clients, while another will hold the actual invoice details. To create the first, start the program, which opens the **Welcome to Lotus Approach** dialogue box.

Next, if this is being done immediately after starting Approach, click the 'Create a New File Using a SmartMaster' tab on the dialogue box and select **Blank Database**. Otherwise, either click the 'Create a new database' icon, shown to the left, or use the **File, New Database** command. Any one of these three methods will cause the **New** dialogue box to be displayed.

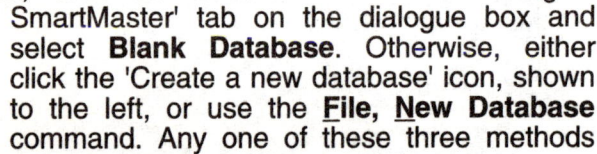

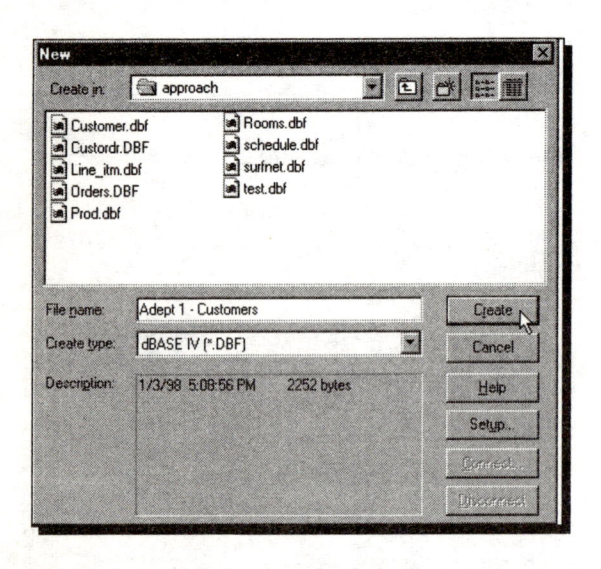

To create a new database, type its name in the **File name** box, say 'Adept 1 - Customers', specify in which folder you want to create it and of what type (the default being dBASE IV), then press the **Create** button. This causes the following dialogue box to be displayed.

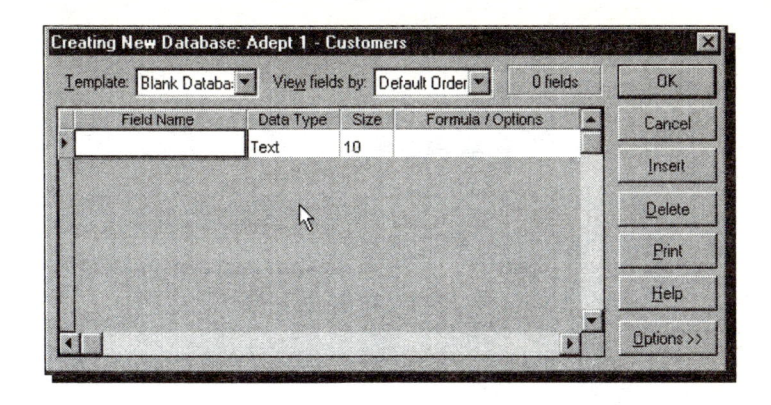

In the **Field Name** box, type the name of each field, then select the **Data Type** and **Size** of each field (see below), according to the following table.

Field Name	Data Type	Size
Customer ID	Text	5
Name	Text	25
Address	Text	15
Town	Text	20
County	Text	15
Post Code	Text	10
Contact	Text	15
Phone	Text	15
Fax	Text	15
Entry Order	Numeric	10

Text is the default choice for the Data Type, while 10 (characters) is the default Size of a field. To change the Data Type, place the cursor within the data type descriptor box which causes a down-arrow button to be displayed. Clicking this button, displays a drop-down list of data types, as shown overleaf.

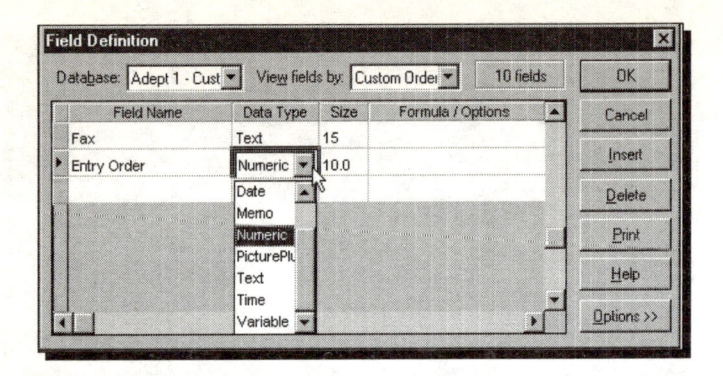

As we intend to use the Entry Order field as a record counter, select 'Numeric' from the drop-down list and change the 'Size' from the default value of 10.2 to 10.0. Furthermore, as this field is a record counter, place the cursor within the Formula/Options column of the Entry Order Field Definition row and press the **Options** button of the dialogue box, to display the following:

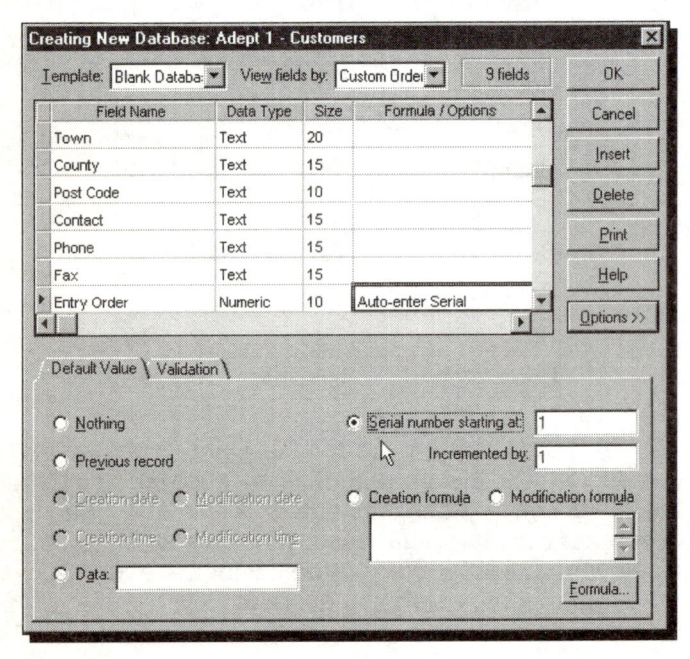

Next, click the **Serial number starting at** radio button and press **OK**. As records are now entered, this field is updated automatically, starting with 1. When you finish entering all the information, press the **OK** button. Your database template is created and displayed, as shown below, ready for you to enter your data.

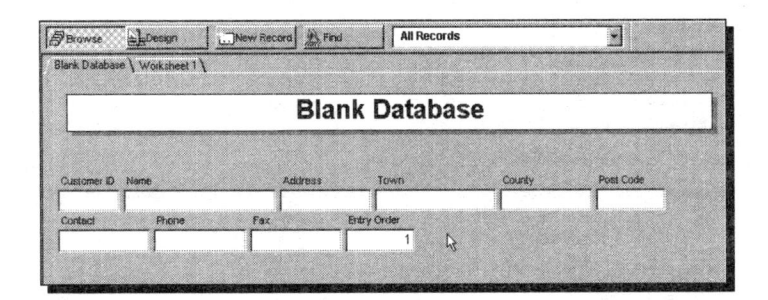

To see the same template in a different view, press the Worksheet 1 tab to display:

Note that in both views, Approach reflects the selected size of your fields. You could even re-design your database template by first reverting to the Blank Database view, then clicking the **Design** button, shown here, and double-clicking on a field. This causes the **Field Name Info** box to be displayed and clicking the **Field Definition** button allows you to change the field names, their type and their size, as shown at the top of the next page.

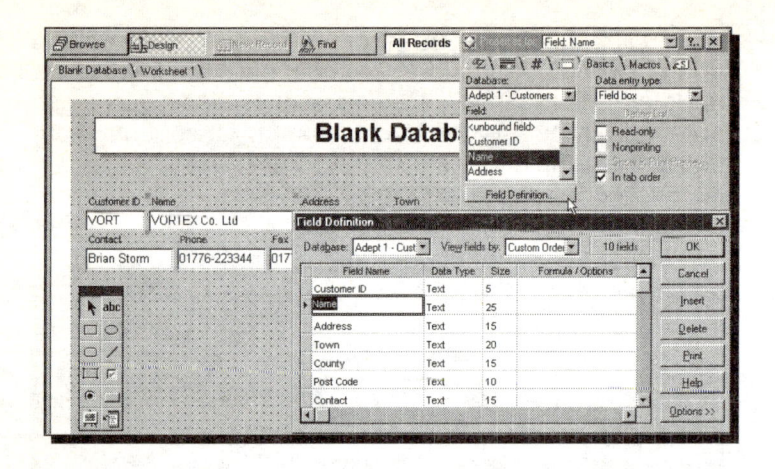

You could use the Drawing Tools skills you acquired in Chapter 5 (page 93), to re-arrange the position of your various fields, maybe as shown below.

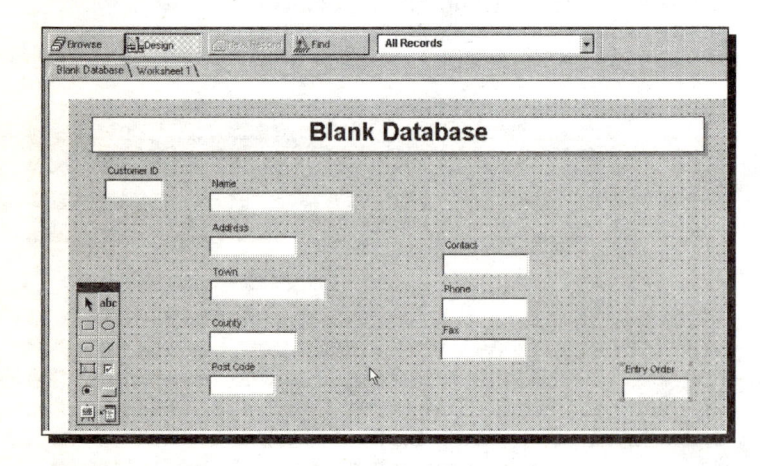

Finally, first click the Save icon (or use the **File, Save** command) to save your design changes, then click the **Browse** button. You are now ready to start entering information, in the displayed 'form' view one record at a time.

Alternatively, you could use the Worksheet view to enter the data shown below plus the additional and related information displayed immediately below it.

Customer ID	Name	Address	Town	County	Post Code
VORT	VORTEX Co. Ltd	Windy House	St. Austell	Cornwall	TR181FX
AVON	AVON Construction	Riverside House	Stratford-on-Avon	Warwickshire	AV152QW
BARR	BARROWS Associates	Barrows House	Bodmin	Cornwall	PL221XE
STON	STONEAGE Ltd	Data House	Salisbury	Wiltshire	SB441BN
PARK	PARKWAY Gravel	Aggregate House	Bristol	Avon	BS552ZX
WEST	WESTWOOD Ltd	Weight House	Plymouth	Devon	PL221AA
GLOW	GLOWORM Ltd	Light House	Brighton	Sussex	BR874DD
SILV	SILVERSMITH Co	Radiation House	Exeter	Devon	EX281PL
WORM	WORMGLAZE Ltd	Glass House	Winchester	Hampshire	WN235TR
EALI	EALING Engines Design	Engine House	Taunton	Somerset	TN173RT
HIRE	HIRE Service Equipment	Network House	Bath	Avon	BA763WE
EURO	EUROBASE Co. Ltd	Control House	Penzance	Cornwall	TR158LK

Contact	Phone	Fax	Entry Order
Brian Storm	01776-223344	01776-224466	1
John Waters	01657-113355	01657-221133	2
Mandy Brown	01554-664422	01554-663311	3
Mike Irons	01765-234567	01765-232332	4
James Stone	01534-987654	01534-984567	5
Mary Slim	01234-667755	01234-669988	6
Peter Summers	01432-746523	01432-742266	7
Adam Smith	01336-997755	01336-996644	8
Richard Glazer	01123-654321	01123-651234	9
Trevor Miles	01336-010107	01336-010109	10
Nicole Webb	01875-558822	01875-552288	11
Sarah Star	01736-098765	01736-098567	12

The widths of the various fields were changed so that all fields could be visible on the screen at the same time. To change the width of a field, place the cursor on the column separator until the cursor changes to the vertical split arrow, then drag the column separator to the right or left, to increase or decrease the width of the field.

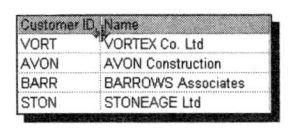

Customer ID	Name
VORT	VORTEX Co. Ltd
AVON	AVON Construction
BARR	BARROWS Associates
STON	STONEAGE Ltd

You can now go back to Design view and change the heading of the form view to 'Customers', and those of the two Tabs to 'Customers' and 'WK Customers' (WK to indicate 'worksheet' view), respectively, as shown below, then save the result as Adept 2 - Customers.

Customers

Browsing and Sorting a Database:

Having entered information into a database, you might need to browse through the database to find a specific record. The best way of doing this is by entering the Worksheet mode (click the WK Customers tab in the case of our database), then make use of the extra SmartIcons which display on the Toolbar, shown below.

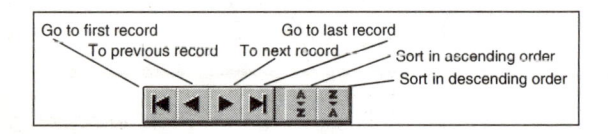

```
Go to first record          Go to last record
     To previous record   To next record
                                          Sort in ascending order
                                          Sort in descending order
```

With the mouse, to sort a database in ascending or descending order of the entries of any field, place the cursor in the required field and click the Sort Ascending or Sort Descending SmartIcon, shown above.

If you want to preserve the order in which you entered your data, then sort by the last field (Entry Order) with its type as Auto Enter Serial. This can be done at any time, even after you finished entering all other information in your table. Sorting a database table in ascending order of an Auto Enter Serial type field, results in the database table displaying in the order in which the data was originally entered in that database.

With the keyboard, to sort a database in ascending or descending order of the entries of any field, place the cursor in the required field, use the **Worksheet, Sort** command, then choose either the **Ascending** or the **Descending** option.

Applying a Filter to a Sort:

If you would like to sort and display only records that fit selected criteria, click the **Find** button, shown here, which displays the screen below. Note that all the field names are displayed, with a row below for you to enter your filter conditions.

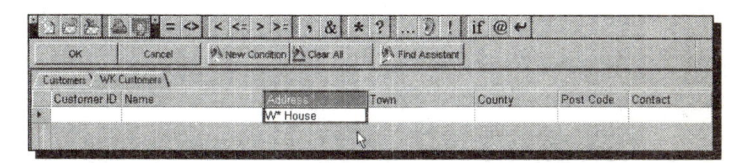

In the above example, we chose to view, in ascending order, the records within the Address field that start with W (we typed W*) followed with the word 'House'. On pressing the <Enter> key, Approach displays only two entries, as seen below.

To sort the filtered data in ascending or descending order of the entries of any field, place the cursor in the required field and click the appropriate Sort SmartIcon. To revert to the display of all the records, click the down-arrow against the **<Current Find/Sort>** box and select *All Records*, as shown above.

If you need to use a more elaborate filter, you can either use the SmartIcons in the Default Find bar (the functions of which are listed overleaf) to help enter your conditions, or use the Find Assistant by clicking the button displayed here and fill in the **Find/Sort Assistant** dialogue box.

193

=	Match similar items
<>	Match items not the same
<	Match items less than
<=	Match items less than or equal to
>	Match items greater than
>=	Match items greater than or equal to
,	Find records when items match either condition
&	Find records when items match both conditions
*	Match any string
?	Match any character
...	Match items within range
≈	Match items that sound like
!	Match items with case sensitive
if	Find records when the expression is true
@	Use @ to preface Approach function in Find
↵	Enter the record or perform the find.

With the Find/Sort Assistant you have the choice of several types of find, as shown below, which are worth investigating.

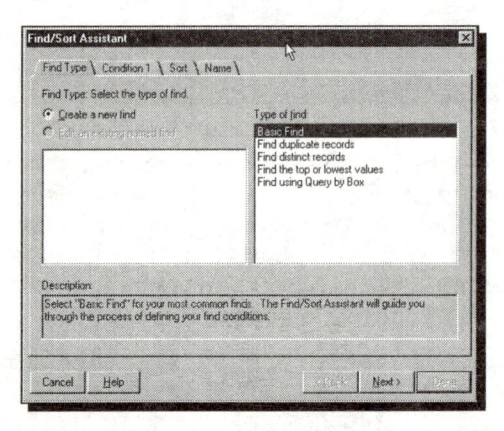

To set up the same find conditions with the keyboard, use the **W‍o‍rksheet, F‍ind** command, then select either the **F‍ind using Worksheet** or the **Find Ass‍istant** option.

194

Find Using a Database Form

Forms can be used to enter, change or view data. They are mainly used to improve the way in which data is displayed on the screen. Forms can also be used to sort records in a database in descending or ascending order of a selected field.

To illustrate the above points, click the Customers tab of our example database to display the following form:

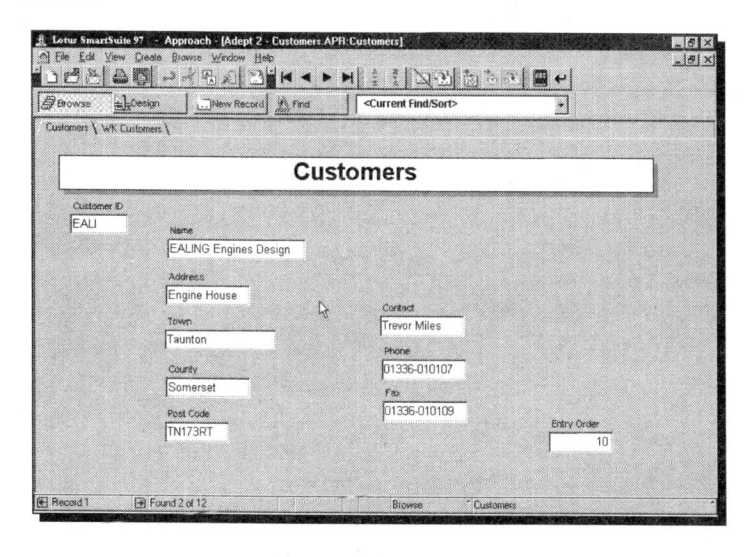

Typing E* in the Customer ID field and pressing the <Enter> key, displays the first of two records (see the bottom of the display). To see the next record, click the 'Go to the next record' button, shown to the left. Entering conditions for a search in a form view are the same as those we discussed in the Worksheet view.

To achieve the same things with the keyboard, use the **Browse, Find** command, then select one of the four displayed options, namely, **Find using Form**, **Find Assistant**, **Find Again**, or **Find All**.

Working with Data

Adding Records in a Database: Whether you are in Worksheet view or Form view, to add a record, first use the **Create Field Definition** command, click the **Options** button, and reset the **Serial number starting at** box to one above the total number of records in your database, as shown below.

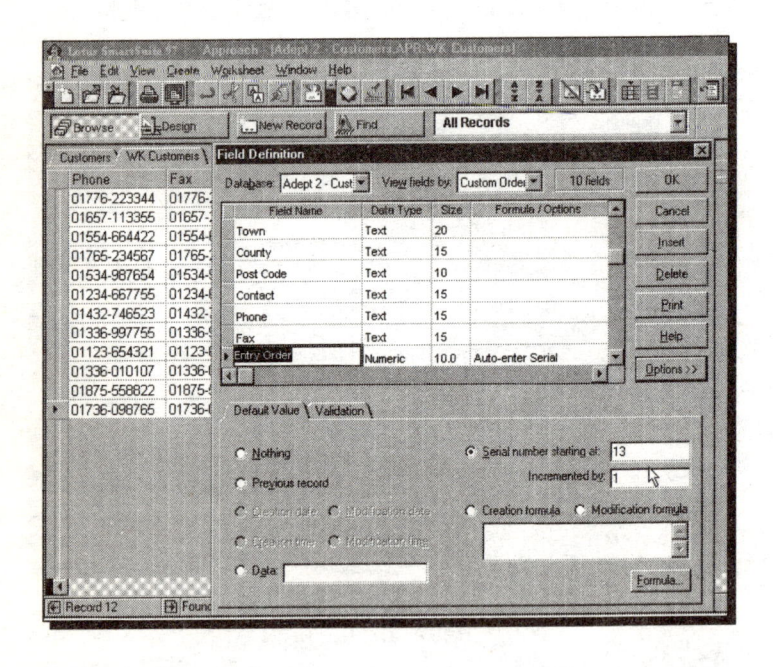

In our example, this has to be reset to 13, as the total number of records in our database is 12.

Next, click the New Record button, shown to the left, which when in Worksheet view causes the cursor to jump to the end of the worksheet on a new line. When in Form view, Approach displays an empty form which can be used to add a new record.

Deleting Records from a Database: Whether you are in Worksheet view or Form view, to delete a record place the insertion pointer inside any of the fields of the record you want to delete and press the Delete the current record icon, shown here.

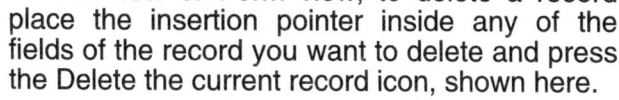

With the keyboard, when in Worksheet view, use the **W̲orksheet, D̲elete, S̲elected Records** command, while when in Form view, use the **B̲rowse Delet̲e Record** command.

Insert and Delete Fields: To insert a field in a database, display it in Worksheet view, click the **Design** button, and use the **C̲reate Field D̲efinition** command. Alternatively, you could click the 'Show Add Field dialog' icon, shown here, and click the **Field D̲efinition** button on the displayed dialogue box. In either case, the following dialogue box will display.

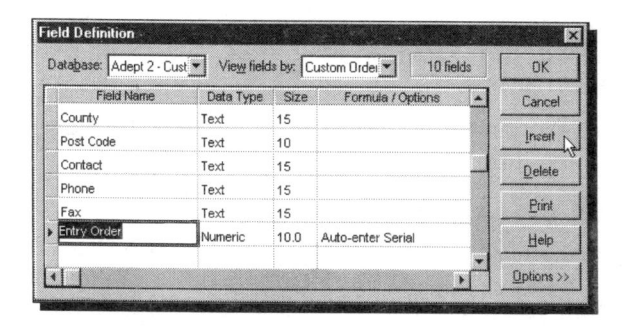

Next, highlight the field above which you want to insert the new field and press the **I̲nsert** button. Finally, type in a field name, specify its size, and press **OK**.

To delete a field from a database, display it in Worksheet view, click the **Design** button, and display the **Field Definition** dialogue box. Next, highlight the field you want to delete and press the **D̲elete** button and press **OK**.

Printing a Database:

You can print a database by clicking the Print icon, the leftmost of the two shown here, or by using the **File, Print** command to display the **Print** dialogue box shown below.

Alternatively, you can preview a database on screen by clicking the Preview icon, the rightmost of the two shown above.

However, printing directly from here, produces a pre-defined print-out whether in Form view or Worksheet view, the format of which you cannot control, apart from the print orientation and paper size. To control these, click the **Properties** button of the **Print** dialogue box which displays the **Print Setup** dialogue box from which you can change the print orientation. Clicking the **Properties** button on the **Print Setup** dialogue box allows you to set the paper size.

For a better method of producing a printed output, see the Report Design section of the next chapter.

12. RELATIONAL DATABASE DESIGN

In order to be able to discuss relational databases, we will create an additional database, which we will call **Adept 2 - Orders**. In the previous chapter we discussed in detail how to create a database so, if need be, refer to it. Below we only summarise the necessary steps you will have to go through to create this new database.

- Start Approach and click the 'Create a New File Using a SmartMaster' tab of the displayed **Welcome to Lotus Approach** dialogue box.

- Select a blank Database template from the displayed SmartMaster list.

- In the **File name** box of the displayed **New** dialogue box, type the **Adept 2 - Orders** and press the **Create** button.

- In the displayed **Field Definition** dialogue box, type the following information.

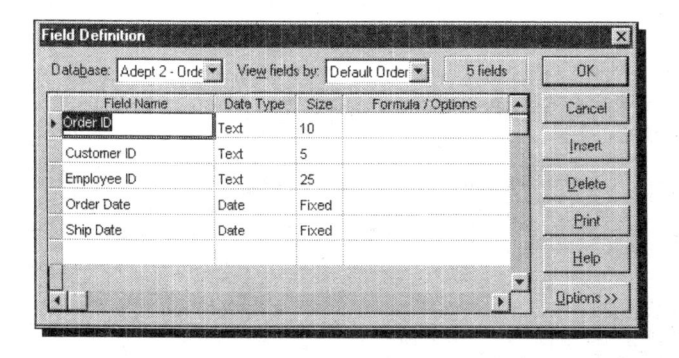

Field Name	Data Type	Size	Formula / Options
Order ID	Text	10	
Customer ID	Text	5	
Employee ID	Text	25	
Order Date	Date	Fixed	
Ship Date	Date	Fixed	

- Use the Form view and click the **Design** button, then change the heading of the form to **Orders** and the Form view and Worksheet view tab names to 'Orders' and 'WK Orders', respectively.

- While in the Design mode of Form view, double-click each data field in turn, and select the field format as 'Date' under the **Format type** and choose an appropriate format under **Current format**, as shown below.

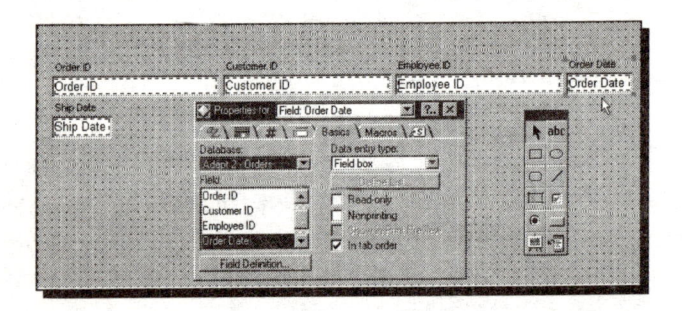

Make sure that the Date format in the Windows 95 Regional Setting is correctly set to correspond to your choice above. If not, use the **Start, Settings, Control Panel** command, double-click the Regional Settings icon, click the Date tab, and select the appropriate **Short date style** from the displayed list.

- Finally, insert the following information in the newly created database.

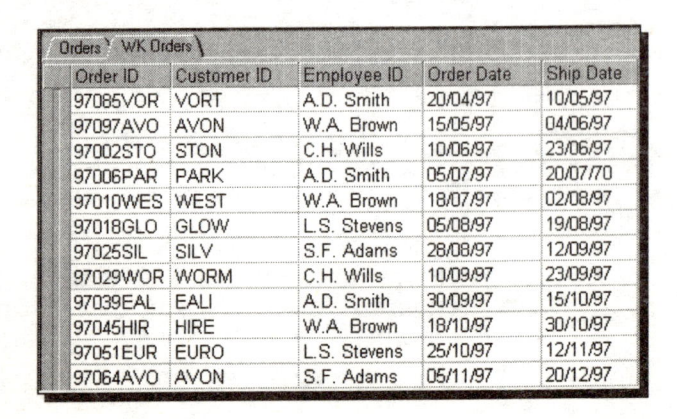

Order ID	Customer ID	Employee ID	Order Date	Ship Date
97085VOR	VORT	A.D. Smith	20/04/97	10/05/97
97097AVO	AVON	W.A. Brown	15/05/97	04/06/97
97002STO	STON	C.H. Wills	10/06/97	23/06/97
97006PAR	PARK	A.D. Smith	05/07/97	20/07/70
97010WES	WEST	W.A. Brown	18/07/97	02/08/97
97018GLO	GLOW	L.S. Stevens	05/08/97	19/08/97
97025SIL	SILV	S.F. Adams	28/08/97	12/09/97
97029WOR	WORM	C.H. Wills	10/09/97	23/09/97
97039EAL	EALI	A.D. Smith	30/09/97	15/10/97
97045HIR	HIRE	W.A. Brown	18/10/97	30/10/97
97051EUR	EURO	L.S. Stevens	25/10/97	12/11/97
97064AVO	AVON	S.F. Adams	05/11/97	20/12/97

Creating a Join

Information held in two or more databases is normally related in some way. In our case, the two databases, **Adept 2 - Orders** and **Adept 2 - Customers**, are related by the Customer ID field. However, before starting to make a join, use the Windows Explorer and copy the three files of each database application (with extensions **ADX, APR** and **dbf** - this last extension could be different if you have not used dBASE) into a different folder. This is a precaution in case you want to Unjoin these databases later and avoid data loss.

To build up relationships between databases, close all databases, then open first the database **Adept 2 - Orders** and while in Browse mode, use the **Create, Join** command which opens the **Join** dialogue box shown below, but with only the **Adept 2 - Orders** database fields showing. Next, press the **Open** button on the **Join** dialogue box and select the **Adept 2 - Customers** database which is then also displayed within the **Join** dialogue box. You can build relationships between databases by dragging a field name from one table into another, as shown below.

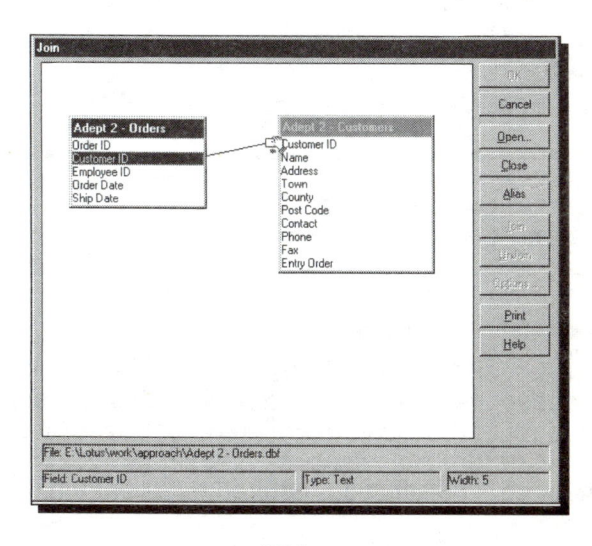

In our example on the previous page, we have dragged Customer ID from the **Adept 2 - Orders** database (by pointing to it, pressing the left mouse button, and while keeping the mouse button pressed, dragging the pointer) to the required field in the other database, in this case Customer ID in the **Adept 2 - Customers** database. Releasing the mouse button joins the two selected fields between the two databases with a line, as shown below.

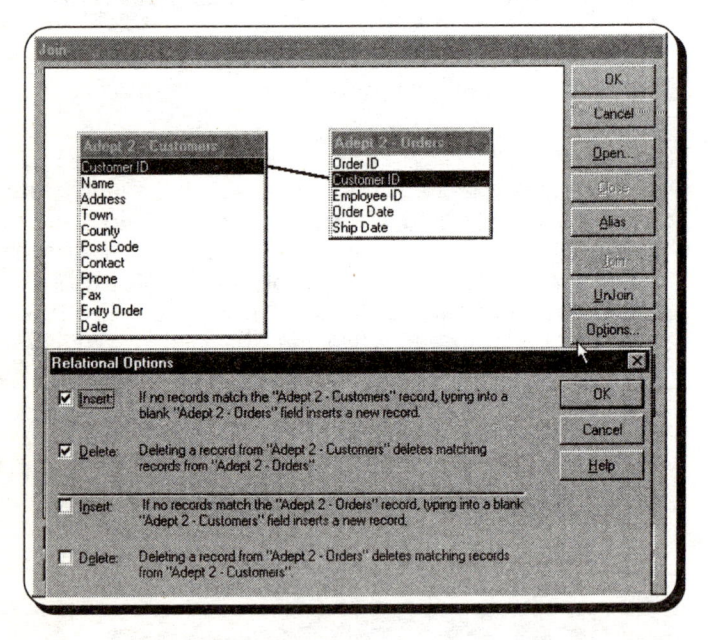

Pressing the **Options** button, opens up the **Relational Options** dialogue box shown above. In this additional dialogue box you can specify what you want to happen when you insert or delete records into or from one database or the other.

In the above join, by using the **Adept 2 - Orders** database first, we have made it the 'Main' database (as it has repeated Customer ID records), while the **Adept 2 - Customers** database becomes the 'Detailed' database - a distinction required by Approach.

Creating a Report

Once you have created a Join between two or more databases, it is possible to create a report which displays selected fields from both databases. Below, we show the steps required to create such a report. First, and with the **Adept 2 - Orders** database displaying, use the **Create, Report** command to activate the Report Assistant, as shown below.

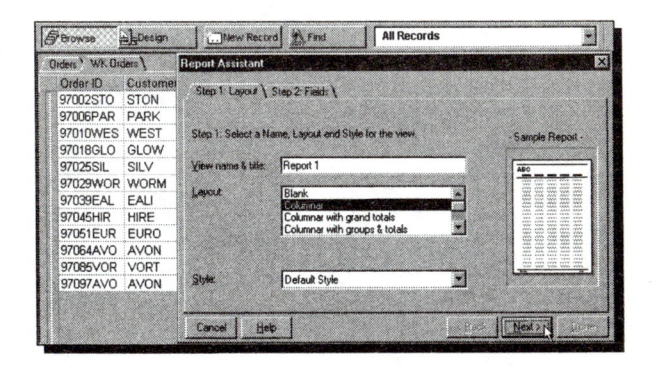

With the Step 1: Layout tab active, select 'Columnar' from the **Layout** list and press the **Next** button.

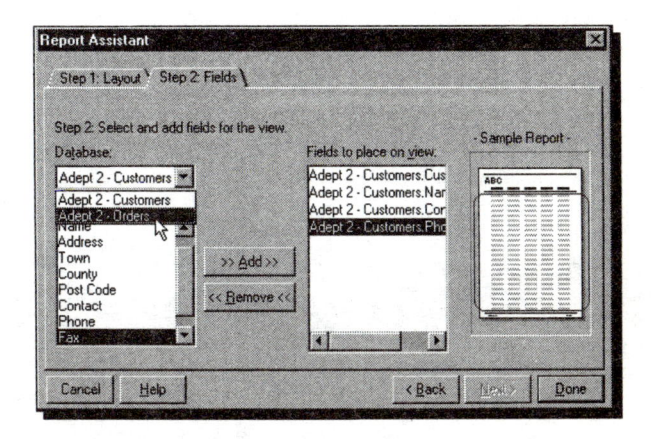

- Customers.Customer ID
- Customers.Name
- Customers.Contact
- Customers.Phone
- Orders.Order Date
- Orders.Ship Date

Next, and with the Step 2: Fields tab active, choose the **Customers** database and select the first four fields shown to the left, pressing the **>>Add>>** button after each selection, then choose the **Orders** database and select the last two fields and press the **Done** button.

In the next dialogue box, shown below, you are asked to specify which of the joined databases is the Main database. Select the **Adept 2 - Orders** database.

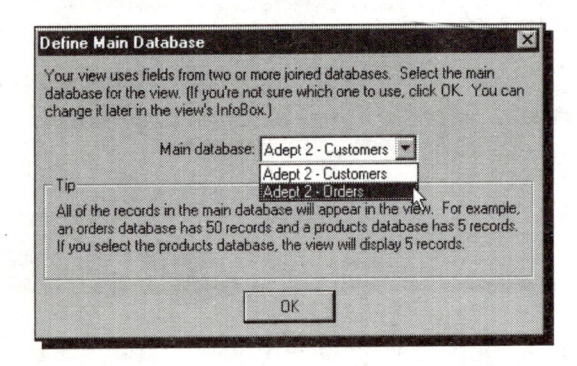

On pressing the **OK** button, **Report 1** appears on the screen in Design form, displaying all the records associated with the **Adept 2 - Orders** database, as shown below.

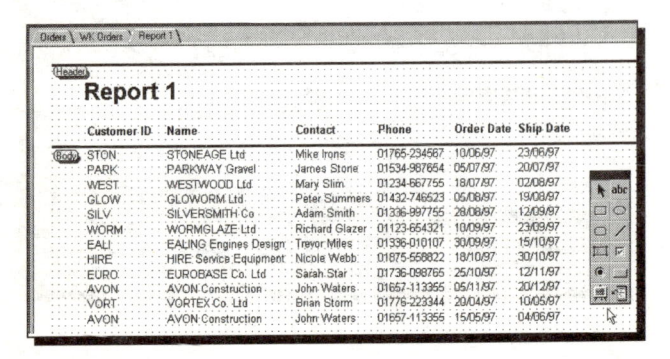

Searching a Report:

You can use all the usual search facilities that you can apply to a database, to search a report. For example, we might want to discuss with our 'Contact' exactly when an order was received from their company and when it was processed. To achieve this, do the following:

- Arrange for the basic **Report 1** to be on your screen.

- Click the **Find** button, which displays the **Find/Sort Assistant** dialogue box with the Find Type tab active.

- Select 'Basic Find' from the list under **Type of find**, as shown below, and press the **Next** button.

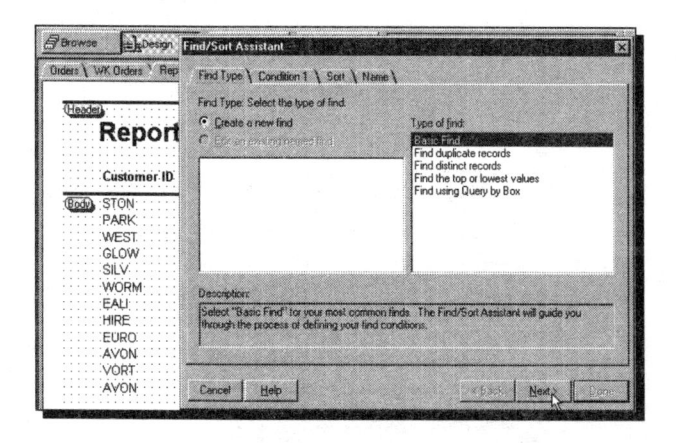

- In the next dialogue box (with the Condition 1 tab active), select 'Customer ID' from the list under **Fields**, and 'is exactly equal to' from the list under **Operator**. Finally, type in the Customer ID you want to search for, which in our case is, say, AVON, as shown overleaf, and click the **Next** button.

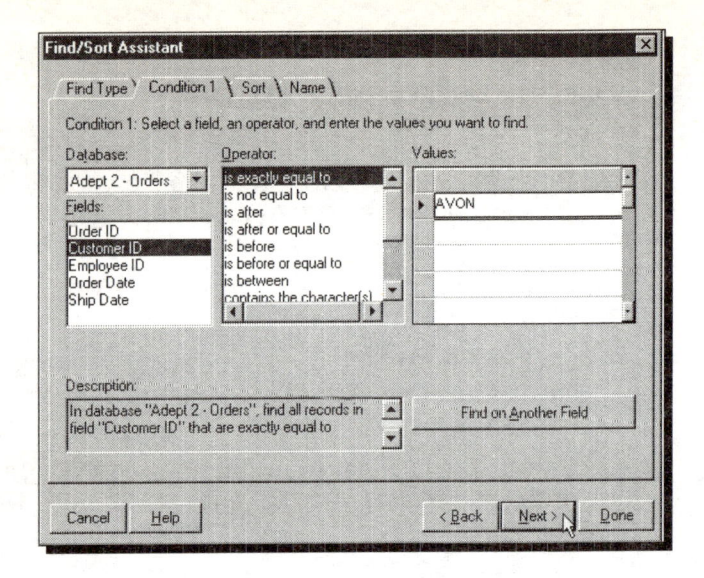

- In the next dialogue box select 'Order Date' for the **Fields to sort on**, as shown below, and press **Next**.

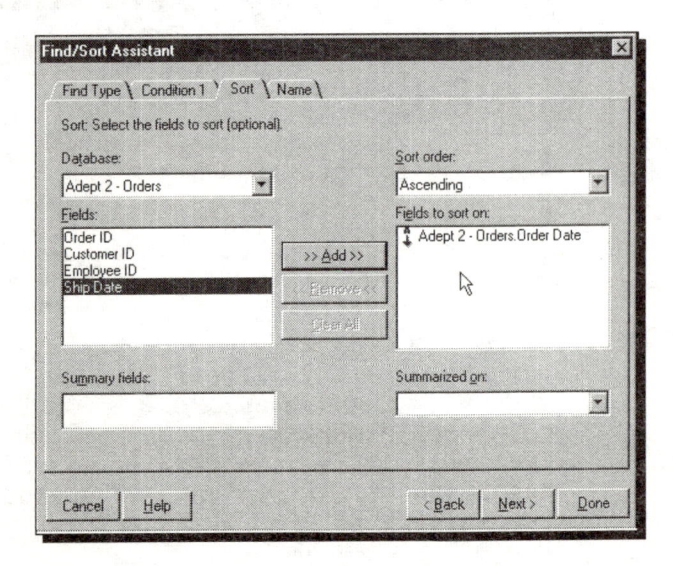

206

- In the next dialogue box you are given the opportunity to give this Find/Sort routine a name for easy access in the future.

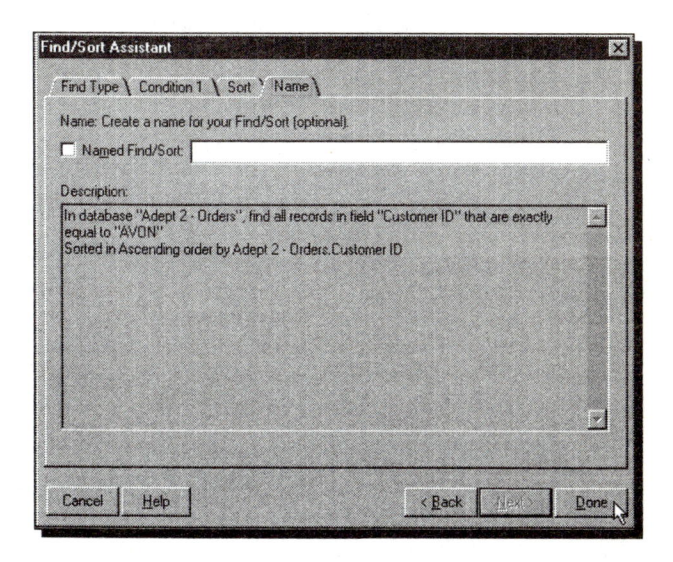

- Finally, pressing the **Done** button, displays the result of our report serch, as follows:

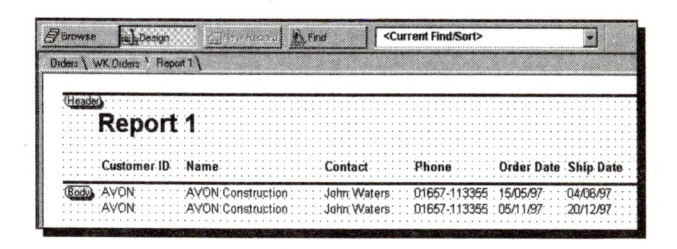

Obviously, you can give a report a more appropriate name, and you can move the displayed fields on the page to suit your requirement. In fact, what you can produce on the screen and on paper, is only limited by your imagination.

Creating an Additional Database

As an exercise, create a third database, using the procedure outlined at the beginning of this chapter, to represent the Invoices sent to your customers. This database should be named **Adept 3 - Invoices** and should have the following field types:

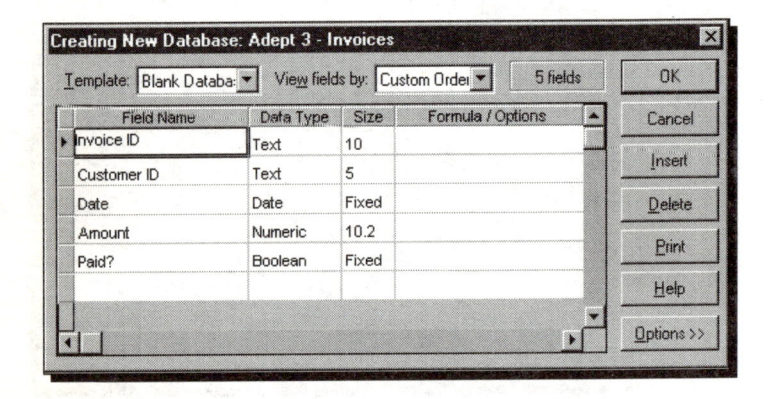

Field Name	Data Type	Size	Formula / Options
Invoice ID	Text	10	
Customer ID	Text	5	
Date	Date	Fixed	
Amount	Numeric	10.2	
Paid?	Boolean	Fixed	

Next, enter the data given below and copy your existing databases to **Adept 3 - Customers** and **Adept 3 - Orders**, as discussed earlier, before attempting to creat appropriate relationships between them.

Invoice ID	Customer ID	Date	Amount	Paid?
AD9701	VORT	10/05/97	120.84	No
AD9702	AVON	04/06/97	103.52	Yes
AD9704	STON	23/06/97	55.98	No
AD9705	PARK	20/07/97	180.22	No
AD9706	WEST	02/08/97	68.52	No
AD9707	GLOW	19/08/97	111.56	No
AD9708	SILV	12/09/97	123.45	Yes
AD9709	WORM	23/09/97	35.87	No
AD9710	EALI	15/10/97	58.95	No
AD9711	HIRE	30/10/97	290	No
AD9712	EURO	12/11/97	150	No
AD9713	AVON	20/12/97	135	No

Finally, do not forget to copy all three databases to a different folder so that you have a ready made backup, before attempting to join these databases.

The relationships between the three databases should be arranged so that one customer has many orders and many invoices, as follows:

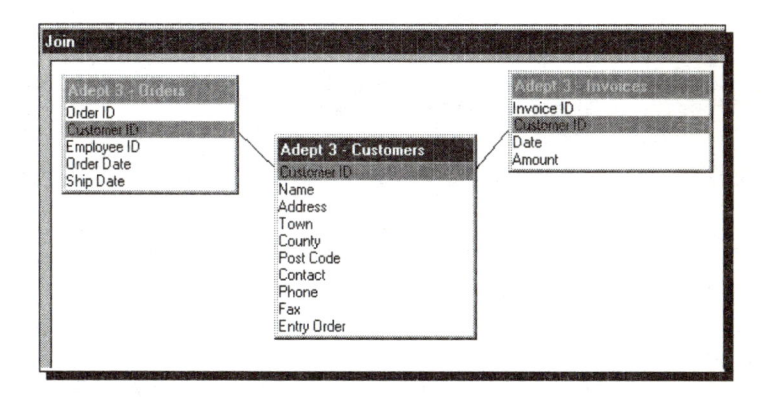

```
Join
┌─────────────────────┐       ┌─────────────────────┐       ┌─────────────────────┐
│ Adept 3 - Orders    │       │                     │       │ Adept 3 - Invoices  │
│ Order ID            │       │                     │       │ Invoice ID          │
│ Customer ID         │───────│ Adept 3 - Customers │───────│ Customer ID         │
│ Employee ID         │       │ Customer ID         │       │ Date                │
│ Order Date          │       │ Name                │       │ Amount              │
│ Ship Date           │       │ Address             │       └─────────────────────┘
└─────────────────────┘       │ Town                │
                              │ County              │
                              │ Post Code           │
                              │ Contact             │
                              │ Phone               │
                              │ Fax                 │
                              │ Entry Order         │
                              └─────────────────────┘
```

It is important that you should complete this exercise, as it consolidates what we have done so far and, in any case, we will be using all three databases in what comes next. So go ahead and try it.

Creating a Crosstab View

You create a *Crosstab View* to display totals in a compact, spreadsheet format. A Crosstab view can present a large amount of summary data in a more readable form. The layout of the extracted data from such a view is ideal as the basis for a report.

For example, suppose we wanted to examine which of our employees was responsible for our customers' orders in each month. The information is contained in the **Orders** database, as follows:

Order ID	Customer ID	Employee ID	Order Date	Ship Date
97085VOR	VORT	A.D. Smith	20/04/97	10/05/97
97097AVO	AVON	W.A. Brown	15/05/97	04/06/97
97002STO	STON	C.H. Wills	10/06/97	23/06/97
97006PAR	PARK	A.D. Smith	05/07/97	20/07/97
97010WES	WEST	W.A. Brown	18/07/97	02/08/97
97018GLO	GLOW	L.S. Stevens	05/08/97	19/08/97
97025SIL	SILV	S.F. Adams	28/08/97	12/09/97
97029WOR	WORM	C.H. Wills	10/09/97	23/09/97
97039EAL	EALI	A.D. Smith	30/09/97	15/10/97
97045HIR	HIRE	W.A. Brown	18/10/97	30/10/97
97051EUR	EURO	L.S. Stevens	25/10/97	12/11/97
97064AVO	AVON	S.F. Adams	05/11/97	20/12/97

From the way this information is presented it is very difficult to work out who was responsible for which order in a given month and how much that order was worth, let alone the total amount of such orders. However, a Crosstab view that lists the names of the Customers ID in rows and the names of the employees as a column heading with the month on which the invoice was raised as a column sub-heading, and the actual amounts of these invoices appearing in the main body of the view, would be an ideal way to present this type of information.

Before you start, however, open the **Adept 3 - Orders** database and make sure that the relevant Customers and Invoices databases are joined appropriately, as discussed in the previous section.

To create a Crosstab view, open the **Adept 3 - Orders** database and use the **Create, Crosstab** command to display the Crosstab Assistant shown below.

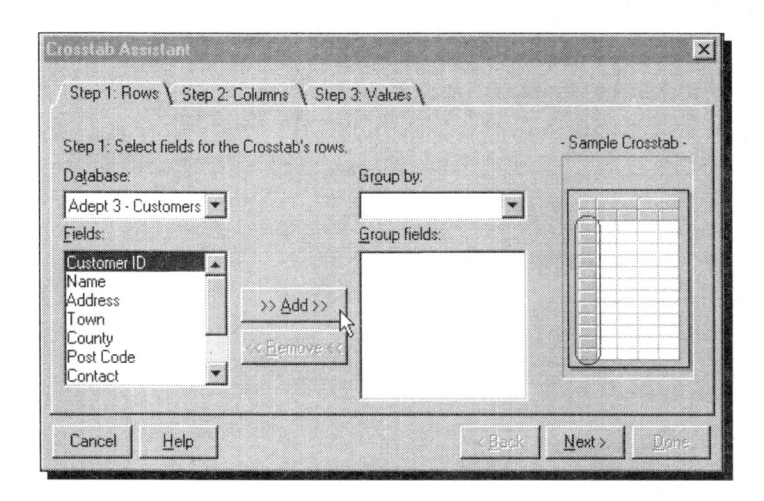

With the Step 1: Rows tab active, select the Customer ID from the Customers database, and click first the **>>And>>** button, then the **Next** button to display the next **Crosstab Assistant** dialogue box shown below.

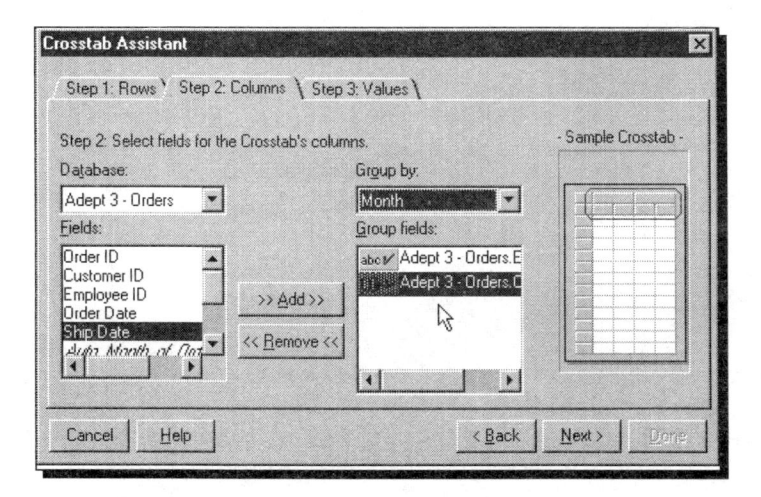

With the Step 2: Rows tab active, select from the **Orders** database, first the Employee ID field and click the **>>And>>** button, then the Order Date field and click the **>>And>>** button. Next, click the down-arrow against the **Group by** box and select 'Month', before pressing the **Next** button to display the third **Crosstab Assistant** dialogue box shown below.

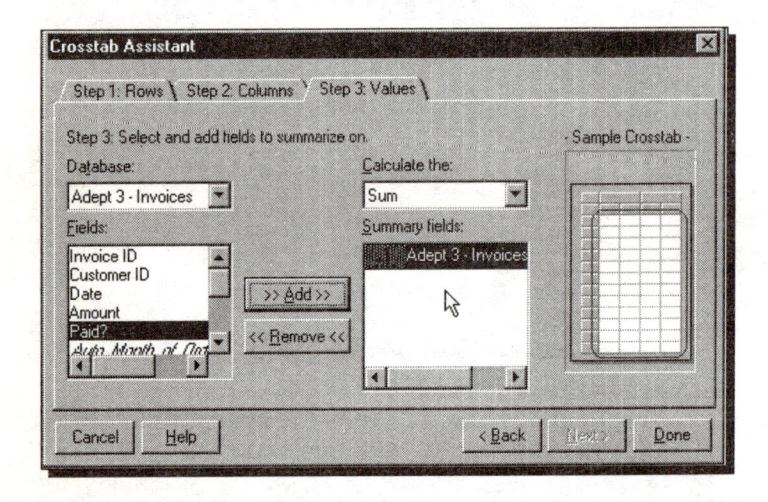

With the Step 3: Rows tab active, select from the **Invoices** database, the Amount field, and press the **Done** button. Finally, specify Adept 3 - Orders as your main database.

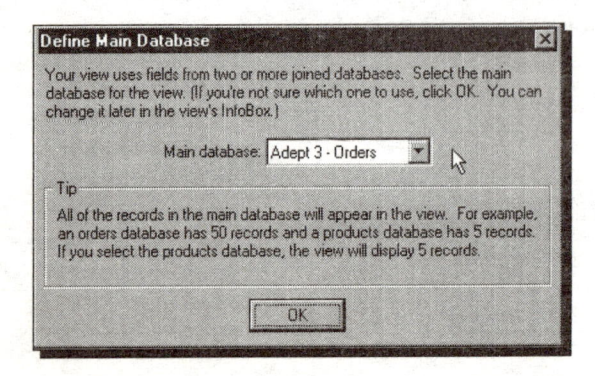

Approach now displays your Crosstab view, as follows:

Orders \ WK Orders \ Report 1 \ Crosstab 1	A.D. Smith				C.H. Wills				L.S. Stevens				S.F. Adams				W.A. Brown				Total
	Apr 97	Jul 97	Sep 97	Total	Jun 97	Sep 97	Total		Aug 97	Oct 97	Total		Aug 97	Nov 97	Total		May 97	Jul 97	Oct 97	Total	
	Amount	Amount	Amount	Amount	Amount	Amount	Amount		Amount	Amount	Amount		Amount	Amount	Amount		Amount	Amount	Amount	Amount	Amount
AVON														238.52	238.52		238.52			238.52	477.04
EALI			58.95	58.95																	58.95
EURO										150	150										150
GLOW									111.56		111.56										111.56
HIRE																			290	290	290
PARK		180.22		180.22																	180.22
SILV													123.45		123.45						123.45
STON					55.98		55.98														55.98
VORT	120.84			120.84																	120.84
WEST																		68.52		68.52	68.52
WORM						35.87	35.87														35.87
Total	120.84	180.22	58.95	360.01	55.98	35.87	91.85		111.56	150	261.56		123.45	238.52	361.97		238.52	68.52	290	597.04	1672.43

As you can see from the previous screen, the required information is tabulated and is extremely easy to read.

Should you require to see the underlying information, select an 'Amount', then click the 'Drill Down to Data' SmartIcon shown here, to let Approach create another worksheet, but displaying only the data associated with the entry you selected.

To see the rest of the information held in the latest worksheet, click its tab to display the folowing:

Customer ID	Auto_Month_of_Order Date	Employee ID	Amount
VORT	01/04/97	A.D. Smith	120.84
AVON	01/05/97	W.A. Brown	103.52
STON	01/06/97	C.H. Wills	55.98
PARK	01/07/97	A.D. Smith	180.22
WEST	01/07/97	W.A. Brown	68.52
GLOW	01/08/97	L.S. Stevens	111.56
SILV	01/08/97	S.F. Adams	123.45
WORM	01/09/97	C.H. Wills	35.87
EALI	01/09/97	A.D. Smith	58.95
HIRE	01/10/97	W.A. Brown	290
EURO	01/10/97	L.S. Stevens	150
AVON	01/11/97	S.F. Adams	103.52

Approach can also display information graphically. Try using the **Create, Chart** command, and see how you can chart your data - the procedure for creating a chart is very similar to that of creating a crosstab view. Try it!

* * *

We hope we have covered enough features of the Approach application in this book to give you the foundations needed to make you want to explore the program more fully by yourself.

* * *

13. THE LOTUS ORGANIZER

Lotus Organizer is an application that lets you organise and manage your time more effectively by allowing you to fill in and see at a glance an appointments and meetings diary. This diary can be viewed with a daily, weekly, or monthly format. Switching from one view to another is simply done by clicking at appropriate icons.

The program also allows you to produce 'To Do' lists, track projects, build a database of contacts, keep a list of telephone calls, scribble on a notepad, and create a list of anniversaries. These various functions are reached by simply clicking the appropriately named tab on the side of the Organizer.

Organizer can be used *online* or *offline*. To work online, your computer must be connected to a shared network resource, which is imperative if you are planning to use the TeamMail features of the Organizer. In that case, your computer must have a connection and a list of users on the system. You work offline if your computer hasn't a connection to a network, in which case the TeamMail features of the Organizer are not available to you.

Starting the Organizer Program

The Lotus Organizer is started in Windows either by clicking the **Start** button then selecting **Programs, Lotus SmartSuite** and clicking the **Lotus Organizer 97** option on the cascade menu, or by clicking the Lotus SmartIcon on the Task Bar, shown here.

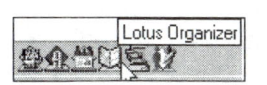

When you start the Organizer, the program first displays its welcoming screen, then it opens up the weekly Calendar, as shown on the next page, with today's date marked in red (in this case the one with the mouse pointer in it).

Parts of the Organizer Screen:

Before we start using the Organizer, let us take a look at its opening screen.

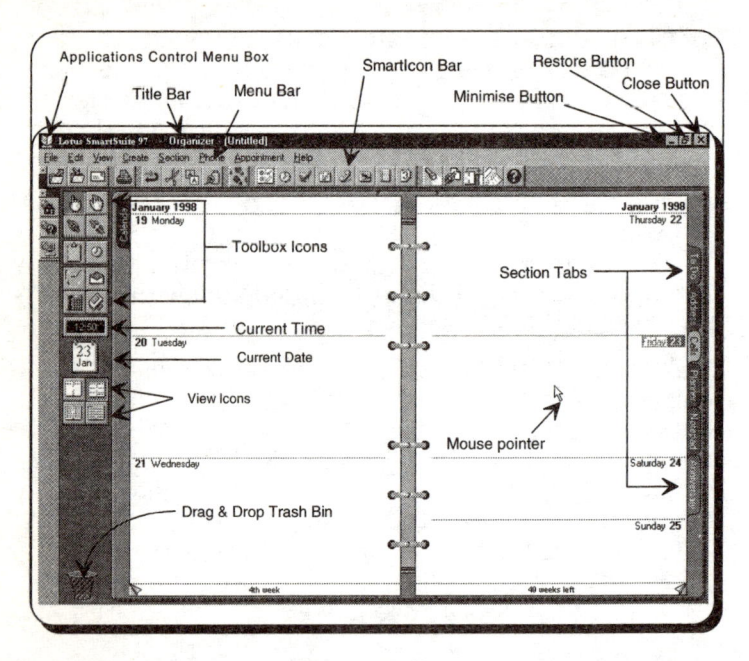

[Screenshot of Lotus SmartSuite 97 Organizer window with labels: Applications Control Menu Box, Title Bar, Menu Bar, SmartIcon Bar, Restore Button, Minimise Button, Close Button, Toolbox Icons, Current Time, Current Date, View Icons, Drag & Drop Trash Bin, Section Tabs, Mouse pointer]

As you can see, this program has some common screen elements with those of other SmartSuite applications, even though at first glance it might look radically different. The central area of the Organizer's window changes the way it displays according to which View or Section tab is active.

To change the displayed Section to another one, say from Calendar to Planner, simply left-click the appropriate tab. However, if you have a sound card which is being used at the time, you might like to silence the noises emitted from the Organizer when you turn its pages or carry out other commands. To do this, use the **File, User Setup** command, then select the **Organizer Preferences** option to display the following dialogue box:

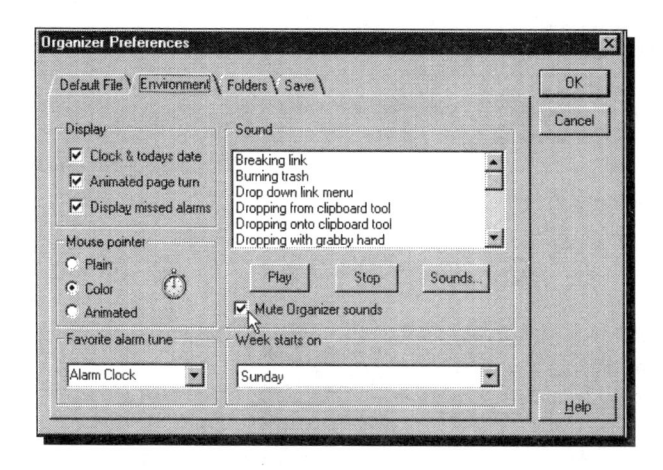

Next, click the Environment tab and check the **Mute Organizer sounds** box, as shown above. As you can see from the above dialogue box, there are other preferences available to you which you might like to explore at this stage.

If you change from the Calendar Section to another one, then return back to Calendar, you will find that the weekly view has changed to a yearly view, as follows:

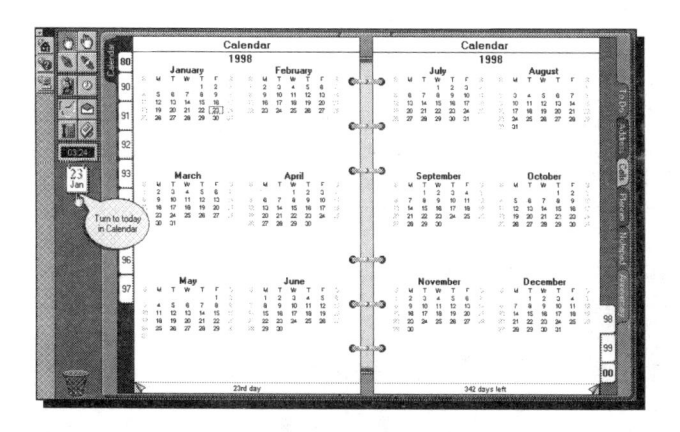

To return to the weekly view, click the Current Date icon on the Toolbar, pointed to above.

217

The Toolbox Icons

The Toolbox icons allow you to perform the tasks described below.

Focus, select, and drag and drop entries	Move an entry
Create links	Break links
Drag an entry here to copy; drag from here to paste	Create an entry
View meeting notices	Send or open mail
Drag an entry here to dial	Print information
View Day per page	View Work per Week
View Week per page	View Months

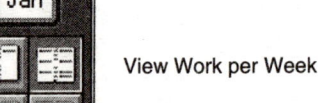

The View and Sort icons (the last four at the bottom of the above screen dump) let you display entries in different ways. They also change depending on what event tab is pressed. To see how these icons change, click a different event tab and place the mouse pointer on each to see their function described in a bubble. For example, in the Notepad Section these four icons change to

View by Page number	View by Title
View by Date	View by Category

Using Help in Organizer

The Organizer Help Program provides on-line help in the same way as the Help programs of the other SmartSuite applications. You can use the **Help, Help Topics** command, to display the dialogue box below.

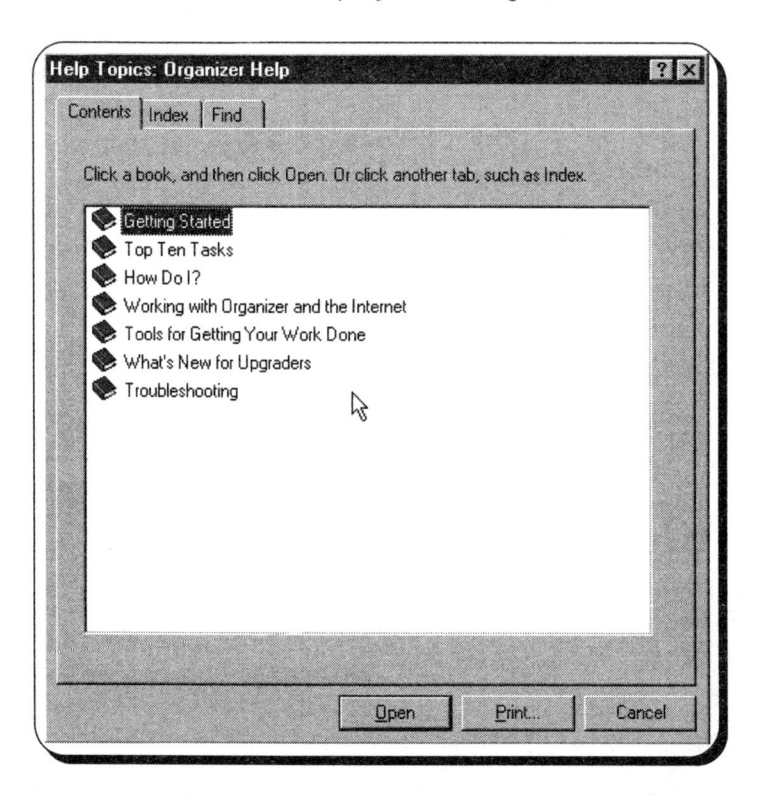

```
Help Topics: Organizer Help                          ? X
┌─────────┬───────┬──────┐
│ Contents │ Index │ Find │
└─────────┴───────┴──────┘

Click a book, and then click Open. Or click another tab, such as Index.

  📕 Getting Started
  📕 Top Ten Tasks
  📕 How Do I?
  📕 Working with Organizer and the Internet
  📕 Tools for Getting Your Work Done
  📕 What's New for Upgraders
  📕 Troubleshooting


                              [ Open ]  [ Print... ]  [ Cancel ]
```

Selecting a book topic from the above list and pressing the **Open** button displays its contents. Selecting one of these, changes the **Open** button to a **Display** button, and pressing this displays the relevant topic on screen. The Index and Find tabs allow you to type in a topic to search for, which can then be displayed. Help topics can be printed on paper by selecting the topic, then clicking the **Print** button.

Viewing Appointments

To look at your appointments, first click the View Month icon to display the following screen:

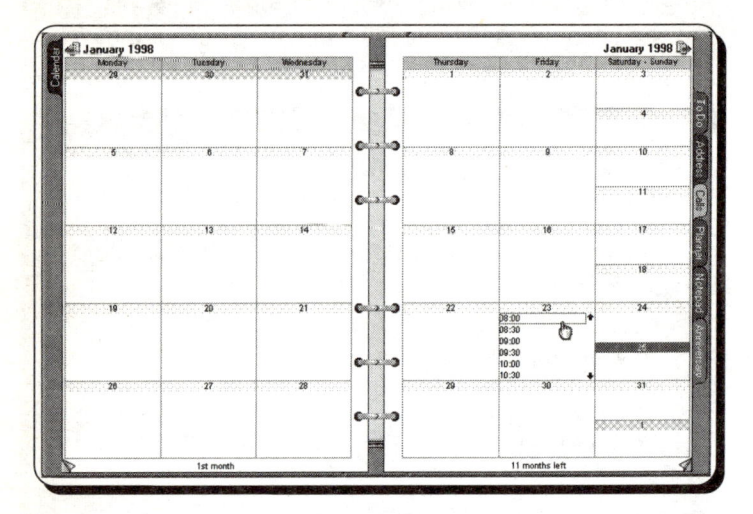

Then select the date you are interested in and click the View Day per page icon to display the following screen:

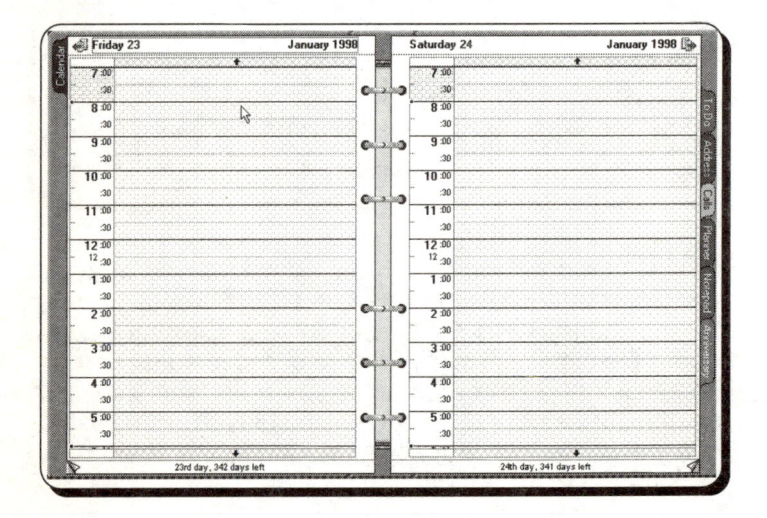

No matter which view you are displaying, you will see at the bottom extreme left and extreme right a turned up part of the page. When the mouse pointer is placed on that area of the screen, it turns to a pointing hand, as shown here, and left-clicking this area can take you backward or forward by the same time period as the one displayed. For example, if you are displaying a weekly view, it will move you through the calendar one week at a time, while if you are viewing a daily view, it will move you through the calendar a day at a time, and so on.

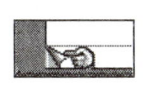

Appointments can be viewed in Organizer in several ways, depending on the details you need to know. In the Daily and Weekly view, you can see the date, time, and the description of an appointment. You also have the facility to use symbols to indicate whether the appointment is recurring, tentative, or private, and whether a reminder has been set or other users have been invited. These facilities can be selected by using the **View, Calendar Preferences** command to display the following dialogue box.

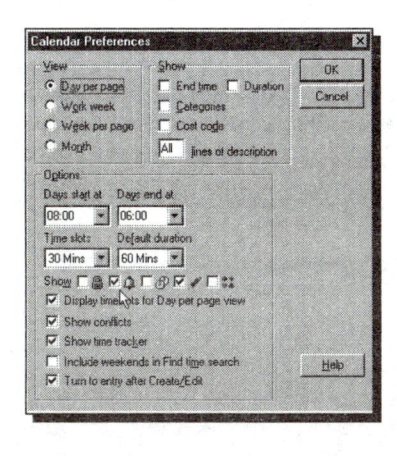

From here you select what information is to be shown on your appointment entries, such as categories, duration, etc. You can also change the starting and ending times of a day, the time slots and the default appointment duration. Finally, you can select which symbols are to be displayed on your diary, to indicate confidential entries, those that have an alarm set, repeating, pencilled-in entries, and type of category.

Entering Appointments:

To start with, let us type in two appointments for meetings; one for 10:00 a.m. on Monday 26 January, the other for the same day and time four weeks later. To do so, click on 26 January on the Monthly Calendar view, then click the One Day per page icon and click the 10:00 a.m. time slot. Next, either double-click the dotted area to the right of the time slot, click the Create an Appointment icon shown here, or use the **Create Appointment** command. Either of these opens the **Create Appointment** dialogue box displayed below in which you can type 'Managers' meeting' in the **Description** box, change the **Duration** from its default value of 1 hour to 2 hours, then select one of the **Categories**, as shown below, and press **OK**.

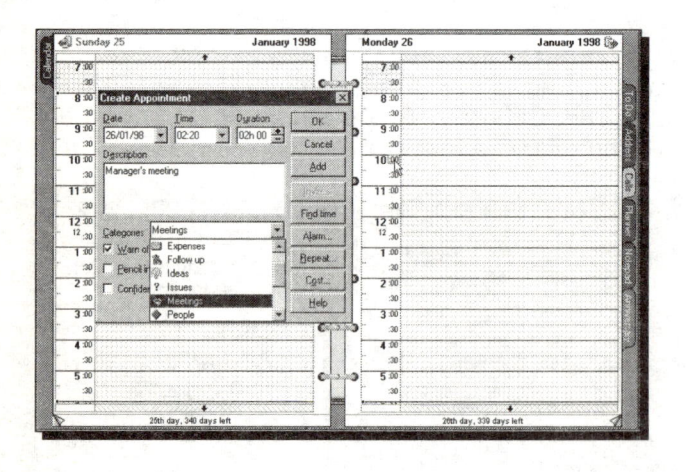

Note that after pressing **OK**, the entry is inserted in your diary, as shown here, and pointing to that entry changes the mouse pointer to a hand. Double-clicking within this entry area, displays the **Create Appointment** dialogue box for the selection of further options.

Since we wanted to repeat this appointment four weeks later, press the **Repeat** button on the **Create Appointment** dialogue box to display the following:

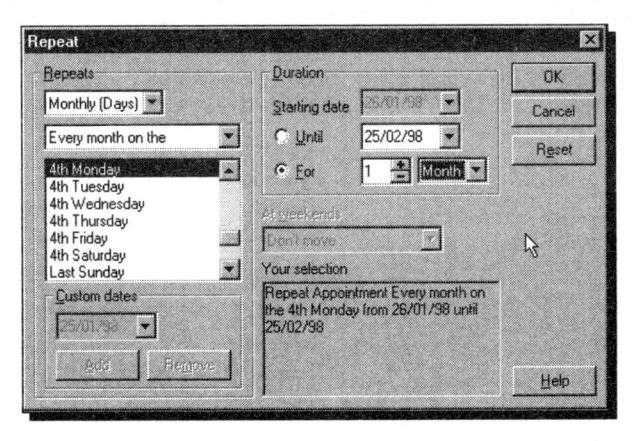

You can use the various options on this dialogue box to make the appointment recurring. Choosing 'Every month on the 4th Monday', and for only '1 month', simply repeats the original appointment 4 weeks later.

Pressing the **OK** button returns you to the **Create Appointment** dialogue box from which you can also choose to set an alarm for this appointment. To do so, click the **Alarm** button to display the dialogue box shown below.

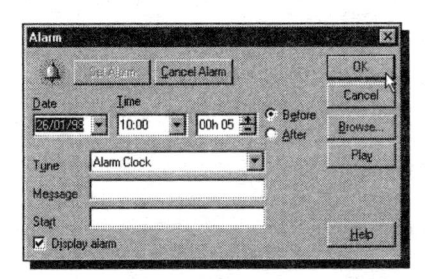

From here, you can set the timing for the alarm, and also the type of **Tune** you prefer to hear. Finally, pressing **OK** on this and its parent dialogue box, causes the alarm and recurring symbols to appear against the appointment entry, provided it has been selected in the **Calendar Preferences** dialogue box discussed earlier.

223

Next, let us assume that you also have a special lunch appointment with your mother on the same day. To enter this information click on 26 January on the calendar on the Daily entry area, against the desired starting time, say 12.30, and fill in the displayed **Create Appointment** dialogue box. Your entry will look as follows:

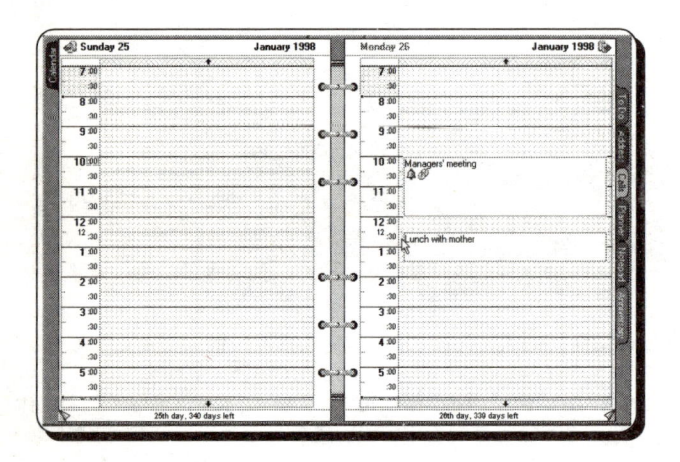

Now let us assume that you made two mistakes with this appointment: (i) you should really have allowed more time for lunch, and (ii) you have not left enough time between the end of your meeting with the managers and the beginning of your lunch date. To correct these, you have two choices: (a) point to the current appointment and when the mouse pointer turns to a hand, press the <Del> key to delete the entry and start afresh, or (b) use the graphics capabilities of the Organizer to first increase the lunch period, then drag the whole period down by half an hour. These two operations are shown below.

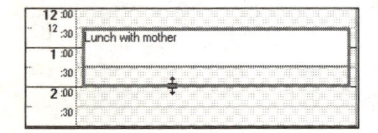

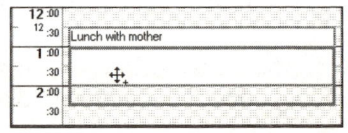

Appointments can also be changed, especially from views other than Daily, by placing the insertion pointer within the entry you want to change and clicking the left mouse button. This displays details of the particular appointment on a thermometer-type band on the spine of the Organizer with starting time, duration and ending time, as shown below.

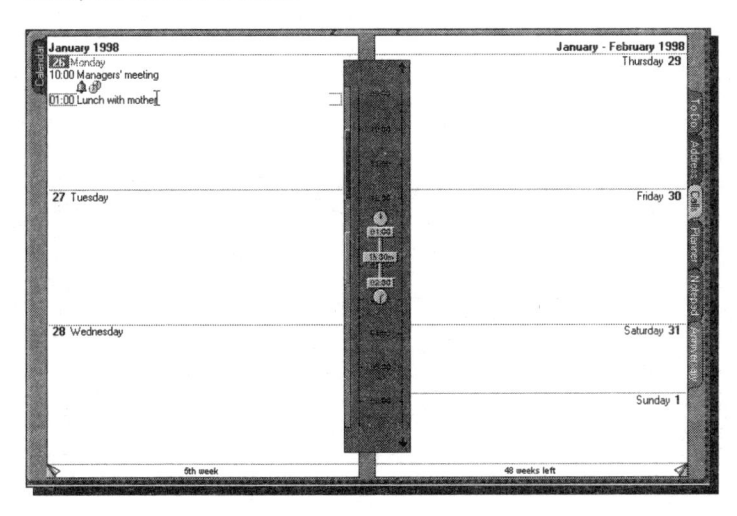

You can change any one of these by dragging either of the two clocks up or down, to increase or decrease the displayed times. Try it!

Printing Information:

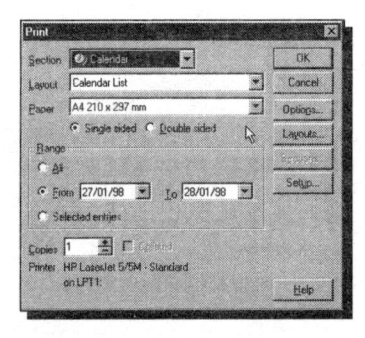

Information held in a diary can be printed on paper. Simply use the **File, Print** command and select an appropriate item from the **Section** and **Layout** list displayed in the **Print** dialogue box. You can also choose the **Paper** size and **Range**.

Other Organizer Facilities

Apart from the Calendar, Organizer contains all the other elements needed to give you an effective time-management tool. These elements are accessed by appropriate tabs situated on the right edge of the screen. The names of these Section tabs can be renamed, if you so wish, by using the **Section, Customize** command which displays the following dialogue box:

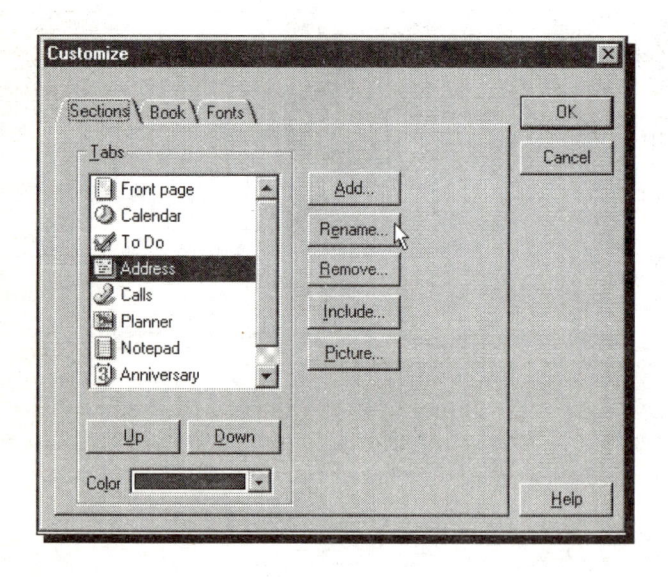

An additional facility allows you to **Add** your own sections based on an existing **Section type**. In this way you can build, say, one address book in which you keep details of friends and family, and another for business contacts.

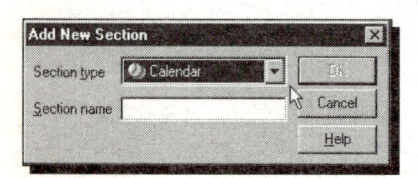

226

To Do List:

Tasks appear in the 'To Do' list, which you can either display in the 'Overdue', 'Current', 'Future', or 'Completed' sub-sections. To create a task, either double-click the 'To Do' page, click the 'Create a task' SmartIcon shown here, or use the **Create, Task** command. Either of these displays the **Create Task** dialogue box shown below, in which you can type a **Description**, set a **Start** and **Due** date, a **Priority**, and other options, including an alarm.

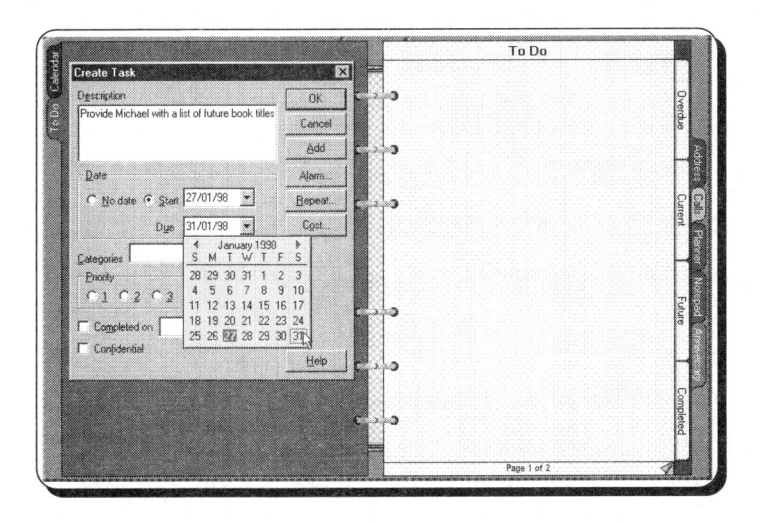

Pressing the **OK** button, inserts the new task in your 'To Do' list under the 'Current' sub-section, as shown here. Note the small square box to the left of the task entry. In this example, it indicates that the task has not been completed. Clicking this square, puts a tick mark inside the square, similar to that in the 'Create a task' SmartIcon, and places this entry in the 'Completed' sub-section.

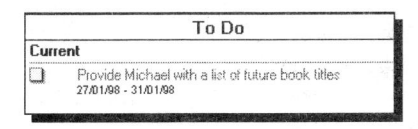

Tasks that have not been completed on time, are automatically transferred into the 'Overdue' sub-section, as shown below right.

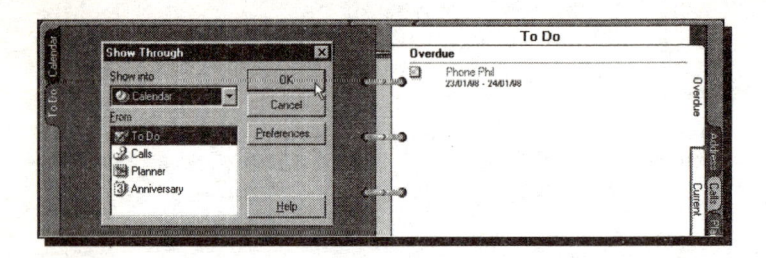

If you want tasks to appear in your diary, use the **S**ection, **S**how Through command, as shown above left. The result when viewed in Calendar is as follows:

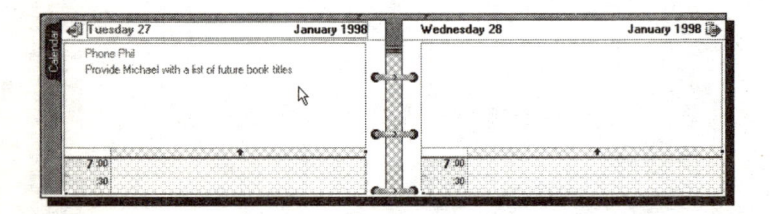

Overdue tasks appear in red, and those in the current sub-section in green.

To delete a task, point to it with the mouse and when the pointer changes to a hand, click the left mouse button to select it, then press the <Del> key. You can delete a task either from the 'To Do' list, or from the Calendar view, if you chose to show it through, as discussed above.

The way information is displayed in the task list can be controlled by you, including grouping and sorting of the various items by priority or start date. To do this, use the leftmost two of the four View and Sort icons on the Toolbox.

Address:

The Address tab displays your contacts in a combined Business and Home list view, as shown below. To create an address, go to an address page, then either double-click an Address page, click the 'Create an Address record' SmartIcon shown here, or use the **Create, Address** command. Either of these displays the **Create Address** dialogue box shown below.

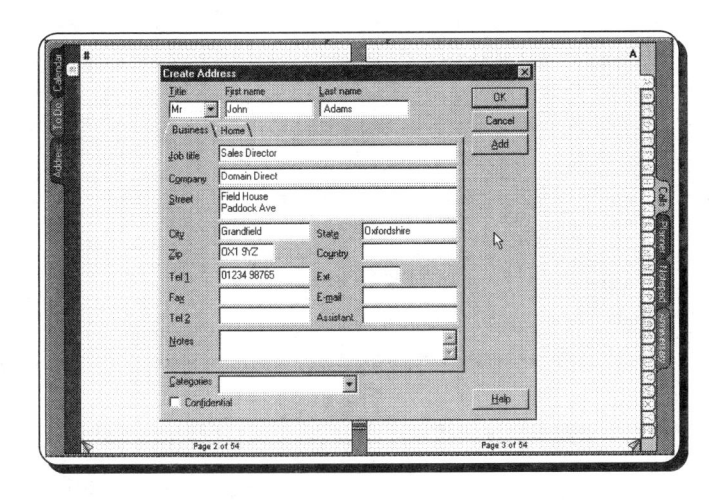

In the contacts entry list shown above, we have chosen to enter information in the Business option of the **Create Address** dialogue box. Pressing the **OK** button, transfers the information into the address book under the **B** (for business) tab. A Home option is also available when entering information by pressing the appropriate tab.

If you have a modem and it is connected to a telephone line, you can get your computer to ring a selected number. Simply place the insertion pointer in the required address entry, and use the **Phone Quick Dial** command. This displays the following dialogue box:

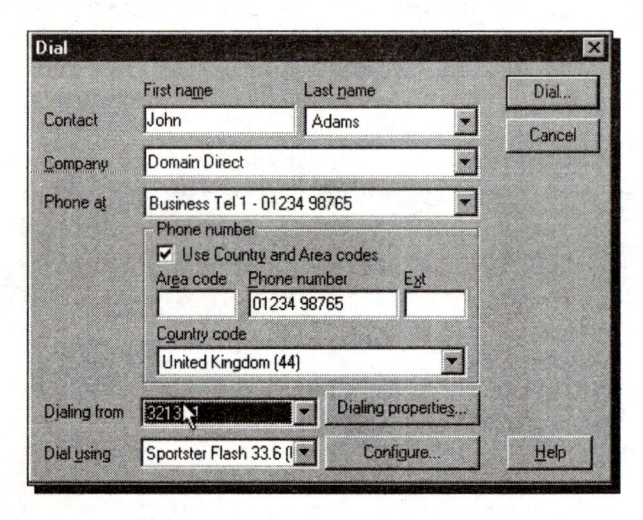

If the **Country code** shown in the **Dial** dialogue box above is incorrect, click the down-arrow against its box to produce an extensive list of alternatives. In fact, every country in the world is listed here. To select one, simply point to it and click the left mouse button.

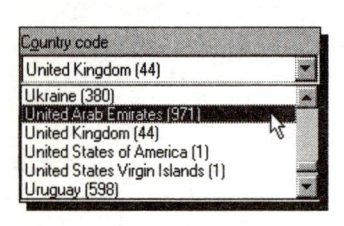

Pressing the **Dial** button starts ringing the selected telephone number.

Note: Had we included the area code in parenthesis when creating an address entry, the area code and the phone number would have appeared in their respective boxes in the **Dial** dialogue box. Try editing the address entry and see the effect.

Calls:

To create a Calls entry, go to the Calls section and either double-click a Calls page, click the 'Create a Calls entry' SmartIcon shown here, or use the **Create Calls** command. Either of these displays the following dialogue box:

If you entered names and addresses in the Address section, they appear in the name and company drop-down boxes. Organizer attempts to match any part of the Address record you specify with the rest of the Address record. For example, if you click the **Last name** drop-down box and select a name from the list, Organizer supplies the person's company name and phone number.

After you select a contact name or company name, you can click either the **OK** button to enter the information in the appropriate Calls page, or the **Dial** button to ring the selected telephone number.

Planner:

To create a Planner entry, go to the Planner section and click the day for the entry, then either click the 'Create an event' SmartIcon shown here, or use the **Create Eve<u>n</u>t** command. In either case, the following dialogue box is displayed:

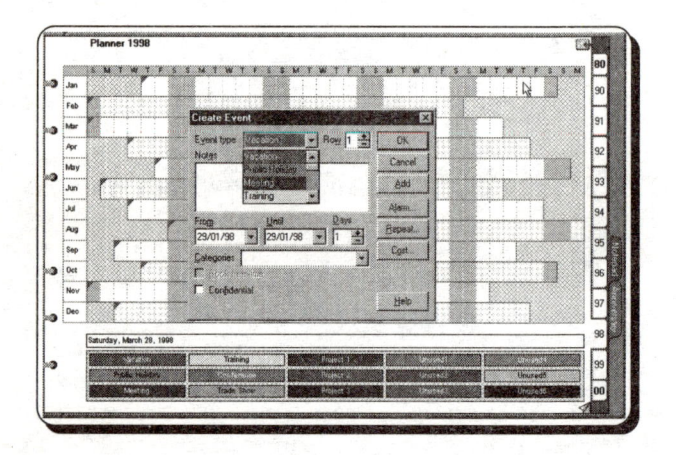

You can select an **E<u>v</u>ent type** from the drop-down list, shown above, the colour of which corresponds with the legend of planner events at the bottom of the dialogue box. Double-clicking anyone of these planner events, displays the Planner Key which can be used to edit any of the listed names.

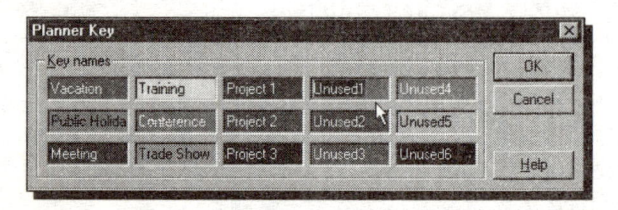

If you are using TeamMail and are connected to a network, you can organise meetings and send requests to participants and then track the status of their response.

Notepad:

To create a Notepad entry, either click the 'Create a page' SmartIcon shown here, or go to the Notepad section and either double-click a page, or use the **Create Page** command. Either of these displays the following dialogue box:

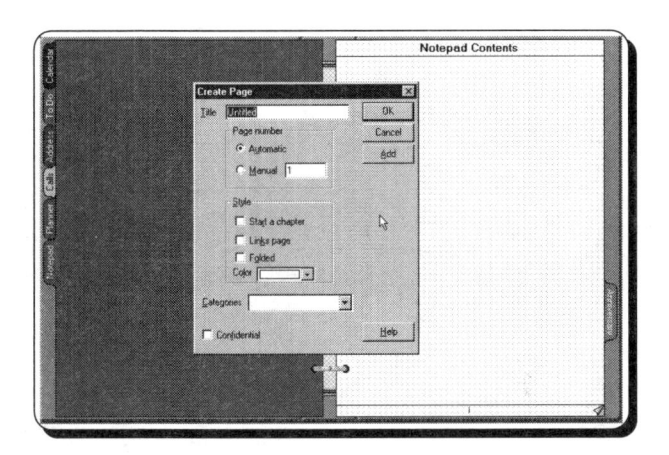

After you've entered a title for the Notepad page, say 'Remember', and selected any of the styles and options in the **Create a Page** dialogue box, click the **OK** button. To add text to your page, go to the named Notepad page, position your mouse pointer on it and click. The I-beam pointer appears, at which point you can start typing the text you want on the page. Below, we illustrate the point by a short sentence.

Remember
Phone Geoffrey tonight - it is his birthday!

Had you included a telephone number, you could use the **Phone, Quick Dial** command later. When you finish entering text, etc., press F2 to save your memo.

Anniversary:

To create an Anniversary entry, either click the 'Create an anniversary' SmartIcon shown here, or go to the Anniversary section and either double-click a month, or use the **Create Anniversary** command. Either of these displays the following dialogue box:

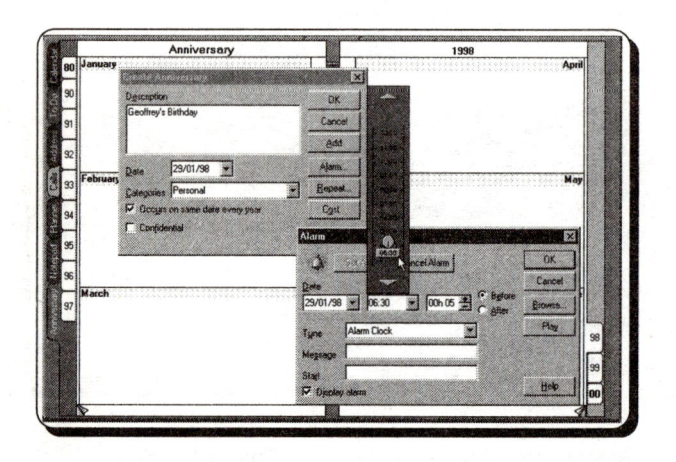

Above we have typed an entry in the **Descriptor** box, set the anniversary **Date** and **Category**, then pressed the **Alarm** button and set the time. Again, had you included a telephone number in your entry, you could use the **Phone, Quick Dial** command when the time came to make the telephone call.

Finally, and at the end of completing any of the Organizer sections, use the **Save As** command and give your diary an original name, such as 'My Diary'! The program adds the extension **OR3** automatically. By default, your diary is saved in the **Lotus\work\organizer** folder. Also by default when you next start the Organizer program, an Untitled file is opened. Use the **File, Open** command to load your saved diary.

14. SHARING INFORMATION

You can link or embed all or part of an existing file created either in a SmartSuite application or in any other application that supports Object Linking and Embedding (OLE). However, if an application does not support OLE, then you must use the copy/cut and paste commands to copy or move information from one application to another via the Clipboard.

In general, you copy, move, link, embed, or hyperlink information depending on the imposed situation, as follows:

Imposed Situation	*Method to Adopt*
Inserted information will not need updating, or Application does not support OLE.	Copy or move
Inserted information needs to be automatically updated in the destination file as changes are made to the data in the source file, or Source file will always be available and you want to minimise the size of the destination file, or Source file is to be shared amongst several users.	Link
Inserted information might need to be updated but source file might not be always accessible, or Destination files needs to be edited without having these changes reflected in the source file.	Embed
To jump to a location in a document or Web page, or to a file that was created in a different program.	Hyperlink

Copying or Moving Information

To copy or move information between programs running under Windows, such as SmartSuite 97 applications, is extremely easy. To move information, use the drag and drop facility, while to copy information, use the **Edit, Copy** and **Edit, Paste** commands. To illustrate the technique, we will copy the file **Project 3.123** created in Lotus 1-2-3 into Word Pro. We will consider the following two possibilities:

Source File Available without Application:

Let us assume that you only have the source file **Project 3.123** on disc, but not the application that created it (that is you don't have Lotus 1-2-3). In such a situation, you can copy the whole or part of the contents of the file to the destination (in our case Word Pro). To achieve this, do the following:

- Start Word Pro and minimise it on the Taskbar.

- Use My Computer (or Explorer) to locate the file whose contents you want to copy into Word Pro.

- Click the filename that you want to copy, hold the mouse button down and point to Word Pro on the Taskbar until the application opens.

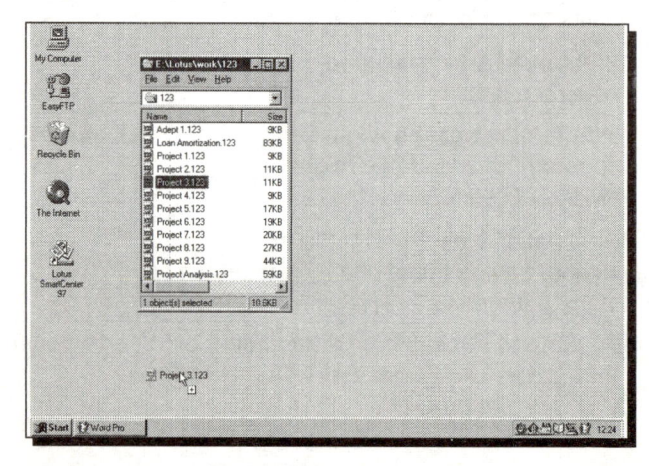

- While still holding the mouse button down, move the mouse pointer into Word Pro's open document and release the mouse button. Word Pro asks you which part of the file you want to insert by displaying the following dialogue box.

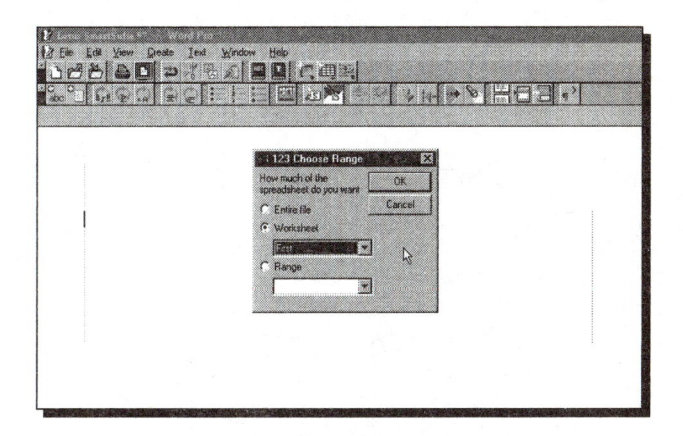

- In the **Choose Range** dialogue box we selected the 'First' worksheet. Pressing the **OK** button, places that part of **Project 3.123** into Word Pro. However, note that only that part of the heading which fits into cell A1 is displayed!

PROJECT

	Jan	Feb	Mar	1st Quarter
Income	£14,000.00	£15,000.00	£16,000.00	£45,000.00
Costs:				
Wages	£2,000.00	£3,000.00	£4,000.00	£9,000.00
Travel	£400.00	£500.00	£600.00	£1,500.00
Rent	£300.00	£300.00	£300.00	£900.00
Heat/Light	£150.00	£200.00	£130.00	£480.00
Phone/Fax	£250.00	£300.00	£360.00	£910.00
Adverts	£1,100.00	£1,200.00	£1,300.00	£3,600.00
Total Costs	£4,200.00	£5,500.00	£6,690.00	£16,390.00
Profit	£9,800.00	£9,500.00	£9,310.00	£28,610.00
Cumulative	£9,800.00	£19,300.00	£28,610.00	

Source File and Application Available:

Assuming that you have both the file and the application that created it on your computer, you can copy all or part of the contents of the source file to the destination file. To achieve this, do the following:

- Start Lotus 1-2-3 and open **Project 3.123**.

- Highlight as much information as you would like to copy and click the copy icon on the Toolbar.

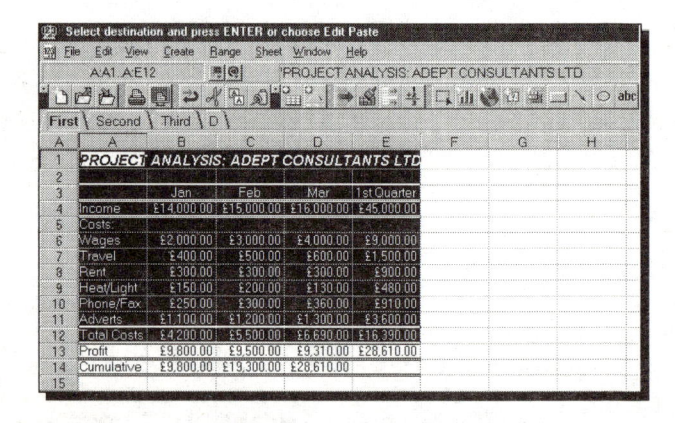

- Start Word Pro and click the Paste icon on the Toolbar. The contents of the Clipboard are inserted in a Word Pro table, as shown below.

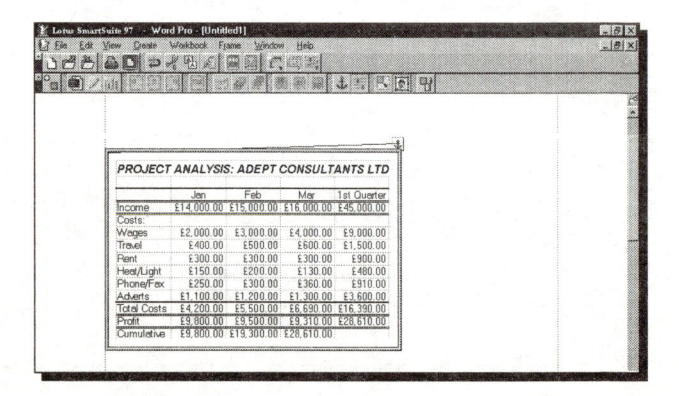

Object Linking and Embedding

Object Linking is copying information from one file (the source file) to another file (the destination file) and maintaining a connection between the two files. When information in the source file is changed, then the information in the destination file is automatically updated. Linked data is stored in the source file, while the file into which you place the data stores only the location of the source and displays a representation of the linked data.

For example, you would use Object Linking if you would want a Lotus 1-2-3 chart included in, say, a Word Pro document to be updated whenever you changed the information used to create the chart in the first place within 1-2-3. In such a case, the 1-2-3 worksheet containing the chart would be referred to as the source file, while the Word Pro document would be referred to as the destination file.

Object Embedding is inserting information created in one file (the source file) into another file (the container file). After such information has been embedded, the object becomes part of the container file. When you double-click an embedded object, it opens in the application in which it was created in the first place. You can then edit it in place, and the original object in the source application remains unchanged.

Thus, the main differences between linking and embedding are where the data is stored and how it is updated after you place it in your file. Linking saves you disc space as only one copy of the linked object is kept on disc. Embedding a logo chosen for your headed paper, saves the logo with every saved letter!

In what follows, we will discuss how you can link or embed either an entire file or selected information from an existing file, and how you can edit an embedded object. Furthermore, we will examine how to mail merge a letter written in Word Pro with a list created either in Approach, 1-2-3, or even Word Pro itself.

Example of Linking or Embedding:

To link or embed an object into an application, do the following:

- Open the container file, say Word Pro, and click where you want to link or embed the object.

- Use the **Create, Object** command, to display the **Create Object** dialogue box, shown below.

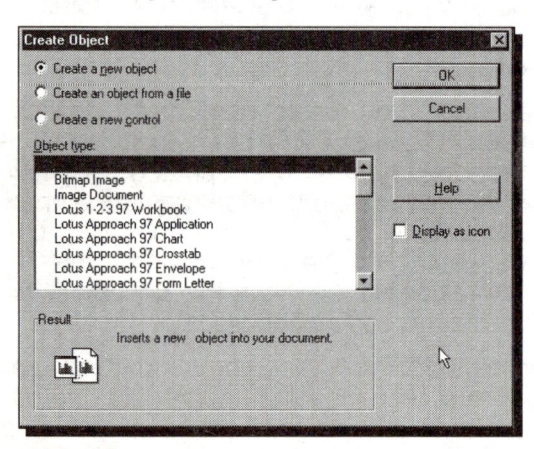

In this dialogue box you have three choices; to **Create a new object**, **Create an object from a file**, or **Create a new control**. You can embed objects from all three options, but you can only link from the second option, because when you select this option, the dialogue box displays a **Link to file** check box. If you check this box the object is linked, but if you leave it unchecked, the object is embedded.

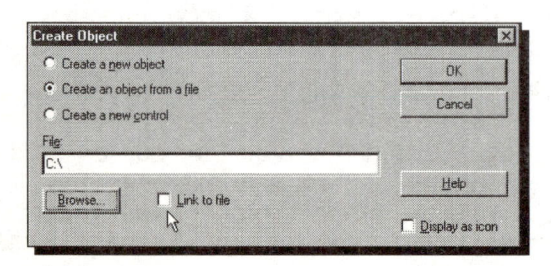

If you want to link or embed a picture file, use the **File, Import Picture** command to display the **Import Picture** dialogue box, shown below.

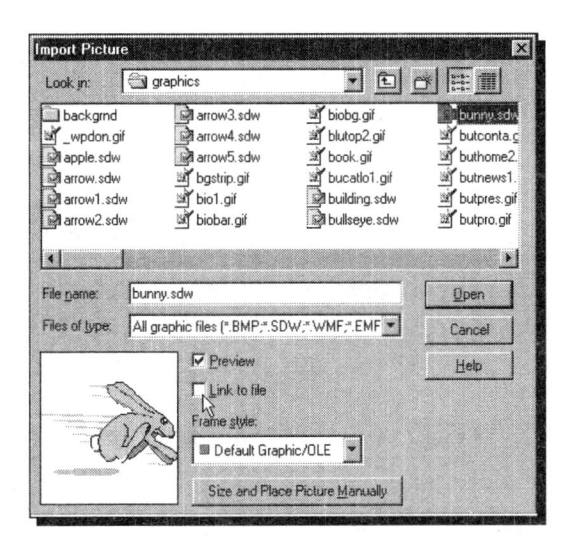

Using the above method you can link or embed the selected picture, depending on whether the **Link to file** box is checked or not, into Word Pro, as shown below. The selected file is **bunny.sdw** and is to be found in Word Pro's **graphics** folder.

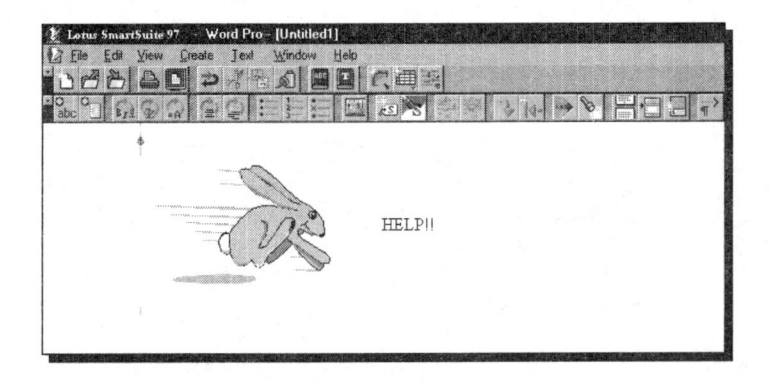

Linking or Embedding Selected Information:

To link or embed selected information from an existing file created in one application into another, do the following:

- Select the information in the source file you want to link or embed.

- Use the **Edit, Copy** command to copy the selected information to the Clipboard.

- Switch to the container file or document in which you want to place the information, and then click where you want the information to appear.

- Use the **Edit, Paste Special** command to open the following dialogue box:

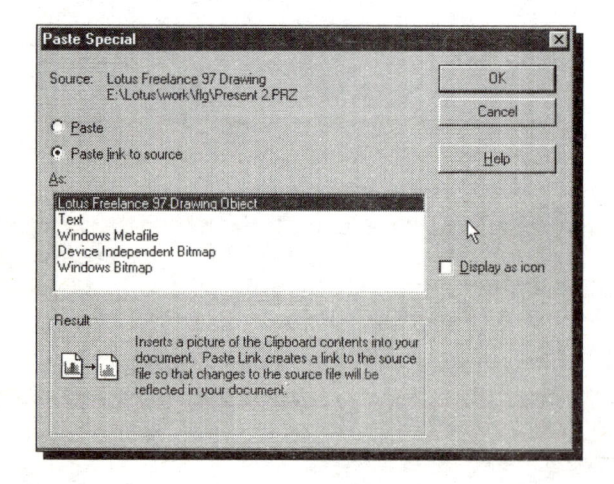

- To link the information, click the **Paste link to source** radio button, or to embed the information, click the **Paste** radio button. In the **As** box, click the item with the word 'Object' in its name. For example, if you copied the information from Freelance, as we have for this example, the Freelance 97 Drawing Object appears in the **As** box. Select this object and press **OK**.

Linking or Embedding into Approach:

When you link or embed an object in a Lotus Approach form or report, the object is displayed in an object frame. To illustrate this point, start Approach and open the Adept 2 - Customers database which we created in Chapter 11. Then do the following:

- Switch to Design view, then use the **Create, Object** command which displays the **Insert Object** dialogue box.

- Click the **Create from File** radio button, then select the **register** folder which is within the **Lotus** folder, and open the **art1.bmp** file.

- Press the **OK** button on the **Insert Object** dialogue box to insert the selected object into the Approach form view, as shown below.

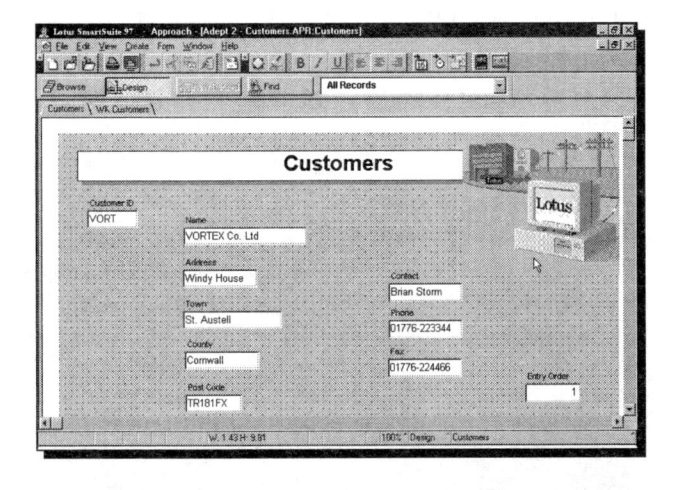

The inserted object was appropriately sized and moved into the position shown above.

Editing an Embedded Object:

If the application in which you created an embedded object is installed on your computer, double-click the object to open it for editing. Some applications start the original application in a separate window and then open the object for editing, while other applications temporarily replace the menus and toolbars in the current application so that you can edit the embedded object in place, without switching to another window. To edit an embedded object in a Lotus Approach database, switch to Design view, then double-click the object to open the application on which it was created.

If the application in which an embedded object was created is not installed on your computer, convert the object to the file format of an application you do have. For example, if your Word Pro document contains an embedded Microsoft Works Spreadsheet object and you do not have Works, you can convert the object to a Lotus 1-2-3 Workbook format and edit it in 1-2-3.

Some embedded objects, such as sound and video clips, when double-clicked start playing their contents, instead of opening an application for editing. To illustrate this, copy the Goodtime video icon from its folder in the Windows 95 CD into Word Pro using the **Create, Object** command (click the **Create an object from file** radio button and the **Display as icon** box on the displayed dialogue box), and **Browse** to the required icon, which is to be found in the **funstaff, videos, highperf** folder. This places a Video Clip in your document, as shown to the left. Double-clicking such an icon, starts the video.

To edit one of these objects, select it and use the **Video Clip, Edit** command. The menu name, in this case **Video Clip**, depends on the selected object.

Hypertext Links

Word Pro publications (these are documents that contain hyperlinks to other locations) or Web pages, that others read on-line are made more interesting by inserting hyperlinks to other items. A hyperlink causes a jump to another location in the current document or Web page, to a different Word Pro document or Web page, or to a file that was created in a different program. You can, for example, jump from a Word Pro document to a Lotus 1-2-3 worksheet or to a Freelance presentation to see more detail.

A hyperlink is represented by a 'hot' image or by display text (which is often blue and underlined) that you click to jump to a different location. To illustrate the procedure, start Word Pro, open the **Pcusers 4** memo, and highlight the word 'Explorer' to be found towards the end of it. Next, use the **File, Internet, Show Web Authoring Tools** command to display the Web Tools bar and either use the **Create, Link** command or click the Create Link button on the Web Tools bar to open the **Create Link** dialogue box which allows you to browse for the destination address.

For our example to work, you need to change the entry in the **Type of link** box to 'Go to another document in this web site' by selecting it from the drop-down list which is displayed when you click the down-arrow against the list box. Next, enter the location of the **explorer.exe** file which is to be found in your **windows** folder.

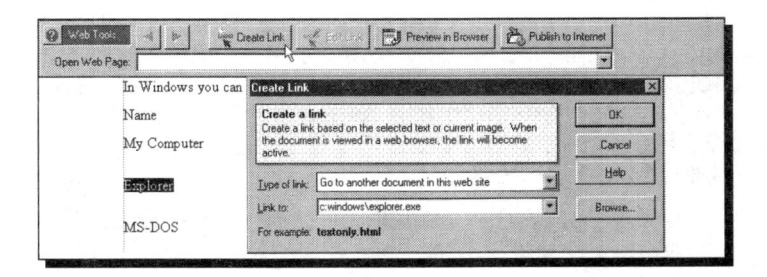

Pressing the **OK** button, underlines the highlighted text and changes its colour to blue. Clicking the **Preview in Browser** button on the Web Tools bar, loads your browser and opens your document in it. Pointing to our hyperlink, changes the mouse pointer to a hand, as shown here to the left, and left-clicking it displays the **Internet Explorer** dialogue box. In this box, click the **Open it** radio button and click **OK** to start the Explorer. When you have finished using the Windows Explorer, close it and then close the Web Browser to return to the hyperlinked Word Pro document. Finally, use the **File, Save As** command, select HTML as the file type and save it under the **PCuser 1** filename. The extension **htm** will be added automatically.

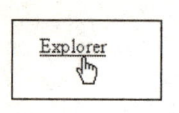

If the location of the file you wanted to hyperlink to is incorrect, or you did not highlight the word to be used as the hyperlink, then errors will occur. To correct such a situation, for the first case click the **Edit Link** button on the Web Tools bar and enter the correct location of the file you want to hyperlink to, while for the second case open the original Word Pro document, and start again.

As a second example, add to the **PCuser 1.htm** file the following lines:

> Hyperlinks can be used for displaying additional information, such as a Lotus 1-2-3 worksheet, or a Freelance presentation.

Next, select the word 'worksheet' in the Word Pro document to use it as the hyperlink to **Project 9.123**. In our case, this file is to be found in the **Lotus\work\123** folder. For the Freelance object, you could select the word 'presentation' to use as the hyperlink to **Present 2.PRZ**. Again, in our case this file is to be found in the **Lotus\work\flg** folder.

Finally, save the result of your work under the filename **PCuser 2.htm**.

Mail Merging Lists

There are times when you may want to send the same basic letter to several different people, or companies. The easiest way to do this is with a Merge operation. Two files are prepared; a 'Data' file with the names and addresses, and a 'Letter' file, containing the text and format of the letter. The two files are then merged together to produce a third file containing an individual letter to each party listed in the original data file.

Before creating a list of names and addresses for a mail merge, you need to select the SmartSuite application that is most suited to the task. For a mail merge, you can use a list you create in Approach, 1-2-3, Organizer, or Word Pro.

- For a long list in which you expect to add, change, or delete records, and for which you want powerful sorting and searching capabilities at your disposal, you should use either Approach or 1-2-3, then specify the appropriate data file in the Mail Merge Assistant (see below).

- To use the list of names and addresses in your Organizer Contact List, you select this list in the Mail Merge Assistant.

- For a small to medium size list of names and addresses in which you do not expect to make many changes, you could elect to create a list in Word Pro itself.

The **Mail Merger Assistant** is a dialogue box in which you specify whether to:

(a) use an existing data file or create a new one, (b) select the current letter, create a new letter, or browse for a letter to merge, and (c) merge, view and print the result. These will be explained next with illustrated examples.

We will illustrate the merge procedure by first using a memo created in Word Pro (**PCuser 1.lwp**) and a data file which can be created in Word Pro, or already exists either in an electronic book such as the Organizer, in 1-2-3 or in an Approach database such as **Adept 1 - Customers**.

No matter which method you choose, first start Word Pro and open the **PCuser 1** memo (or your own letter), then provide two empty lines at the very top of the memo/letter by placing the insertion pointer at the beginning of the memo and pressing <Enter> twice. Then select these two empty lines and choose the Default Text paragraph style.

Next, use the **Text, Merge, Letter** command, which displays the **Mail Merge Assistant** dialogue box shown below.

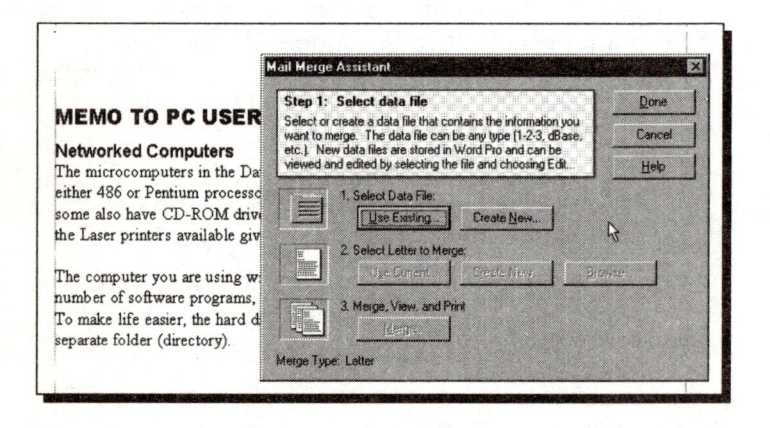

In this box, you define in three successive steps:

1. The data file to be used,
2. The letter to merge, and
3. The merging, viewing, and printing of the two.

Getting an Address List:

In step 1, you can select either to open (or import) an existing list of addresses which might be found in Approach, 1-2-3, Word Pro, Organizer, etc., or create your data source (the list of addresses) in Word Pro.

In what follows, we will examine both options, first by using an existing file, then by creating a new file in Word Pro. Once an existing address file is opened, or a new data file is created in Word Pro, the process of merging your data with your document is the same. We, therefore, start by clicking the **Use Existing** button of the Mail Merge Assistant, selecting the type of file - dBase (*.DBF) since we will be using an Approach database, and browsing to the required file (in our case **Adept 1 - Customers**, to be found in the **approach** folder), as shown below.

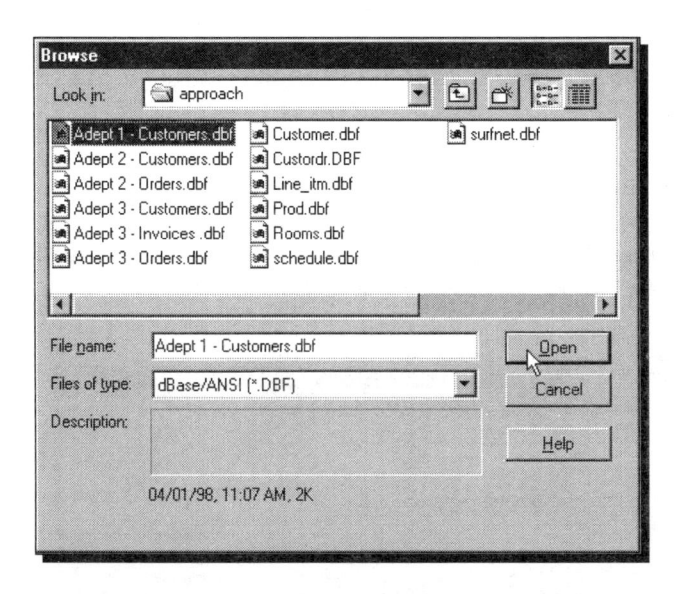

Pressing the **Open** button, displays a further dialogue box asking you if we want to open the entire file or part of it. Select the former and press the **OK** button.

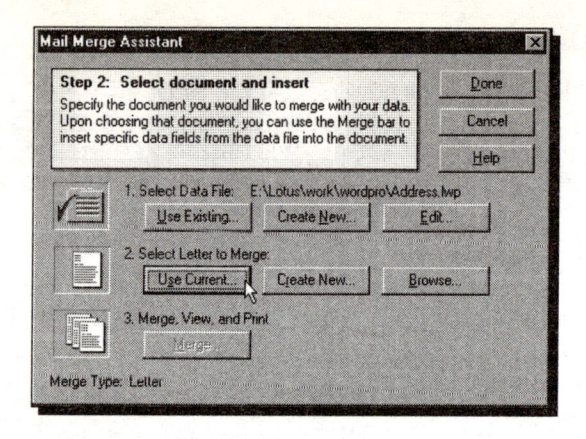

Note that the displayed dialogue box above now has a tick against the **Select Data File** option, and we are now ready to specify the letter to be used for the merge process. However, before we go on, let us examine what would have happened, had we pressed the **Create New** button on the **Mail Merge Assistant** dialogue box.

Creating an Address List in Word Pro:

Had we pressed the **Create New** button on the **Mail Merge Assistant** dialogue box, the following dialogue box would have been displayed.

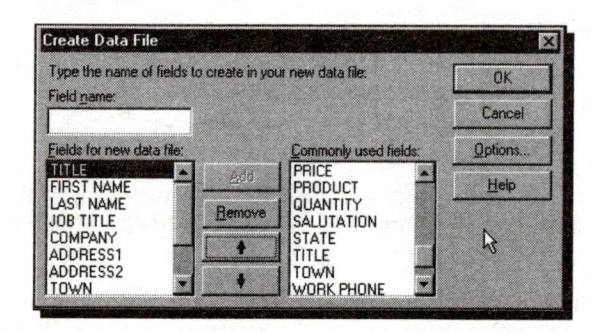

As you can see, Word Pro provides commonly used field names for your address list. Unwanted field names can be deleted from the list by selecting them and pressing the **Remove** button. To add your own field name, type it in the **Field name** box and press the **Add** button. The two arrow buttons below the **Remove** button can be used to move a selected field in the list to the top or bottom of the list by pressing the up-arrow or down-arrow, respectively.

Having compiled the required field names for your list, press the **OK** button to display the **Data File** dialogue box shown below.

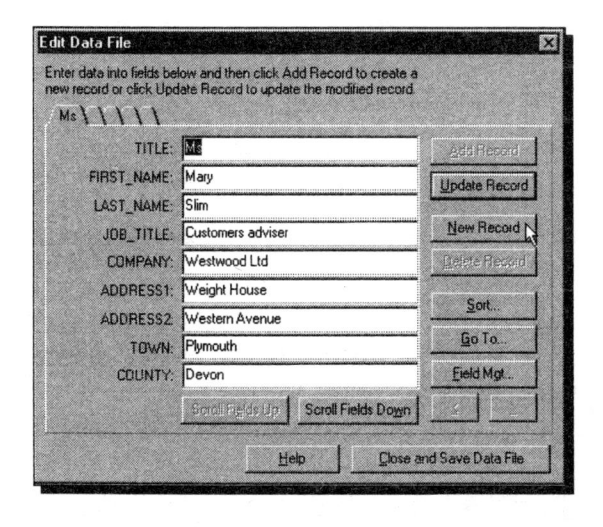

Here you can create a new data list. We have typed in only one fictitious entry in order to demonstrate the process. Pressing the **Close and Save Data File** button, displays a **Save As** dialogue box, in which you can name your data list, say **Address**. Word Pro automatically adds the **.lwp** file extension.

What follows is common to all existing data files, no matter in which application you chose to create it.

Selecting a Letter to Merge:

If the letter you want to use for your mail merge is not already opened, either create a new letter, or browse to open one, then click the **Use Current** button on the **Mail Merge Assistant** dialogue box. This causes the fields of your selected database to appear at the top of your screen, as shown below.

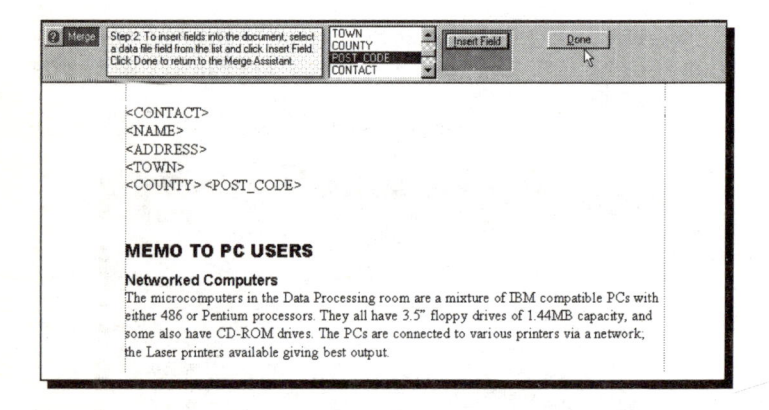

```
Merge   Step 2: To insert fields into the document, select    TOWN        Insert Field    Done
        a data file field from the list and click Insert Field. COUNTY
        Click Done to return to the Merge Assistant.            POST_CODE
                                                                CONTACT

        <CONTACT>
        <NAME>
        <ADDRESS>
        <TOWN>
        <COUNTY> <POST_CODE>

        MEMO TO PC USERS
        Networked Computers
        The microcomputers in the Data Processing room are a mixture of IBM compatible PCs with
        either 486 or Pentium processors. They all have 3.5" floppy drives of 1.44MB capacity, and
        some also have CD-ROM drives. The PCs are connected to various printers via a network;
        the Laser printers available giving best output.
```

Next, select in turn the fields, Contact, Name, Address, Town, County, and Post_Code, pressing the **Insert Field** button after each selection. The first four are placed on the document on separate lines (by pressing <Enter> after each selection), while the last two are placed on the same line, but separated by a space.

Once you have completed the field selection, press the **Done** button to display the **Mail Merge Assistant** dialogue box in which two of the three selection steps are now ticked, as shown on the next page.

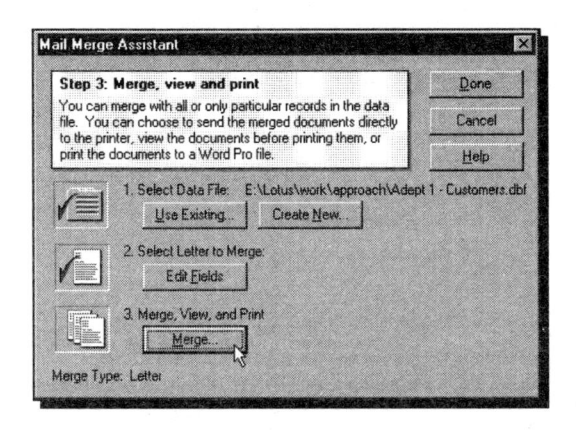

All that is required now is to click the **Merge** button. This opens the **Merge, View and Print** dialogue box which allows you either to merge all the records or to merge a selection of them.

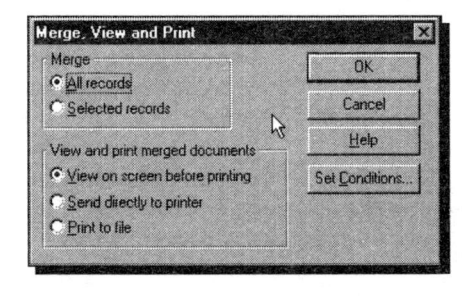

What appears on your screen now is the merged information incorporating the first database record on your letter, the first few lines of which are shown on the next page.

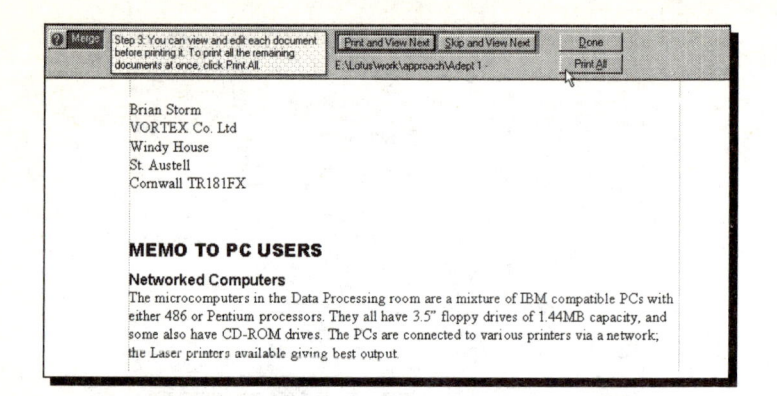

> **Merge** — Step 3: You can view and edit each document before printing it. To print all the remaining documents at once, click Print All.
>
> [Print and View Next] [Skip and View Next] [Done]
> E:\Lotus\work\approach\Adept 1 - [Print All]
>
> Brian Storm
> VORTEX Co. Ltd
> Windy House
> St. Austell
> Cornwall TR181FX
>
> **MEMO TO PC USERS**
>
> **Networked Computers**
> The microcomputers in the Data Processing room are a mixture of IBM compatible PCs with either 486 or Pentium processors. They all have 3.5" floppy drives of 1.44MB capacity, and some also have CD-ROM drives. The PCs are connected to various printers via a network; the Laser printers available giving best output.

You can view, edit, or print your merged letters at will. When you try to exit Word Pro, you will be asked whether you would like to save the merged document, if you have not saved it already. That's all there is to it. You will possibly find it takes as little time to do, as it did to read about it!

APPENDIX - GLOSSARY OF TERMS

Application	Software (program) designed to carry out a certain activity, such as word processing.
Association	An identification of a filename extension to a program. This lets Windows open the program when its files are selected.
ASCII	A binary code representation of a character set. The name stands for 'American Standard Code for Information Interchange'.
Bit	A binary digit; the smallest unit of information that can be stored, either as 1 or as 0 (zero).
Bitmap	A technique for managing the image displayed on a computer screen.
Browse	A button in some dialogue boxes that lets you view a list of files and folders before you make a selection.
Byte	A grouping of binary digits (0 or 1) which represent information.
CD-ROM drive	A device which when installed on your PC, allows the use of CDs.
Cell	The intersection of a column and row in a spreadsheet, or a table, which can hold information.

Check box	A small box in a dialogue box that can be selected (✓), or cleared (empty).
Click	To quickly press and release a mouse button.
Client	A computer that has access to services over a network. The computer providing the services is a server.
Client application	A Windows application that can accept linked, or embedded, objects.
Clipboard	A temporary storage area of memory, where text and graphics are stored with the cut and copy actions.
Close	To remove a dialogue box or window, or to exit a program.
Command	An instruction given to a computer to carry out a particular action.
Configuration	A general purpose term referring to the way you have your computer set up.
CPU	The Central Processing Unit; the main chip that executes all instructions entered into a computer.
Cursor	The blinking line indicating where the next input can be entered.
Database	A collection of related information or data, organised for a specific theme.

Dial-up connection	A popular form of Internet connection for the home user, over standard telephone lines.
Default	The command, device or option automatically chosen by the system.
Desktop	The Windows screen working background, on which you place icons, folders, etc.
Device driver	A special file that must be loaded into memory for Windows to be able to address a specific procedure or hardware device.
Device name	A logical name used by the operating system to identify a device, such as LPT1 or COM1 for the parallel or serial printer.
Dialogue box	A window displayed on the screen to allow the user to enter information.
Dimmed	Unavailable menu options shown in a different colour.
Disc	A device on which you can store programs and data.
Disc file	A collection of program code, or data, that is stored on disc under a given name.
Document	A file produced by an application program.
Double-click	To quickly press and release a mouse button twice.

Drag	To press and hold down the left mouse button while moving the mouse, to move an object on the screen.
Drive name	The letter (followed by a colon) which identifies a floppy disc drive, a hard disc drive, or a CD-ROM drive.
Embedded object	Information in a document that is 'copied' from its source application. Selecting the object opens the creating application from within the document.
Field	A single column of information of the same type.
File	The name given to an area on disc containing a program or data.
File extension	The optional three-letter suffix following the period in a filename. The extension is used to identify the filetype.
File list	A list of filenames contained in the active folder/directory.
Filename	The name given to a file. In Windows 95 & 97 this can be up to 255 characters long.
Filespec	File specification made up of drive, path and filename.
Floppy disc	A removable disc on which information can be stored magnetically. The two main types are a 5¼" flexible disc, and a 3½" stiff disc.

Folder	An area on disc where information relating to a group of files is kept.
Font	A graphic design representing a set of characters, numbers and symbols.
Function	A built-in formula which performs specific calculations in a spreadsheet or database cell.
Function key	One of the series of 10 or 12 keys marked with the letter F and a numeral, used for specific operations.
Graphics card	A device that controls the display on the monitor and other allied functions.
Hardcopy	Output on paper.
Hard disc	A device built into the computer for holding programs and data. It is sometimes referred to as a fixed disc.
Hardware	The equipment that makes up a computer system, excluding the programs or software.
Help	A Windows system that gives you instructions and additional information.
Highlight	The change to a reverse-video appearance when a menu item or area of text is selected.
Host	A computer acting as an information or communications server.

HTML	HyperText Markup Language; the format used in documents on the Web.
Hypermedia	Hypertext extended to include linked multi-media.
Hypertext	A system that allows documents to be cross-linked so that the reader can explore related links, or documents, by clicking on a highlighted word or symbol.
Icon	A small graphic image that represents a function or object. Clicking on an icon produces an action.
Insertion point	A flashing bar that shows where typed text will be entered into a document.
Interface	A device that allows you to connect a computer to its peripherals.
Internet	The global system of computer networks.
Key combination	When two or more keys are pressed simultaneously, such as <Ctrl+Esc>.
Kilobyte	(KB); 1024 bytes of information or storage space.
LAN	Local Area Network; PCs, workstations, or minis, sharing files and peripherals within the same site.
Linked object	A placeholder for an object inserted into a destination document.

Links	The hypertext connections between Web pages.
Local	A resource that is located on your computer, not linked to it over a network.
Megabyte	(MB); 1024 kilobytes of information or storage space.
Megahertz	(MHz); Speed of processor in millions of cycles per second.
Memory	See RAM.
Menu	A list of available options in an application.
Menu bar	The horizontal bar that lists the names of menus.
Microprocessor	The calculating chip within a computer.
MIDI	Musical Instrument Digital Interface - enables devices to transmit and receive sound and music messages.
Monitor	The display device connected to your PC.
Mouse	A device used to manipulate a pointer around your display and activate a certain process by pressing a button.
Multimedia	The use of photographs, music, sound, and movie images in a presentation.
Network server	Central computer which stores files for several linked computers.

Password	A unique character string used to gain access to a network, or an application document.
PATH	The location of a file in the directory tree.
Peripheral	Any device attached to a PC.
Pixel	A picture element on screen; the smallest element that can be independently assigned colour and intensity.
Port	An input/output address through which your PC interacts with external devices.
Print queue	The list of print jobs waiting to be sent to a printer.
Program	A set of instructions which cause the computer to perform certain tasks.
Processor	The electronic device which performs calculations.
RAM	Random Access Memory. The PC's volatile memory. Data held in it is lost when power is switched off.
Record	A row of information in a table relating to a single entry and comprising one or more fields.
Resource	A directory, or printer, that can be shared over a network.

Right-click	To click and release the right mouse button, which often opens a context sensitive menu in a Windows application.
Scroll bar	A bar that appears at the right side or bottom edge of a window.
Server	A networked computer that is used to share resources.
Shared resource	Any device, program or file that is available to network users.
Site	A server, or a collection of linked Web pages at a single location.
SmartIcon	A small graphic image that represents a function or object. Clicking on such an icon produces an action.
Software	The programs and instructions that control your PC.
Spreadsheet	An electronic page made of a matrix of rows and columns.
SVGA	Super Video Graphics Array; it has all the VGA modes but with 256 colours.
Table	A two-dimensional structure in which data is stored, like in a speadsheet.
Template	A file blank you can create to contain common text and formatting to use as a basis for new documents.

Text file	An unformatted file of text characters saved in ASCII format.
Tool	SmartSuite 97 application, such as the Drawing facility or the Toolbox in Organizer.
Toolbar	A bar containing icons giving quick access to commands.
Toggle	To turn an action on and off with the same switch.
TrueType fonts	Fonts that can be scaled to any size and print as they show on the screen.
Web	See World Wide Web.
Web Page	An HTML document that is accessible on the Web.
Wildcard character	A character that can be included in a filename to indicate any other character (?), or group of characters (*).
World Wide Web	A network of hypertext-based multimedia information servers. Web browsers, such as the Internet Explorer, can be used to view any information on the Web.
Zoom	Enlarged view focusing on a portion of the page so that you can see the fine details of your page layout.

INDEX

A

Absolute address ... 147
Adding
   drawings 174
   records (Approach) 196
   SmartIcons 59
   SmartSuite comp'nts 10
Address
   Organizer 229
   Word Pro 250
Aligning
   paragraphs 60
   text (1-2-3) 126
Anchoring frames 89
Anniversary (Organ'r) 234
Annotating a chart .. 164
Annotations (Word Pro) 68
Application button 19
Appointments 220
Approach
   file 179
   program 181
   reports 203
   screen 183
AutoSum icon 136
Ask the Expert option 15

B

Bar chart 151
Blank
   database 186
   workbook 113
Browsing a database 192
Bullet insert 65

C

Calendar
   preferences 221
   printing 225
Calls (Organizer) ... 231
Cell pointer 115, 116
Changing
   cell width 127
   default options 33
   field names 189
   fonts (1-2-3) 126
   fonts (Word Pro) .. 22
   margins (Word Pro) 31
   page layout 31
   paragraph style ... 26
   print options 32
   text (Word Pro) ... 44
   text alignm't (1-2-3) 126
   time periods 224
   views 28
Character font 22
Charts (1-2-3) 151
Chart
   annotation 164
   command 153
   improvement 111
   SmartIcons 154
   types 109
Clip Art 173
Clipboard 47
Close
   button 19, 21
   document 36
Column
   letter (1-2-3) 115, 116
Command buttons ... 20
Contacts (Organizer) 229

Copy command ... 38, 41
Copying
    blocks of text 41
    information 236
    sheets 144
Creating
    address list 250
    charts 153, 159
    crosstab view 210
    database applicat'n 186
    database join 201
    database report .. 203
    document template 73
    drawings 94
    frames 86
    notes (Word Pro) . 68
    paragraph style 26, 71
    queries (Approach) 195
    reports (Approach) 203
    table charts 106
    tables (Word Pro) . 98
Crosstab view 210
Currency format 127
Current
    sheet (1-2-3) 115, 116
    style (Word Pro) .. 19
Customising
    1-2-3 chart 159
    Approach form ... 190
    Organizer sections 226
Cut command 38, 42

D

Data types 187
Database
    criteria 194
    design 186, 199
    elements 179
    forms 195
    query 195
    sorting 192

Date & time insert 67
Default
    options 31
    printer 32
    template 26, 71
Deleting
    blocks of text 43
    buttons 38
    fields (Approach) . 197
    frames 94
    records (Approach) 197
Design
    presentation 171
    view (Approach) .. 189
Dictionary 47
Display views 28
Divider tab 19, 21
Document
    basics 17
    command button .. 19
    closing 36
    editing 37
    formatting 55
    info box 19, 23
    print preview 53
    printing 49
    properties 31
    screen displays ... 27
    styles 26
    templates 26, 73
    views 27, 53
Draft mode 27
Drag & Drop text 30
Drawing 86
Drawing tools 93
Drop capitals 76

E

Edit
    command 38
    line 116, 119

Editing
  charts 111
  embedded objects 244
  documents 37
  drawings (Word Pro) 94
  tables (Word Pro) 104
Embedding
  information . 240, 243
  objects 244
Enhancing
  text (Word Pro) ... 79
  screen show 176
  worksheets 141
Entering
  appointments 222
  expressions 101
  formulae (1-2-3) . 134
  information (1-2-3) 124
  text (Word Pro) ... 24
Exiting 1-2-3 130
Explorer 245
Expressions in tables 101

F

Field (Approach) 179
File commands 34
Filling in a
  range by example 133
  worksheet 131
Find & Change 44
Find
  Assistant 193
  command 44
  tab 13
Finding records 195
Font
  change 22, 126
  selection 19, 56
  size 22

Footers in
  1-2-3 142
  Word Pro 81
Forms (Approach) .. 195
Formatting
  buttons 58, 60
  documents 55
  entries (1-2-3) ... 132
  features 76
  page tabs 69
  quick keys 60
  styles (Word Pro) . 71
  tabs 70
  text 55, 58
Frames (Word Pro) 86, 89
Freezing panes 149
Freelance Graphics
  screen 166
  screen show 175
  view tabs 167
Full screen mode 28
Functions (1-2-3) ... 135

G

Getting address list . 249
Go To
  1-2-3 118
  Word Pro .. 19, 23, 25
Grouping worksheets 121

H

Hanging indents .. 63, 72
Hardware requirements 4
Headers in
  1-2-3 142
  Word Pro 81
Help
  button 16
  command 12
Hypertext links 245
Hyphenation 78

I

Icons Setup 58
Importing information 240
Indentation 62
Inserting
    annotations 68
    bullets (Word Pro) 65
    chart (1-2-3) 153
    Clip Art image ... 173
    date & time 67
    drop capitals 76
    fields (Approach) ..197
    hypertext links ... 245
    page break 46, 79
    graphic 92, 241
    special characters 77
    worksheet 146
Insertion point(er) . 19, 22
Installing
    SmartSuite 97 5
    SmartSuite comp'ts . 7

J

Justifying text 60

K

Key navigation
    1-2-3 117
    Word Pro 25

L

Landscape orientation 31
Layered drawings 95
Layout mode . 27, 52, 53
Line spacing 61
Linking
    information 240
    into Approach 243
    files 150
    sheets 146

Lotus 1-2-3
    charts 151
    navigation 117
    screen 115
    spreadsheet 113
Lotus Organizer 215
    help 219
    screen 216
LPT1 port 49

M

Mail
    merge 247
    merge Assistant . 252
Making a join 201
Margins (Word Pro) .. 31
Meetings 220
Menu bar
    Approach 183
    1-2-3 115
    Freelance 168
    Organizer 216
    Word Pro 19, 21
Minimise button ... 19, 21
Misspelled words box 23
Mouse pointers ... 10, 19
Moving
    around a document 25
    around a workbook 117
    between sheets .. 119
    blocks of text 42
    frames 88
    fields (Approach) . 179
    information 236
    toolbars 58
Multiple
    bar charts 159
    columns on page . 84
    workbook sheets . 103

N
Naming charts (1-2-3) 156
Navigating a
   Word Pro document 25
   Word Pro table ... 99
   workbook 117
New document 36
Notes (Word Pro) 68
Notes pages 172
Notepad (Organizer) 233
Numbering pages . 66, 79

O
Online help 12
OLE 235, 239
Open
   file 36, 50, 131
   workbook ... 113, 129
Orientation 31
Organizer
   help 219
   preferences 216
   screen 216
   toolbox icons 218
Outline
   mode (Word Pro) . 29
   view (Freelance) . 171

P
Page
   breaks (Word Pro) 46
   set-up (1-2-3) 138
   set-up (Word Pro) . 31
   margins 31
   numbering 79
   orientation 31
   properties 80
   preview (1-2-3) .. 140
   scrolling buttons 19, 23
   sorter mode 28
   tabs 69, 170

Pane freeze 149
Paragraph
   alignment 60
   spacing 61
   styles 26, 71
Parallel printer port .. 49
Paste command .. 38, 41
Paste special .. 152, 242
Pie chart 162
Planner (Organizer) . 232
Portrait orientation ... 31
Pre-defined charts .. 109
Presentation
   design 171
   printing 177
Preview document 53, 140
Print
   Calendar 225
   database 198
   document 49
   icon 50
   options 32
   orientation 31
   preview 53, 140
   properties 52
   settings 49
   worksheet area .. 138
Printer ports 49
Program icons 9
Properties
   document 33
   table 100

Q
Query (Approach) ... 195
Quick
   format (1-2-3) 131
   menus (1-2-3) ... 157
   key formatting . 58, 60

R

Range
- filling (1-2-3) 133
- properties (1-2-3) 125

Record (Approach) . 179

Relational
- database 199
- facilities 180

Relative address 147

Removing
- Approach fields .. 197
- SmartSuite comp'nts 10

Renaming sheets ... 120
Repeat appointments 223
Replace command ... 44
Report Assistant 203
Restore button 19, 21
Replacing text 44
Row number ... 115, 116

S

Save command . 34, 128

Saving
- charts (1-2-3) 156
- to file (Word Pro) . 34
- workbooks 128

Screen display
- 1-2-3 115
- Approach 183
- Freelance 116
- Organizer 216
- Word Pro 19

Screen show 175
Scroll arrows/bars 19, 22
Search & Replace ... 44
Searching for records 205
Section tabs 216

Selecting
- cells 122
- letter to merge ... 252
- range of cells 123
- style 22
- template 26, 73
- text 39

Sharing information . 235

Sheet
- linking 146
- order 103

Shortcut
- icon 9
- menus (1-2-3) ... 122

Show view 175
SmartCenter 9
SmartIcons 58, 154, 168
SmartMasters 18, 26, 114

SmartSuite
- components 10
- icons 58
- installation 5

Software requirements . 4

Sort
- filter 193
- view 170

Sorting a database .. 192
Spacing paragraphs . 61
Speaker notes 172
Spell Checker ... 37, 47
Split boxes (1-2-3) .. 116
Special views 30
Spreadsheet charts . 151

Starting
- 1-2-3 113
- Approach 181
- Freelance 165
- Organizer 215
- Word Pro 17

Status bar 19, 22

Style
- box 22
- formatting 70

Suite start tool 9
Sum function .. 102, 135

T

Tab
- scrolling (1-2-3) .. 116
- types (Word Pro) . 70

Table
- charts 106
- creation 98
- editing 104
- navigation 99
- sizing 100

Tasks (Organizer) .. 227
Templates 26, 73

Text
- alignment (1-2-3) 126
- copying 41
- deleting 43
- Drag & Drop 30
- editing 37
- enhancement 60
- finding & changing 44
- formatting 55
- in frames 91
- indentation 62
- moving 42
- orientation 91
- properties 55
- selecting 39
- searching 44

Thesaurus 48
Title bar 19, 20, 21
To Do list (Organizer) 227
Toolbox (Organizer)) 218
Types of charts 109

U

Undo
- command 43, 55
- entry (1-2-3) 137

Unfreezing panes ... 149

V

Video clip 244
View
- icons (Organizer) 216
- modes 28
- preferences 29
- tabs (Freelance) . 167
- worksh't (Appr'ch) 189

Viewing
- appointments 220
- documents 27
- workbook sheets . 123

Views
- Approach ... 189, 191
- Freelance 167
- Word Pro 30

W

Web tools 245
Wildcard characters
- Approach 193
- Word Pro 45

Window command .. 123
Word Pro
- basics 17
- document 24
- help 12
- properties command 33
- screen 19
- settings 31
- special views 30
- templates 26, 73
- toolbar 19, 21

Word wrap 24
Workbook 125
- navigation 117
- opening 129
- saving 128

271

Worksheet
- 3-dimensional 144
- copying 144
- enhancing 141
- grouping 121
- linking 146
- order 103
- printing 138
- view (Approach) . 191

Z
Zoom
- full page 53
- mode (Word Pro) . 28

COMPANION DISCS TO BOOKS

COMPANION DISCS are available for most computer books written by the same author(s) and published by BERNARD BABANI (publishing) LTD, as listed at the front of this book (except for those marked with an asterisk). These books contain many pages of file/program listings. There is no reason why you should spend hours typing them into your computer, unless you wish to do so, or need the practice.

ORDERING INSTRUCTIONS

To obtain companion discs, fill in the order form below, or a copy of it, enclose a cheque (payable to **P.R.M. Oliver**) or a postal order, and send it to the address given below. **Make sure you fill in your name and address** and specify the book number and title in your order.

Book No.	Book Name	Unit Price	Total Price
BP		£3.50	
BP		£3.50	
BP		£3.50	
Name		Sub-total	£.............
Address		P & P (@ 45p/disc)	£.............
....			
....			
		Total Due	£.............
Send to: P.R.M. Oliver, CSM, Pool, Redruth, Cornwall, TR15 3SE			

PLEASE NOTE

The author(s) are fully responsible for providing this Companion Disc service. The publishers of this book accept no responsibility for the supply, quality, or magnetic contents of the disc, or in respect of any damage, or injury that might be suffered or caused by its use.

NOTES

To freeze column headers: p 149